Antiochus the Great

Antiochus the Great

Michael J. Taylor

Pen & Sword
MILITARY

First published in Great Britain in 2013
and republished in this format in 2021 by
Pen & Sword Military
an imprint of
Pen & Sword Books Ltd
Yorkshire – Philadelphia

ISBN 978 1 39908 524 3

Typeset in Ehrhardt by Mac Style
Printed in the UK by CPI Group (UK) Ltd, Croydon, CR0 4YY

Pen & Sword Books Limited incorporates the imprints of Atlas,
Archaeology, Aviation, Discovery, Family History, Fiction, History,
Maritime, Military, Military Classics, Politics, Select, Transport, True
Crime, Air World, Frontline Publishing, Leo Cooper, Remember When,
Seaforth Publishing, The Praetorian Press, Wharncliffe Local History,
Wharncliffe Transport, Wharncliffe True Crime and White Owl.

For a complete list of Pen & Sword titles please contact

PEN & SWORD BOOKS LIMITED
47 Church Street, Barnsley, South Yorkshire, S70 2AS, England
E-mail: enquiries@pen-and-sword.co.uk
Website: www.pen-and-sword.co.uk

Or
PEN AND SWORD BOOKS
1950 Lawrence Rd, Havertown, PA 19083, USA
E-mail: Uspen-and-sword@casematepublishers.com
Website: www.penandswordbooks.com

Contents

Abbreviations

Prosopography: Grainger, John, *A Seleucid Prosopography and Gazetteer*, Brill, 1997.

Roman War: Grainger, John, *The Roman War of Antiochos the Great*, Brill, 2002.

Syrian Wars: Grainger, John, *The Syrian Wars*, Brill, 2010.

Hellenistic World: Austin, M. M., *The Hellenistic World from Alexander to the Roman Conquest.: A Selection of Ancient Sources in Translation*, (2nd Edition), Cambridge, 2006.

Coming of Rome: Gruen, Erich, *The Hellenistic World and the Coming of Rome*, University of California Press, 1984.

Samarkhand: Kuhrt, Amelie and Sherwin White, Susan, *From Samarkhand to Sardis: A New Approach to the Seleucid Empire*, University of California Press, 1993.

Royal Economy: Aphergis, G.G. *The Seleukid Royal Economy: The Finances and Financial Administration of the Seleukid Empire*, Cambridge, 2004.

RC: Wells, Bradford, Royal Correspondence in the Hellenistic Period, London, 1934.

Asia Minor: Ma, John, *Antiochus III and the Cities of Western Asia Minor*, Oxford, 1999.

Antiochos der Grosse: Schmitt, Hatto, *Untersuchungen zur Geschichte Antiochos des Grossen und seiner Zeit*, Franz Steiner Verlag, 1964.

Mediterranean Anarchy: Eckstein, Arthur, *Mediterranean Anarchy: Interstate War and the Rise of Rome*, University of California Press, 2006.

Rome Enters the Greek East: Eckstein, Arthur, *Rome Enters the Greek East*. University of California Press, 2008.

Hellenistic Monarchies: Habicht, Christian, *The Hellenistic Monarchies: Selected Papers*, University of Michigan Press, 2006.

SEHHW: Rostovetzeff, M. *The Social and Economic History of the Hellenistic World* (2nd Edition), Oxford: Clarendon Press, 1953.

Institutions: Bickerman, E.J., *Institutions Des Seleucides*, Paris, 1938.
LCL: Translation taken from the Loeb Classical Library, 1st Edition.
NRSV: Biblical translation taken from the New Revised Standard Version.

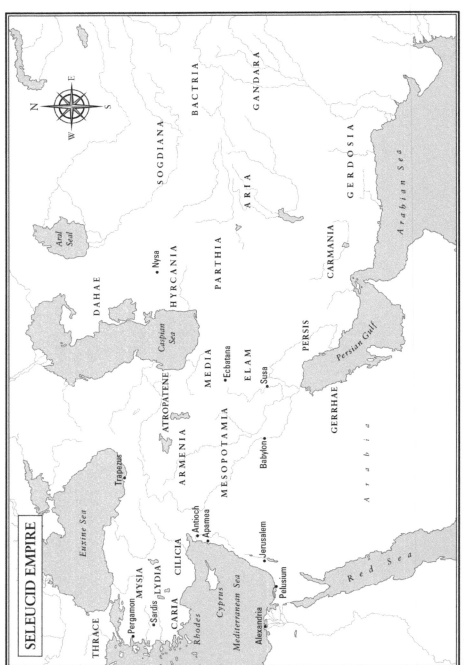

SELEUCID EMPIRE

N E S W

THRACE

Euxine Sea

Trapezus•

Pergamon•
MYSIA
Sardis•
LYDIA
CARIA
CILICIA

Rhodes

Cyprus

Mediterranean Sea

Alexandria

Pelusium•

Red Sea

•Antioch
•Apamea

•Jerusalem

ARMENIA
ATROPATENE

MESOPOTAMIA

Babylon•

Arabia

MEDIA
•Ecbatana
ELAM
•Susa

GERRHAE

Aral
Seal

DAHAE

Caspian
Sea

HYRCANIA

•Nysa

PARTHIA

PERSIS

Persian Gulf

CARMANIA

Arabian Sea

SOGDIANA

BACTRIA

GANDARA

ARIA

GERDOSIA

Map 1

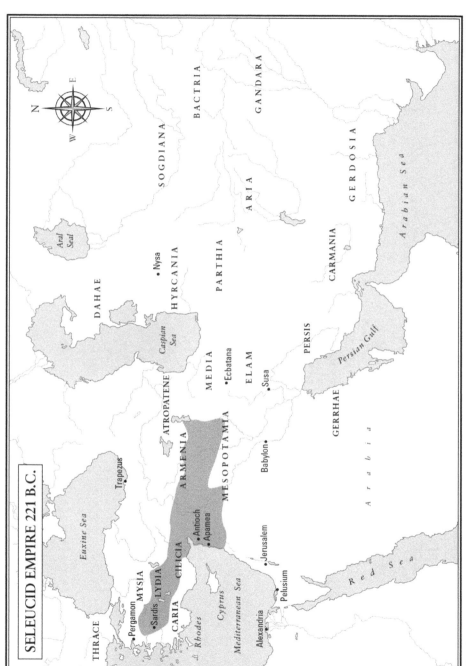

SELEUCID EMPIRE 221 B.C.

N
W E
S

THRACE

Pergamon
Trapezus

MYSIA

Euxine Sea

Sardis
LYDIA

CARIA

CILICIA

Antioch
Apamea

Rhodes

Cyprus

ARMENIA

MESOPOTAMIA

Jerusalem

Alexandria

Mediterranean Sea

Pelusium

Red Sea

DAHAE

Caspian
Sea

ATROPATENE

Babylon

Arabia

ARIA

GANDARA

GERDOSIA

Arabian Sea

Aral
Seal

SOGDIANA

BACTRIA

Nysa

HYRCANIA

PARTHIA

MEDIA

Ecbatana

ELAM

Susa

PERSIS

Persian Gulf

CARMANIA

GERRHAE

Map 2

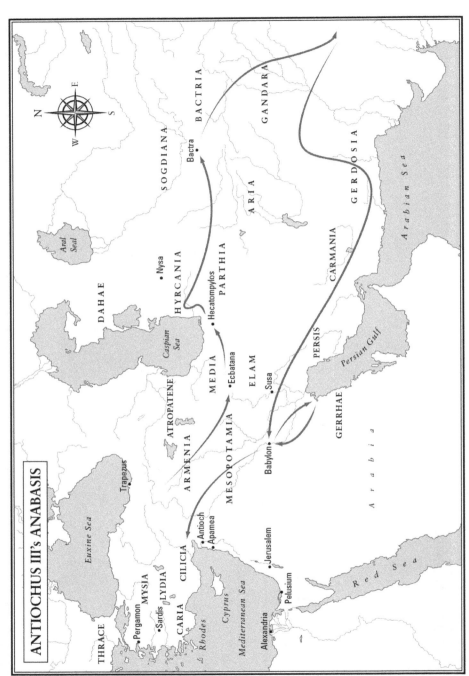

ANTIOCHUS III's ANABASIS

Map 3

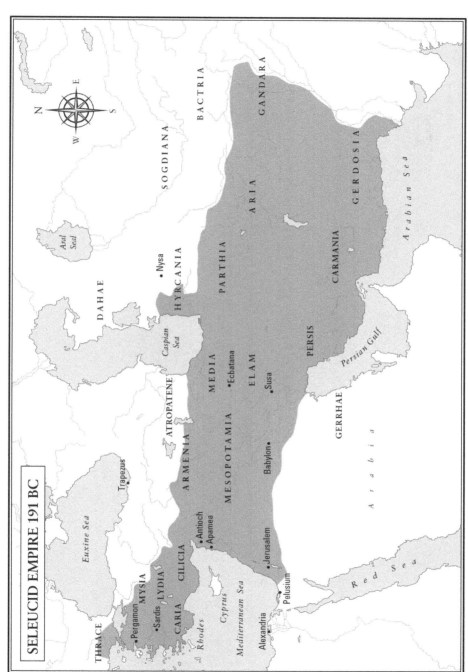

SELEUCID EMPIRE 191 BC

THRACE
MYSIA
Pergamon
Sardis LYDIA
CARIA
Rhodes
CILICIA
Antioch
Apamea
Trapezus
Euxine Sea
Cyprus
Mediterranean Sea
Alexandria
Pelusium
Jerusalem
Red Sea
ARMENIA
ATROPATENE
MESOPOTAMIA
MEDIA
Ecbatana
ELAM
Babylon
Susa
Caspian
Sea
Aral
Sea
DAHAE
HYRCANIA
Nysa
SOGDIANA
BACTRIA
GANDARA
PARTHIA
ARIA
GERDOSIA
PERSIS
CARMANIA
Persian Gulf
GERRHAE
Arabia
Arabian Sea

N
E
S
W

Map 4

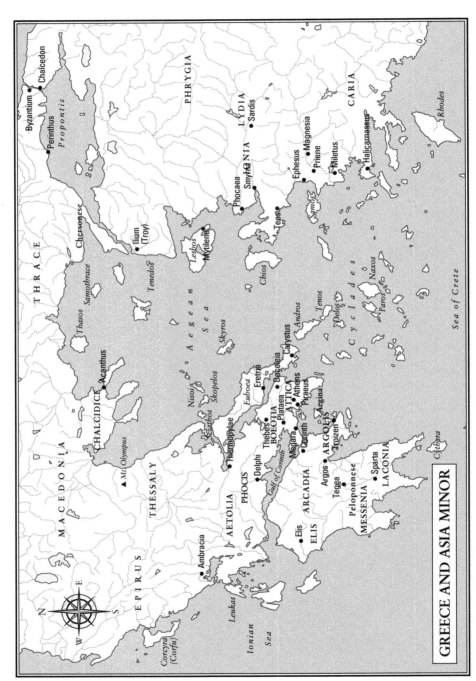

GREECE AND ASIA MINOR

Map 5

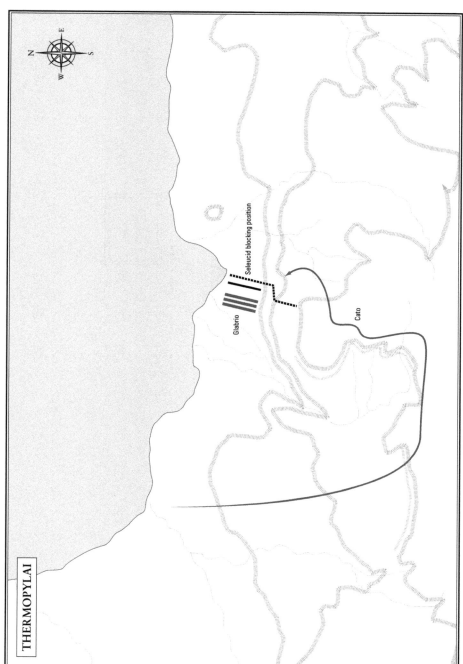

THERMOPYLAI

Seleucid blocking position

Glabrio

Cato

N
E
W
S

Map 6

BATTLE OF MAGNESIA

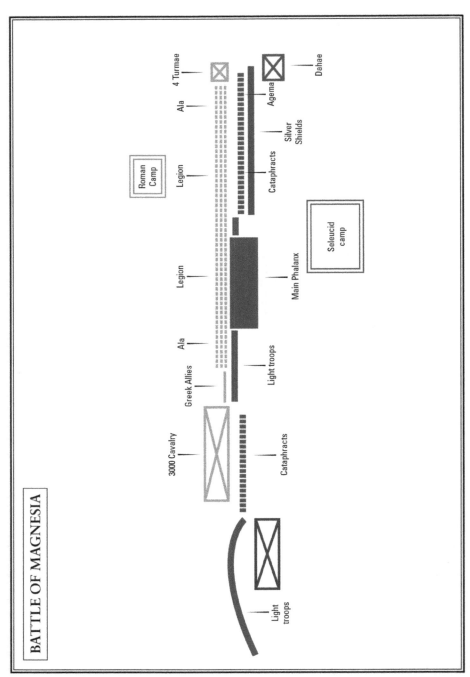

Map 7

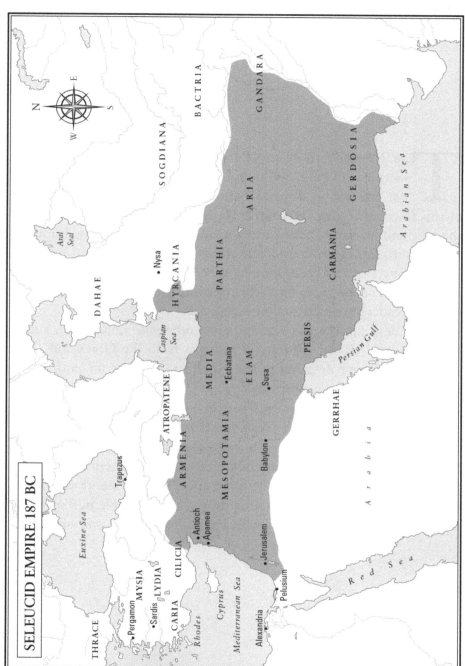

SELEUCID EMPIRE 187 BC

N E S W

THRACE
Pergamon
MYSIA
Sardis · LYDIA
CARIA
Rhodes
Cyprus
Mediterranean Sea
Alexandria
Pelusium

Euxine Sea
Trapezus

Antioch
Apamea
CILICIA
Jerusalem

Red Sea

Arabia

GERRHAE

Arabian Sea

Persian Gulf
GERDOSIA
PERSIS
CARMANIA

ARMENIA
MESOPOTAMIA
Babylon·
ELAM
Susa·
MEDIA
Ecbatana·
ATROPATENE

Caspian Sea
Aral Sea

DAHAE

HYRCANIA
· Nysa
PARTHIA
ARIA

SOGDIANA
BACTRIA
GANDARA

Map 8

Preface

The last modern biography of Antiochus III was written in German in 1964, by Hatto Schmitt. This present book does not attempt to displace Schmitt's academic study of the life of this fascinating king. It is rather designed as a narrative overview of the king and his times, aimed at the widest possible audience. Endnotes are designed less to drive academic arguments, than to acknowledge the heavy lifting that has been done by other scholars, and to provide the reader with a useful guide for further reading. I have, whenever possible, directed readers to quality online resources.

Translations are my own, except when otherwise noted. As a rule, I have translated all but the longest excerpts from the Greek and Latin sources, but I have deferred to the expertise of others for both Greek inscriptions and the cuneiform tablets.

I owe my gratitude to my ever-patient editor at Pen and Sword, Phil Sidnell. I would also like to thank the Brittan Travel Fund in the UC Berkeley Department of Classics, the generosity of which allowed me to visit many relevant sights in Greece through the American School of Classical Studies in Athens. The often anonymous photographers who contribute their shots to Wikimedia proved indispensible in illustrating this book. Special thanks to my wife, Kelsey, for her love and support.

Introduction

On a cold, damp morning in the autumn of 190 BC, twenty-five thousand Roman and Italian soldiers were ordered to march out of their fortified camp and form themselves for combat. They were very far from home, marshalling upon a foreign plain in the fabled land of Asia. Some of the citizen-soldiers had listened to the debates in Rome to wage war here, watching as some elite politicians counselled diplomatic patience while others demanded immediate war. A few soldiers had even voted in the citizens' assembly to formally declare a state of war between the Roman people and King Antiochus. Many had volunteered for service after rumours of the King's magnificent wealth excited hopes for even a small share of the spoils, yet most were conscripts, peasant boys who had little reason to know or care about a distant king and the vast eastern empire he ruled.

A few were able to hear the fine words of their general, as he rode about at dawn haranguing his troops, laying out the rewards of victory and the bitter consequences of defeat. Their commander had chosen to fight in the horseshoe of two rivers, so that water blocked all hope of retreat.

Intermittent rain fell on the soldiers as they shivered in ranks, and the enemy battleline was obscured by a dense bank of fog. As the sun rose, burning off the mist, the teenaged skirmishers in the front line saw before them an enormous horde, the combined strength of Asia. Dense ranks of pikemen presented an impenetrable mass of iron, ash-wood and bronze, above which loomed the shadow of elephants. From a distance it seemed that the Romans confronted not an army, but rather the walls and towers of an impregnable city. More dangerous was a long line of cavalry, both horse and rider heavily armoured, specifically massed to crash through the Roman legions. Among the metal-clad troopers was the hostile King himself, prepared to personally lead the charge against the Roman invaders. Scanning his foe, the King identified a weakness in the Roman line, and on his command his cavalry surged forward: 16,000 hooves pounded across the plain. Any Roman who believed the bellicose rhetoric promising an easy victory over the effeminate Greeks and Asians knew now that he had been badly deceived. Panic gripped the over-stretched Roman infantry line, and the legionaries turned and fled back toward the ramparts of their camp. The entire Roman left wing collapsed before the horsemen of Media, Phrygia, and Syria. In hot pursuit of the fleeing Roman infantrymen was the Great King himself, Antiochus III.

Chapter One

The Seleucid Empire

By almost any metric, the empire ruled by Antiochus III from 223 to 187 BC was impressive. He ruled as king (*basileus*) over the most populous empire in the Mediterranean world, constituting, by one modern estimate, between ten and twenty million subjects. In terms of landmass, no rival Mediterranean state could come close. At the kingdom's peak, Antiochus III held sway over nearly 1.5 million square miles of territory, an area that encompasses the modern countries of Syria, Lebanon, Israel, Palestine, Jordan, Armenia, Iraq, Kuwait, Iran, Afghanistan and Azerbaijan, as well as parts of Turkey, Uzbekistan and Turkmenistan.

From this vast population and territory, the King drew immense resources. His military at its peak mustered over 120,000 soldiers and sailors; his annual revenues may have approached 20,000 silver talents (roughly 600 tons of silver bullion).[1] At the military arsenal in Apamea, the royal stables housed some 30,000 mares, 3,000 stallions, and a royal elephant corps.[2]

The Seleucid Empire facilitated cultural and economic exchange between East and West by its very scope.[3] Antiochus III found himself negotiating with Bactrian kings, Indian dynasts, Jewish high priests, Greek town councillors, and Roman senators. In Bactria, in the northeast corner of the empire, one could find rock carvings of Delphic maxims and inscribed tracts of Buddhist piety.[4] Antiochus III sponsored a Greek style-library in Antioch, in imitation of the great Library in Alexandria; his son Antiochus IV would host Italian-style gladiatorial games in the same city.[5] That the Seleucid kings were able to maintain such a far-flung territorial empire speaks well of their energy, intelligence, and skill.

The House of Seleucus: 323–223 BC

Antiochus III was a king who was keenly aware of the history of his dynasty, and who was not ashamed to start wars or seize territories based on historical claims.[6] Indeed, as a young king he had inherited not simply control of territory or the loyalty of the army, but the heavy burdens of the past: old dynastie feuds, unfulfilled territorial ambitions and unavenged affronts.

The realm of Antiochus III was a young empire, forged in the violent wars of Alexander's successors (*diadochoi*). Antiochus III's great-great grandfather, a Macedonian officer named Seleucus, was one of these ambitious successors.[7] As a young man Seleucus had served in the ominous shadow of Alexander, whose brutality and charisma subsumed the otherwise ferocious personalities of his subordinates. With Alexander dead, his generals finally gave expression to their latent prowess and suppressed ambition. Yet Seleucus had never been in the upper echelons of Alexander's command structure, which perhaps explains why he survived for as long as he did, managing to escape both the purges of the officer corps initiated by Alexander, as well as the first bloody spasms of successor warfare.

A tenuous calm prevailed in the immediate aftermath of Alexander's death in 323 BC. His mentally handicapped half-brother Philip III Arrhidaeus was paraded as a successor. Alexander's Bactrian wife Roxanne gave birth shortly afterward, and the baby, Alexander IV, was also named king. Ambitious Macedonian officers were assigned to govern various occupied regions in what was effectively a 'power-sharing' agreement designed to avert immediate civil war. A Macedonian general named Perdiccas, the senior member of Alexander's inner circle, was assigned to oversee the kings in Babylon as regent. Seleucus was protégé and junior ally of Perdiccas. However, Perdiccas subsequently bungled an engagement on the Nile against Ptolemy, the recalcitrant satrap of Egypt.[8] Seleucus led a mutiny that murdered the discredited Perdiccas in his tent. As a reward, he obtained the satrapy of Babylon.

Another round of internecine war followed.[9] By 316 BC, a veteran officer emerged as the most powerful successor warlord: a one-eyed (*monophthalmos*) man named Antigonus, aided by his impetuous son Demetrius, nicknamed 'the besieger' (*Poliorcetes*). Between them, Antigonus and Demetrius controlled much of Syria and Anatolia (Turkey) as well as the islands of the Aegean Sea and a chain of fortified strongholds in Greece.[10] Antigonus soon struck against the hapless

Seleucus, who had no means to resist from his small Babylonian fiefdom. Outlawed on trumped-up corruption charges, Seleucus fled to Egypt, where he was received and recruited by Ptolemy. Seleucus became an admiral in the Ptolemaic fleet, and for the rest of his life used an anchor as his personal emblem. After his death, the anchor became a lasting symbol of Seleucid royal authority, stamped on everything from coins to sling bullets.[11]

In 312 BC, Ptolemy defeated Demetrius Poliorcetes at Gaza, giving his ally Seleucus a chance to reclaim Mesopotamia. Borrowing a tiny force of 1300 cavalry from Ptolemy, Seleucus re-entered Babylon. To reassure his troops, who were terrified of ambush and annihilation, Seleucus told them that the ghost of Alexander the Great had promised success to him in a dream.[12] Antigonus did not let this incursion go unnoticed. His forces invaded Mesopotamia but were repulsed after bloody street fighting in Babylon. Safely reinstalled in his satrapy, Seleucus looked to the east: a prudent course, as the other successors were locked into death struggles to the west. From 306 to 302 BC, Seleucus moved his army across Iran toward modern-day Pakistan, emulating the endless march of Alexander. Where Alexander actively fought against the Indian dynast Porus and ravaged communities down the Indus River Valley, Seleucus practised canny diplomacy. He negotiated a peace treaty with the rising Indian dynast Chandragupta, who was known by the Greeks as Sandracottus. Chandragupta was in the process of building his own sub-continental empire, and he was eager to avoid future incursions against his northern border by menacing hordes of adventurous Macedonians. In exchange for lasting peace, Chandragupta gave Seleucus a vital military asset: a herd of 500 trained war-elephants.[13] The war-elephant was still a new variable on the Hellenistic battlefield, first encountered during Alexander's campaign into India. These animals inspired tremendous fear in men who were not familiar with their enormous size and bizarre appearance. They were particularly effective against cavalry, as their size and smell spooked even the steadiest of warhorses. Now Seleucus had more of these tank-like creatures than any of his rivals.

By 309 BC, Alexander IV, the posthumous son of Alexander the Great, had been murdered in Macedonia.[14] In the absence of an officially titled successor, the warlords felt increasingly comfortable assuming the title and trappings of kingship. The first successors to do so were Antigonus and Demetrius, following a victory off the coast of Cyprus in 306 BC. The others quickly followed suit. Seleucus was first listed as king in Babylon in 305/4 BC.[15]

The tremendous power wielded by Antigonus and Demetrius prompted rival warlords to unite in a grand coalition against father and son. Seleucus allied himself with Cassander, the king of Macedonia, and Lysimachus, who had crowned himself king of Thrace.[16] These three allies and their combined armies of approximately 75,000 men clashed with the 80,000-man army of Antigonus and Demetrius in the Battle of Ipsus in 301 BC. Demetrius led a successful cavalry charge, but in his zeal to emulate Alexander he over-pursued on the flanks. His father lost the infantry fight and the Antigonid centre collapsed. Antigonus One-Eyed, then eighty years old, fell fighting, riddled with spears. Demetrius boarded ship and fled with the remnants of his army to occupy his few remaining citadels in mainland Greece.[17]

Seleucus and his allies then rapaciously divided the empire of Antigonus 'as if it was the great carcass of a slaughtered beast'.[18] Ptolemy took control of the islands of the Aegean Sea and the Lebanon-Judea-Palestine region, called 'Koile' or 'hollow' Syria because of the Biqua Valley formed by the Lebanon and Anti-Lebanon mountains. Lysimachus expanded his holdings in northern Anatolia, and Seleucus took just about everything else. He set about an ambitious program of city-building in his new domains in Syria. He founded Antioch on the banks of the Orontes River, named in honour of his father. Antioch-on-the-Orontes would become the primary royal residence and one of the most splendid cities of antiquity.[19] To populate the city, Seleucus transplanted 5300 settlers from Antigoneia, recently established by his defeated rivals.[20] The depopulated city named after Antigonus One-Eyed was then razed to the ground. Seleucus also established the garrison town of Apamea in southern Syria as his most important military base. Apamea stood on the new boundary between the territories of Seleucus and those of Ptolemy. Seleucus founded two major cities on the Mediterranean Sea: Seleucia Pieria, intended as his new Mediterranean capital, and the port Laodicia-on-the-Sea, named after his mother.[21]

Ptolemy and Seleucus by now had had a long history of personal cooperation, but in the bloody and unstable politics of the successors, friendship and alliance were decidedly transient. Koile Syria proved a major sticking point between the two men. Seleucus claimed that the two men had agreed that Koile Syria would go to him, and was furious when Ptolemy furtively occupied it while the rest of the coalition was busy fighting Antigonus and Demetrius.[22] In all likelihood, the agreement between Seleucus and Ptolemy had been diplomatically vague. Koile Syria was strategically important to Ptolemy; it provided a number of points where a modest defensive force might bottle up any attempt to invade Egypt from the north, while Seleucus coveted it for its natural resources and wealthy cities.

Seleucus by now had an adult son, Antiochus, a budding general who worked closely with his father.[23] The two men expressed their close cooperation in a most unusual way. Seleucus had since married a young woman named Stratonice, the daughter of Demetrius Poliorcetes (her name means 'Victorious Army'). Demetrius was humbled by Ipsus, but still had fortresses and fleets that would make him a useful counterbalance to his tenuous northern ally Lysimachus.[24] For Seleucus it was a political marriage, his second. He did not put away his first wife, Apame, but rather practised a form of traditional royal polygamy that prevailed in the Macedonian court.[25] Soon young Antiochus became deeply enamoured with the comely Stratonice, who was now his stepmother. In some circumstances, this could have prompted his execution. Seleucus, however, used what could have been a scandalous affair to strengthen the impending dynastic succession. The father divorced the lovely Stratonice and generously married her to his son.[26] An additional realist calculation may have influenced the King's decision: he had recently fallen out diplomatically with Stratonice's father, Demetrius Poliorcetes, making his marriage alliance to her less politically useful.[27] Whatever Stratonice thought of this arrangement, she quickly began producing male heirs. Seleucus proclaimed Antiochus I co-king in 292 BC, and gave his son operational control over the Eastern satrapies.

Demetrius Poliorcetes would eventually join his daughter in the Seleucid court, under less than ideal circumstances. In 287 BC, Demetrius was expelled from Macedonia, and decided to gamble his remaining force of mercenaries on a final adventure into Anatolia. Disease destroyed his dwindling ranks, and his demoralized army soon melted away. Seleucus captured Demetrius and confined him to gentlemanly captivity. Demetrius, who had always been a high-functioning alcoholic, soon drank himself to death.[28]

In 281, Lysimachus, the potentate of Thrace, a former ally turned enemy, also invaded Anatolia. Seleucus marched north to meet him, and triumphed in the Battle of Corupedium. Lysimachus fell fighting, and his kingdom perished with him. Seleucus now stood ready to reunite the ancestral kingdom of Macedon with the Persian lands won by Alexander's spear. He landed in Macedonia, where he was proclaimed king. But in the tumultuous world of the successors, this triumph was fleeting. The bastard son of Ptolemy I, called Keraunos ('the Thunderbolt') joined Seleucus in his entourage, but then coaxed the old king aside and stabbed him to death. Keraunos briefly proclaimed himself king of Macedonia, only to be killed shortly afterwards by an invading horde of Gauls.[29] Macedonia descended into a decade of chaos; order would finally be restored when Demetrius' son Antigonus Gonatas scored a crushing victory over the Gauls and reclaimed the kingship of Macedonia.

With the death of Seleucus, his son Antiochus I became the sole ruler of a suddenly troubled empire. Central Syria revolted during the time it took Antiochus to make the journey from the Upper Satrapies in the east to the heart of the kingdom. Meanwhile, the Bithynians proclaimed their independence, and their self-proclaimed king invited a band of Gauls to cross into Asia in order to distract the Seleucids from his rebellion.

These Gauls were part of the onslaught that struck Macedonia and Greece in 279 BC. Antiochus I confronted them with an army spearheaded by his impressive elephant corps, and the lightly armed Gallic warriors were routed in the so-called 'Battle of the Elephants'.[30] Victory over the barbarians allowed Antiochus I to portray himself as champion of Hellenism and civilization-at-large, as the Gauls became known as barbarians to the Hellenistic world: a race so violent and bestial, according to some fervid descriptions, that they would rape corpses and pluck infants off their mothers' breasts in order to eat them.[31] Yet it is unclear whether Antiochus was militarily capable of completely annihilating the Gauls, or that he wished to do so. Rather, Antiochus I and his successors confined them to a sizable reservation in central Anatolia, maintaining them as autonomous allies, as well as a convenient pool for mercenary recruitment. Most Seleucid armies would ultimately contain a large contingent of Galatian hires.

Antiochus I also embarked on what would prove to be a series of wars with Ptolemaic Egypt, over the territory of Koile Syria. The First Syrian War, fought in the mid 270s BC, was brief, inconclusive and poorly documented. Seleucid ambitions against Ptolemaic holdings in Koile Syria would be passed down through the line of kings.[32]

Antiochus I was succeeded by his son Antiochus II, the product of his 'love-match' with Stratonice.[33] Antiochus II was, in fact, the second son of this union; the first son, named Seleucus, had been executed on unknown charges.[34] Information on Antiochus II's reign is limited. He fought another short war with Ptolemy II of Egypt (the Second Syrian War), but again failed to make any significant territorial gains. Antiochus II was guilty, however, of some deleterious dynastic mismanagement. His first wife and cousin, Laodice, was a member of the Seleucid royal family (one source suggests she was his half-sister),[35] and she diligently bore her husband two sons and three daughters. But in his desire to make peace with Ptolemaic Egypt, Antiochus II divorced her and repudiated their children. Laodice was not cast out of the court, as the divorce settlement provided her with ample estates to allow her to continue to live in grand style.[36]

In her place, Antiochus II married Berenice, the daughter of Ptolemy II by his sister Arsinoe. While Berenice bore a son and heir, Antiochus II died soon after, leaving his kingdom to a baby. This dynastic situation was made more complicated by the fact that an alternative and fully adult heir was available: Seleucus II, the natural son of Antiochus II and Laodice.[37] Seleucus II had a powerful ally in his wronged mother, for Laodice still had many influential supporters in the Seleucid court.

Yet Berenice had one very powerful advocate: her brother Ptolemy III, who had recently come to power in Egypt. Ptolemy III marched north with his army. The military details are sparse, but it is clear he won several major victories. He captured Apamea, Antioch, and Seleucia Pieria, while Seleucus II retreated into Mesopotamia. Laodice fled north, where she was instrumental in organizing further resistance from Anatolia. Ptolemy

III celebrated in Antioch, even publishing an official account of a joyous reunion with his sister and nephew.[38]

The official history was a lie. Berenice and her infant son were already dead, murdered by partisans of Laodice. While the Ptolemaic phalanx reached Babylon, Ptolemy III was eventually forced to withdraw and return to Egypt in response to internal unrest at home. No doubt bereaved by the death of his sister and nephew, he was nonetheless much enriched, carrying home over 1500 talents of looted silver bullion. He retained one great territorial prize: control of Seleucia Pieria, the Seleucid port and naval base, some twenty kilometres down the Orontes river from Antioch itself. The loss of Seleucia Pieria was a symbolic as well as strategic loss, as the city contained the tomb of Seleucus I. Once fortified and garrisoned with Ptolemaic troops, Seleucia Pieria would become a thorn in the side of the Seleucids for the next twenty-five years.

Seleucus II and his mother had lost plenty of battles, but they emerged victorious in the Third Syrian War, which is often called the Laodicean War in honour of the iron lady who propelled her teenage son to power. Yet the crisis of Ptolemaic invasion had consequences through the east. Two satraps revolted: Andragoras of Parthia and Diodotus of Bactria. The rebels immediately faced a nomadic invasion by the Parni, led by their ferocious chieftain Arsaces I. Diodotus managed to expel the Parni from Bactria, but they soon swept into Parthia, killing the rebellious satrap Andragoras and establishing an independent kingdom of their own. Seleucus II marched east and claimed victories, but he accomplished little. Both Arsaces' Parthia and Diodotus' Bactria remained independent kingdoms.[39] Seleucus II most likely acquired the epithet Callinicus ('Glorious victory') during these campaigns, a title that dramatically overstated his actual successes. In 238, a major revolt broke out in Babylon, although it seems to have been contained by 235.

In a capstone to these woes and disorders, Seleucus II's younger brother, Antiochus Hierax ('the Hawk') revolted and proclaimed himself king in Asia Minor.[40] Hierax commanded a powerful army, and allied himself with various local powers: the king of Pontus, the king of Bithynia and the bellicose Galatians. Hierax won the first round, repulsing Seleucus' attacks in the so-called War of the Brothers, which lasted from 239 to 236 BC.

In the midst of this civil war, a new kingdom emerged in eastern Anatolia. A local dynast named Attalus, who had previously sworn fealty to the Seleucid king, now proclaimed himself king of an independent state based around the fortified city of Pergamon. Attalus I attacked Hierax and drove him from his base Asia Minor. Hierax fled into exile, and ultimately was murdered by brigands in Thrace. His revolt, along with the creation of the Attalid kingdom (the third independent kingdom hewn from Seleucid territory in less than ten years), demonstrates the fragility of the Seleucid realm, which was vulnerable to both territorial fragmentation and dynastic instability.

A less dramatic breakaway occurred in Caria in the 240s, under a local official named Olympichos. While he did not claim the royal title, his actions were increasingly autonomous, as he issued decrees in his own name, without reference to the Seleucid king, and later conducted direct diplomacy with the kings of Macedonia. After the island city of Rhodes suffered a devastating earthquake in 226 BC, he made a contribution to the reconstruction of the city under his own authority as a 'dynast' (*dunastes*), independent of the contribution made by the Seleucid king.[41] Olympichos was no usurper, but simply a local dynast operating in the power vacuum created by the virtual collapse of Seleucid authority in Asia Minor in the 240s and 230s. Whenever the Seleucid dynasty was riven by internal confusion, hundreds of officials like Olympichos simply carried on, collecting taxes, maintaining local garrisons and providing the basis for regional law and order.

Seleucus II Callinicus had two sons. The elder of these was named Seleucus III Keraunos, another 'Thunderbolt'.[42] The youngest was Antiochus, who was not expected to become king.[43] It was Seleucid royal custom to name the eldest son Seleucus after the dynasty's founder and the younger son Antiochus. As a rule, Antiochoi only succeeded in the event of the premature death of their older brother.

Seleucus III, then a young man of twenty, marched his army north to wage war against Attalus' breakaway kingdom of Pergamon. Attalus I had done his father a great favour by efficaciously disposing of Hierax, but he had his own ambitions on the Anatolian territory traditionally claimed by the Seleucids. Having revoked his ancestors' token loyalty, he now became a standing enemy of the dynasty.

Seleucus III's campaign quickly floundered and he was murdered by his army, perishing without a son. Thus the teenaged Antiochus assumed the diadem and became the *basileus* (king) of a very troubled realm in 223 BC. Modern historians have dubbed him Antiochus III, adopting the medieval European habit of using Roman numerals to distinguish Hellenistic kings with the same name. He would not have been called this by contemporaries, but was rather expected to acquire an appropriately magnificent epithet to distinguish himself: Seleucus I had dubbed himself *Nicator* (Victor), his son Antiochus I took the title *Soter* (Saviour), while his grandson Antiochus II adopted the hyperbolic epithet *Theos* (God). Antiochus' father Seleucus II referred to himself as *Callinicus* (Beautiful Victory), while his brother Seleucus III also claimed the title of *Soter* (Saviour) during his fleeting reign.[44]

Antiochus was related by blood to Seleucus I, but he maintained psychic kinship to two other royal lines. The first and most important line for the purposes of royal propaganda was the connection to Alexander the Great. Almost all Hellenistic kings were obsessed with the physical image of Alexander, the ultimate role model and prototype for Hellenistic kingship. Before Alexander, a copious and virile beard was the sign of a mature Greek man. But Alexander had died before he reached the age where it was customary for Greek men to grow a beard, and his youthful clean-shaven state was copied by his successors even into old age. As a result, beards went out of fashion in the Mediterranean for the next 450 years.[45] Of all Hellenistic kings, Antiochus III could claim to come closest to emulating Alexander's mighty deeds as well, in particular an ambitious march east to the border with India. Antiochus ultimately rewarded himself with the ultimate self-tribute: he took the cognomen *Megas* – 'the Great'.[46]

Yet Antiochus III ruled a vast Near Eastern realm. Of all Alexander's boorish and parochial lieutenants, Seleucus I was perhaps the most sensitive to native cultures that remained in lands conquered by the Macedonian spear. Alexander had famously forced his reluctant Macedonian officers to marry Iranian wives in an effort to create a bi-cultural ruling aristocracy. This exercise in social engineering failed miserably; when Alexander died, every man except one divorced his barbarian wife. Seleucus maintained his union with the Bactrian princess named Apame; she was the mother of Antiochus I, and the great-great grandmother of Antiochus III. Apamea, the formidable garrison city, was named in her honour.

With a sense of cross-cultural relations, Seleucus I and his progeny reached out to the native cultures of the land they ruled. In many ways, this choice was also a strategic necessity. Seleucus I started out with only a tiny army of 20,000 ethnic Greeks and Macedonians, and the population that identified itself as Greek or Macedonian may not have exceeded a few hundred thousand even in Antiochus III's day. This was not enough to control the native population by force alone, and accommodation of native practices and communities would be critical for survival.

In particular, Seleucus and his followers won the goodwill and cooperation of the priests of Babylon. The rolls of Babylonian kings show a continuity that spans from the Persian kings to Alexander to Seleucus and his sons. Thus, Antiochus was as much the heir of Cyrus, Darius and Xerxes as he was of Alexander. He assumed another royal title, one that carried historical baggage: *Basileus Megas*, or 'Great King', the same title that Greeks had given the Persian emperor. Kings of Babylon had been accustomed to refer to themselves as the 'Great King' (GAL LUGAL), while the Persian king Darius I called himself 'the great king, king of kings, king of countries containing all kinds of men, king in this great earth far and wide'.[47]

Seleucid geography

The Seleucid Empire encompassed vast expanses of land. This was a great handicap, as ancient empires generally required large bodies of water to transport materials and people. Rome relied on the unifying waters of the Mediterranean Sea, while Han China was bound together by the far reaches of the Yellow and Yangtze rivers. Land transport, whether of grain, bullion, bureaucrats, or troops, was prohibitively expensive and arduous: the cheapest form of transportation was by sea. As a general rule, it cost six times as much to transport goods by river as it did by sea. However, once goods were loaded onto wagons or pack animals, the price skyrocketed even further. It cost 60 times as much to cart goods overland than to transport them by sea; more to transport a bushel of grain 50 miles by land than it did to ship it 3000 miles across the entire length of the Mediterranean.[48]

And yet, the Seleucids for much of their history were landlubbers, lacking an active Mediterranean navy. While Seleucus I had initially planned to establish his primary capitals at Seleucia Pieria, on the Syrian coast, Ptolemaic naval superiority forced him to make inland Antioch his main royal residence. While the Seleucids did maintain a modest naval presence on the Red Sea, which controlled a lucrative trade with the spice fields in Yemen and far-flung routes in India, they largely ceded the Mediterranean Sea to other powers. They controlled the island of Ikaros in the Persian Gulf (modern-day Failaka off Kuwait) as a colony and naval base, although Arab traders and pirates constantly challenged their position. Antiochus III would attempt to develop Seleucid naval power with mixed results.

In landlocked and arid terrain, rivers shaped the patterns of both trade and agriculture. In Syria, the Orontes River watered the fertile agricultural lands of the Amuk plain that fed the growing population of Antioch and linked the capital city to the port at Seleucia Pieria and arsenal at Apamea. The Amuk plain was famous in ancient times for the olives and orchards; Syria was a leading exporter of dried fruit. In addition to agricultural bounty, the Orontes river and surrounding area also supported large urban populations: Antioch was a city on par with Ptolemaic Alexandria, Carthage, and Rome.

In the southern part of the empire lay Koile Syria, still not yet part of the Seleucid realm, but much coveted. The Lebanon and Anti-Lebanon mountains, parallel north–south ranges that formed the 'hollow' of the Biqua Valley, contained some of the finest timber in the Mediterranean, including the famous cedar stands of Lebanon. Further south lay modern-day Israel and the fields watered by the Jordan River: the coastal plain of the Gaza strip, now one of the densest urban areas in the world, was then splendid cropland fed by rains coming off the sea. Gaza was particularly known for fertile vineyards and excellent wines. The Phoenician coast contained merchant cities of great antiquity, most notably Tyre, Sidon Gaza and Arados. The Phoenician coast was also a major production centre for purple dye made of crushed murex shells.

Moving east to modern day Iraq, the Tigris and Euphrates rivers bounded the fertile crescent of Mesopotamia (literally 'between the rivers'). Today, salinization has reduced the fertility of this region, but then it was arguably the best agricultural land in the world. The fertile crescent was the site of some of the earliest human agriculture and the first urban civilizations. The most important native city in the area was Babylon, once the seat of a sizeable empire and home to important priestly authorities. Seleucus I established a royal residence near Babylon at Seleucia on the Tigris, replete with an opulent set of monumental buildings. Both the Tigris and the Euphrates could be used for transport, although their swiftness generally made them one-way highways.

Beyond the fertile crescent lay the Iranian Plateau, once the heartland of the Persian Empire, particularly the satrapies of Persia and Media, an enormous tract of land transected by the Zagros mountain range. While Iran lacked unifying rivers such as the Orontes, Tigris, and Euphrates, mountain passes knit the region together. The mountains themselves provided their own rugged form of connectivity, as the scarcity of upland environments mandated vigorous low-level trade for inhabitants to maintain the necessities of life. The plains of Iran also bred fine horses, skilled riders, and tough warriors.

Linked to great steppes of Eurasia, the Iranian plateau was vulnerable to waves of nomadic peoples sweeping down from the north. While the Caucasus mountains between the Black and Caspian seas provided a formidable natural barrier to Steppe invaders, Iran was vulnerable to infiltration east of the Caspian. In the Middle Ages, Iran would suffer from the incursions of nomadic armies led by Genghis Khan and Timor the Lame. In the third century BC, the menacing nomads were called the *Parni*, but they eventually acquired the name of the satrapy they infiltrated: Parthia.

Governance

How did the Seleucid kings manage to govern this enormous landmass, especially given the slow communications that plagued the ancient world? It is unlikely that the speediest of messengers would make 150–200 miles in a day on horseback. For purposes of comparison, riders on the nineteenth-century American pony express rarely covered more than 200 miles a day, and this was with a fresh horse every ten miles. Such a breakneck pace without renewal would quickly kill both horse and man. Estimates for the speed of the later Roman Imperial post suggest a distance of no more than 50 miles a day; there is no reason to suggest the Seleucids managed anything better.[49] At this speed it could take forty days (under the best circumstances) to send a message 2000 miles from Antioch to Bactria, and almost three months before the timeliest of replies.

Solutions to the problem of governance and slow communication had been identified. After all, the Seleucids controlled much of the same territory formerly occupied by the Achaemenid Persians, and they naturally adopted many elements of the Persian system. Key to Persian governance was a system of decentralized provinces, ruled by officials called satraps. The term satrap was a Greek bastardization of the Old Persian word *chsacapava*, 'protector of the kingdom'. By the reign of Antiochus III the Greek term *strategos* (general) was preferred (or occasionally *eparchos*, 'governor'), but the term 'satrap' was still used unofficially.[50] *Strategoi* served at the pleasure the king, and generally were of Greek or Macedonian descent. Given the slow pace of communication, satraps enjoyed relative autonomy, as long as they kept peace and forwarded a steady stream of tax revenue to the royal treasury. Satraps maintained military garrisons and even convened mini-courts. Yet because of their independence, the risk that a satrap would revolt and claim more power (or independence) was high; the best control against satrapal over-reach was nepotism: placing trusted friends or relatives in satrapies.[51]

The Seleucids also mimicked the Persian custom of multiple royal capitals. The Achaemenids had maintained administrative centres with royal residences along the king's imperial circuit: the most important Persian capitals were Sardis, Persepolis and Susa. In a similar way, Seleucid royal centres at Sardis, Antioch, and Seleucia-on-the-Tigris, anchored the key regions (respectively) of Anatolia, Syria and Mesopotamia. Antiochus III later envisioned a royal centre at Lysimacheia to control Thrace, with his cadet son installed as governor, and established a semi-permanent residence at Ephesus, on the Ionian coast of Asia Minor.

The extensive frontier of the empire often required the king to fight multiple wars simultaneously. Although the king would often personally lead an army in the most critical area of operations, he had to be willing to trust sizeable military forces to other generals and geographic areas. These independent generals posed a greater risk to the king than did the satraps. Satraps controlled only modest and scattered garrisons, but a general with a field army could prove very dangerous indeed. In selecting generals, personal loyalty at times eclipsed military competence. When possible, Seleucid kings tapped close relatives to command field armies – preferably sons, but also brothers and cousins. Unfortunately, relatives with royal blood in their veins were also prone to revolt, as evidenced by Antiochus Hierax against Seleucus II, and later Achaeus, the rebel cousin of Antiochus III.

The Seleucid king lived in a world with no newspapers or equivalent to mass media. He had no organized intelligence source and frequently lacked good information when making critical decisions. Information about the outside world filtered in through contacts in court, tradesmen, ambassadors, and mercenary captains.[52] Diplomatic links were also crucial sources: the Seleucids would have maintained such links with neighbouring counties and sought to reinforce them when necessary through marriage or other means. A few books circulated that could fill in knowledge gaps concerning nations farther away. For example, if Antiochus III wanted to learn about the barbarian people called the Romans, he could read the history of Rome written by the senator Fabius Pictor, who had recently published a treatise (c. 200 BC) in Greek to explain his society to Hellenic audiences. Nonetheless, when analysing the decisions made by ancient leaders, it is important to remember that they operated with very limited information, frequently basing critical decisions on little more than hearsay or rumour.

The Mediterranean world of Antiochus III

The Seleucid Empire was one of five major powers that emerged following the end of the wars of the Successors. Two others were also 'Hellenistic' powers, ruled by Macedonian dynasties descended from successor warlords. The descendants of Seleucus' old ally Ptolemy controlled Egypt (the dynasty is sometimes referred to as the 'Lagids,' after Ptolemy I's father Lagos). Macedonia was controlled by the descendants of Antigonus One-Eyed and Demetrius the Besieger, known as the 'Antigonids' by modern historians.

In a twist of historical coincidence, all three Hellenistic states acquired young kings at approximately the same time. Nineteen-year-old Antiochus III became king in 223 BC, Ptolemy IV assumed the diadem in Egypt in 221 BC at the age of twenty-three, and seventeen-year-old Philip V obtained full regal powers in Macedonia in 221 upon the death of his regent and co-king, his uncle Antigonus III Doson. The youth of these kings was not seen necessarily as a liability by their contemporaries. After all, Alexander the Great had become king at the age of nineteen. Beauty and adolescent brashness were admired features in Hellenistic kings. Indeed, fat and middle-aged Hellenistic kings tended to display themselves as young and vigorous men, harkening back to the youth and vigour of Alexander, who died at the age of thirty-three.[53]

A long tradition of friendship prevailed between the Antigonid and Seleucid kings, dating back to the political match between Stratonice and Seleucus. Antiochus III would have a grandson named Demetrius, a traditional Antigonid dynastic moniker. This friendship and natural alliance was helped along by the fact that neither side shared a contested border. But Seleucid relations with the Ptolemies were another matter entirely, as has been discussed previously. Although Ptolemy I and Seleucus I had cooperated against Antigonus One-Eyed and Demetrius the Besieger, contestations around the shared borders of their empire would lead to generations of warfare.

The Antigonid relations with the Ptolemies also proved frequently hostile. Although based firmly in Egypt, the Ptolemies controlled a great maritime empire that included the Aegean islands, Cyprus, territories on the coast of Asia Minor and Thrace, on the doorstep of the Macedonian king. Furthermore, Ptolemaic kings had traditionally sought to undermine Macedonian imperial authority by supporting the independent aspirations of Macedonian subject peoples. In the 260s, Ptolemy II funded Athens and Sparta in their revolt against Macedonian hegemony.[54] In the 220s, Ptolemy III would bankroll the ambitions of the upstart Spartan king Cleomenes, who was defeated by Macedonian troops in 222.

In terms of population, the King of Macedonia ruled over approximately 300,000 ethnic Macedonian subjects.[55] He could raise field armies of between 20,000 and 40,000 men, yet was required to devote thousands of additional soldiers to garrison duties. Macedonia was the traditional policeman of Greece's northern border and took responsibility for keeping the barbarian Illyrian, Dardanian, and Danubian tribesmen from rampaging the south. The King of Macedonia also controlled tremendous natural resources, including some of the best timberlands in the eastern Mediterranean. Silver and gold mines financed expensive military operations; according to one source, the Macedonian king received at least 1000 silver talents a year from his mines alone (1 talent = 6000 drachmas, or roughly 26 kilograms; a silver talent could purchase enough grain to feed 100 people for an entire year).[56]

Despite the natural resources in Macedonia, the Ptolemaic king of Egypt controlled the finest and most productive agricultural land in the Mediterranean: the Nile valley. Every year, Nile floods deposited rich layers of silt, giving Egypt spectacular crop yields. Between four to seven million peasants worked the land to harvest this agricultural bounty. The Ptolemies were also effective and systematic tax collectors; their yearly income is given at between 12,000 and 14,800 silver talents.[57] The bounty of the Nile allowed the Ptolemies to maintain a maximum of 90,000 troops in field armies and garrison and to deploy an impressive fleet.

Like the Seleucid king, the Antigonid and Ptolemaic kings were absolute monarchs. They ruled with no checks on their power; all claimed to rule land that was 'spear-won' (*doriktetos chora*). In physical appearance, the *basileus* distinguished himself with a cloth band knotted around his head called a diadem; it is still disputed whether the symbol originated in the Macedonian or Persian court.[58] He carried a sceptre, a Greek royal symbol since the time of Iliad, and wore an expensive purple robe, dyed with a purple laboriously extracted from crushed murex snails. Favourite courtiers of the king were also distinguished by their expensive purple robes, which the king might personally rip from the body should a courtier fall from the king's favour.[59]

Classical Greek political theory was traditionally hostile to the idea of absolute kingship, which in its extreme form was believed to degenerate into violent hubris: paranoid monarchs fearing competition and butchering the talented men of their realm.[60] While Plato chose a king to lead the ideal state of his *Politikon* (Republic), the said king had also experienced a rather unusual philosophical epiphany.

With the rise of Alexander and his successors, however, political theorists made necessary and politic adjustments. As warlords became kings, a new theory of kingship arose, a philosophical and political strain that emphasized the special competence of the king in military and administrative spheres. Indeed, most successors delayed coronation until they achieved a major success on the battlefield.[61] The most famous expression of this new view of kingship is found in the Suda, a Byzantine encyclopaedia that preserves earlier threads of Greek thought:

> Monarchy: It is neither descent nor legitimacy which gives monarchies to men, but the ability to command and army and to handle affairs competently. Such was the case with Philip and the successors of Alexander. For Alexander's natural son was in no way helped by his kinship with him, because of his weakness of spirit, while those who had no connection with Alexander became kings of almost the whole inhabited world. (Suda s.v. basileia; Austin *Hellenistic World*, 45).

The implications of such a view were chilling to a king who failed as a general and administrator. He could expect to be liquidated and replaced. However, dynastic continuity proved a strong force in most of the Hellenistic kingdoms. Among the Ptolemies, strong-willed ministers compensated for the failings of weak or immature monarchs. In Macedonia, the boy king Philip V was not murdered, but assigned his uncle Antigonus Doson as regent and co-king. It was the elites of the Seleucid Empire who displayed the strongest proclivity to assassinate kings who failed as generals and administrators, as happened to Antiochus' brother Seleucus III. A similar fate would befall his son Seleucus IV.

In the Western Mediterranean, two non-Hellenic and non-monarchical powers dominated the scene: the Republic of Rome, which headed a powerful Italian confederacy, and the African city-state of Carthage, which dominated the fertile agricultural lands in modern day Tunisia and Libya. The two powers were allies for much of their earlier histories, but collided in 264 BC over the island of Sicily. The resulting war from 264 to 242 BC was a narrow Roman victory. Carthage devoted her subsequent military energies to carving out an empire in Spain to compensate for territories lost in this first war. When young Antiochus III assumed power in 223 BC, a tenuous peace prevailed between the powers. It would not last long.

When the second war with Rome broke out, Carthage raised enormous multi-ethnic armies, fielding upwards of 170,000 men in 215 BC. Carthage also benefited from ample mineral resources in Spain; the prosperous mines around New Carthage alone could generate upwards of 1300 talents a year.[62]

In contrast to Carthage's Iberian bounty, Rome possessed only modest mineral resources. Italy lacks significant gold and silver veins, but possesses impressive iron deposits in Etruria (modern day Tuscany) and on the island of Elba. Without question, Rome's most bountiful resource was an enormous pool of tough, warlike peasants. In all, some three million free persons inhabited the Italian peninsula in the late third century BC; there were approximately 270,000 adult male Roman citizens in 225 BC. Rome's Italian coalition could contribute roughly 700,000 adult males of military age, including citizens and allies (*socii* – hence our word 'social').[63] In 212 BC, during the second war with Carthage, Rome mustered 25 legions and allied wings, containing between 160,000 and 200,000 men.

Unlike their Hellenistic counterparts, both Rome and Carthage were republics. This does not mean that they were democracies in the modern sense; rather they were governed through 'mixed' constitutions, with senior magistrates (consuls in Rome, suffets in Carthage), a powerful aristocratic body (approximately 300 senators in Rome, 104 'judges' in Carthage), and citizen assemblies that elected magistrates and declared war. This mixed form of governance was much admired by ancient political philosophers; Aristotle praised the constitution of Carthage highly, which he compared favourably to the constitution of Sparta.[64] The Greek historian Polybius, heavily influenced by Aristotle's analysis, later emphasized the efficacy of the checks and balances in the Roman system.[65]

The two western republics were tremendously powerful, and by 218 they were again at war. A Greek statesmen speaking before a peace conference in 217 warned assembled dignitaries that they must beware of a 'cloud now looming in the west'.[66] It is unclear whether he meant Rome or Carthage, although at this point Carthage, led by the brilliant tactician Hannibal, had invaded Italy and was unquestionably gaining the upper hand. Any prudent statesman would certainly be wary of the eventual victor in the coming clash. But up to that point, neither Rome nor Carthage had expressed any predatory designs on the Eastern Mediterranean: Carthage focused her expansionism against Sicily and inland Spain; Rome had been occupied for most of the third century with forging and defending the empire in Italy. While raids by Illyrian pirates had prompted two interventions east across the Adriatic Sea, the Romans promptly withdrew their forces once they had overthrown the offending Illyrian dynast.[67] Roman expansionism was focused mostly in northern Italy (then dubbed Cis-Alpine Gaul), where land-hungry Roman armies and colonists pushed into the fertile territory of the Po River Valley, occupied by tough Gallic tribes. Given the Romans' focus on the Italian peninsula, few could have predicted that Antiochus III would confront armies of invading Romans in Asia Minor.

Both Carthage and Rome maintained polite and peaceful relations with the Hellenistic powers. Carthage's Libyan possessions bordered on Ptolemaic holdings in Cyrene, but the two shared an amicable border. The Carthaginians maintained relations with the Seleucids that were friendly enough for the Carthaginians to obtain Indian elephants in their herds. Hannibal's favourite elephant was named 'Surus', or 'the Syrian', possibly bred in the Seleucid elephant farm at Apamea.[68]

Diplomatic contacts between Rome and Ptolemaic Egypt were initiated in the 270s, after Rome repelled the invasions of the Epirote warlord Pyrrhus. The Ptolemaic empire maintained a policy of polite neutrality during the 1st Punic War (264–242 BC).

Relations between Rome and the Seleucid Empire came much later. At some point during the third century BC, the Roman senate wrote a letter to a king Selecus, requesting that he respect the city of Ilium (Troy).[69] Most likely the Seleucus in question was Antiochus III's father, Seleucus II, who campaigned in the region in the early 220s.[70] The city of Ilium held a special significance for the Romans, as they claimed descent through the Trojan hero Aeneas and were accustomed to using mythic genealogies to drive diplomacy with Hellenistic powers.

In addition to the five major powers, a number of small states that played a role during Antiochus' reign deserve mention, the dynasts of Anatolia in particular. The most important of these was the Attalid kingdom of Pergamon. Attalus I was the first of his dynasty to call himself a king, but his father Eumenes I and great-uncle Philatairos were both powerful regional dynasts who appeased distant Seleucid overlords by refraining to assume the royal title.

On the northern coast of Anatolia, facing the Black Sea, were the kingdoms of Bithynia and Pontus, and in the eastern highlands of Anatolia lay the rugged kingdom of Cappadocia. All three were ruled by native families, who nonetheless adopted a Hellenic veneer and surrounded themselves with most of the trappings of Hellenistic kingship. Pontus, in particular, maintained close ties with the Seleucid empire, including a tradition of intermarriage with the Seleucid royal family.

In theory, the Greek city-states within mainland Greece and along the coast of Asia Minor were independent entities. During the wars of the successors, various warlords had proclaimed the slogan 'freedom (*elutheria*) for the Greeks' in order to gain the support of these proud if increasingly impotent communities.[71] In reality, however, only a few city-states managed to hold their own in the tumultuous environment of the third century BC, and freedom was generally interpreted loosely, so that 'free' cities endured royal garrisons and paid tribute (*phoros*) to the royal fisc.

A prominent exception to this increasing dependence was Rhodes, an island city-state that maintained its independence through a well-organized navy. When an earthquake struck Rhodes in 222 BC, the mighty Hellenistic kings scrambled to outdo each other in lavishing relief aid upon the shattered island.[72] The reason for such competitive generosity was not difficult to discern: despite the damage, the Rhodian navy remained a potent force in the Mediterranean.

Most other Greek city-states realized that they must unite or perish. A number of federal leagues emerged, uniting city-states with one another for protection. The two most prominent were the Achaean league in the Peloponnesus and the Aetolian League, based in central Greece. The power of both leagues quickly eclipsed that of Athens and Sparta, the traditional hegemons of southern Greece since the fifth century. Cities in these leagues managed their own domestic affairs but combined their military and financial resources to conduct foreign policy. These leagues traditionally had limited interaction with the Seleucid Empire, as their primary focus was countering the menacing presence of the neighbouring Macedonian king.[73]

Sources

This book is billed as a biography, yet it cannot promise a biography in the modern sense of the world. The biography of a modern political leader would likely try to delve into the psychological nature of the subject and his motivations. It might explore how experiences in childhood and youth found themselves reflected in later adult life, or how public actions were shaped and shaded by private emotions and relationships. It would give access to introspective moments away from the public spotlight and explore personal relations with family, friends, and even enemies. In support of these goals, most modern biographies have tremendous amounts of data to draw upon: diaries, letters, memoirs, interviews, and public speeches. But evidence for the ancient world is sparse, even for a king as powerful as Antiochus III.

No ancient biography of Antiochus III survives. This is perhaps fortunate. Ancient biography was notoriously unreliable, frequently combining gossip, slander, and unfounded suppositions. The genre was usually more concerned with moralizing than systematically analysing political or individual developments. For ancient figures with surviving biographies, the infamous Roman emperor Nero for example, it can be difficult to distinguish reliable information from the literary constructs of the biographer. A modern biographer of Antiochus III carries no such baggage.

Unfortunately, our information about Antiochus comes from references in just a handful of ancient sources.[74] The most important of these sources is Polybius, a Greek historian who wrote between 160 and 140 BC.[75] At once a victim and an admirer of Roman imperialism, Polybius was a high-ranking official in the Achaean League, who spent almost two decades as a hostage in Rome after 167 BC. His book was designed to explain to fellow Greek aristocrats that resistance to Rome was futile, even if honourable co–existence might be possible.

While enduring a genteel captivity in Rome (he was granted significant freedom of movement around Italy), Polybius befriended a number of important senators, and busied himself writing a history that would explain Rome's domination of the Mediterranean. Even though his 'universal' history has not survived intact (indeed, most of the details concerning Antiochus' life after 200 BC are lost), Polybius rates as one of the most important and most reliable historians of antiquity. He was the prime source for later historians, most notably the Roman historian Livy (Titus Livius), who authored an epic history of Rome between 27 BC and AD 15. Livy had access to Roman historians active during Antiochus' lifetime (including Fabius Pictor and Claudius Alimentius), as well as Roman archival records from the third and second century BC. Still, for eastern affairs, Livy relied overwhelmingly on Polybius.

Polybius had access to two particularly important connections concerning the Seleucid Empire. The first, a Seleucid prince named Demetrius, was the grandson of Antiochus III. Demetrius also spent time as a hostage in Rome, where he became close friends with Polybius (the two men were kept in gentlemanly captivity). No doubt Demetrius gave Polybius sound information concerning family history and the arrangement of current Seleucid institutions. Polybius' second contact was Scipio Aemilianus, a young Roman nobleman who had ties to two of the most noted aristocratic families in Rome: he had been born into the patrician Aemilii, and adopted into the patrician Cornelii Scipiones. While Scipio Aemilianus was too young to recall the war between Rome and Antiochus III, he likely provided access to documents and oral family core regarding the Roman generals who conducted the war against Antiochus: Scipio Africanus and Scipio Asiaticus, his adoptive grandfather and great-uncle.

Despite the accounts of Polybius, it is also necessary to rely on later literary sources, many of which were written in the second century AD during the intellectual 'second sophistic' period of the High Roman Empire. One of the most prolific writers of this period was Plutarch, who wrote from c.75 to 120 AD. A Greek with Roman citizenship, Plutarch penned many works, including a series of linked biographies comparing Greek and Roman notables. Although he did not write a biography of Antiochus III, his biographies of the Roman statesmen Titus Quinctius and Marcus Porcius Cato 'the Elder' shed significant light on the confrontation between Antiochus and Rome.[76] Another Greek historian of High Imperial Rome was Appian of Alexandria, a Roman citizen and *procurator* who was writing c. 150 AD. His primary opus was a lengthy history of Rome delineated mostly by various periods of conflicts, including a section on Seleucid conflicts entitled *Syrian Wars*.[77]

Last, we have the history of Justin, who wrote in Latin in the third century AD. Justin, however, was summarizing a much earlier work, written by the Roman historian Pompeius Trogus nearly two hundred years earlier. Trogus was quite interested in the history of the Near East and delved deeply into the sweep of Seleucid history: it is regrettable that only Justin's 'cliff notes' of his work survive.[78]

These historical narratives are important but still limiting; several other types of evidence are critical to understanding the Seleucid Empire. The first is epigraphy, the study of inscriptions. Multiple inscriptions survive that record decrees and letters from Antiochus III; these sources allow us to hear Antiochus III in his own voice, even if that voice is in the formal, regal language of royal correspondence.[79] Additionally, a series of astrological diaries, maintained by the astronomer priests of Babylon, provide a non-Greek view of Seleucid rule and prove helpful on questions of chronology.[80] These diaries comment on grain prices, military activities, and the activities of the king and his officials within the city. Surviving material evidence such as coins give us a sense of what Antiochus might have looked like, and illustrate the dynastic image he wished to project to his people.[81] In an age with no printed material and severely limited literacy, coins were one of the most effective forms of political propaganda.

Chapter Two

The War with Molon

The teenage king

The exact date of Antiochus' accession to the throne is unclear, but it occurred after July 223 BC, when his brother Seleucus III (referred to as king in Babylon) died during the campaign season. Babylonian astronomical tablets record the year 222 BC as Antiochus' first full year on the throne.[1] The year of Antiochus' birth is also unclear. Polybius indicates that he was just over fifty in the year 191 BC, which would indicate that he was born in 241 BC or slightly earlier. By any calculation, Antiochus was a young man, likely around nineteen years old, when he became the king of the Seleucid Empire.[2]

According to Polybius, Antiochus had been sent to live 'in the interior' while a youth, which suggests either the royal city of Seleucia-on-the-Tigris or possibly Babylon. An early stay in Babylon during adolescence might explain the close relationship he developed with the great Babylonian temple of Esagila. During this time, there is no evidence that Antiochus was given any significant responsibilities as a cadet brother of the king, although he probably enjoyed a number of empty honours and notional titles.[3]

The death of Seleucus III led to a power vacuum and serious rebellion in the east, which was in full force by the summer of 221 BC. The revolt was lead by Molon, the satrap of Media, joined by his brother Alexander the satrap of Persia.[4] Together, these two brothers controlled two of the most important eastern provinces, the heart of the old Achaemenid Empire. Soon, Molon was also styling himself as king, and even minting coins with the appellation 'King Molon'. The revolt of Molon and Alexander was similar to the revolt of the Parthian and Bactrian satraps in the late 230s, representing the centrifugal tendencies of the empire's peripheral regions in times of dynastic instability.

While Alexander the Great had proven that a nineteen-year-old king could be decisive, canny, and cruel, he was the exception rather than the rule. Groomed from an early age to succeed his father, Alexander had been entrusted with important military commands and consequential decisions by the age of sixteen. Antiochus III had none of this grooming or experience. He was the little brother of the king, a symbolic royal lieutenant rather than a trusted advisor, and the untimely death of Seleucus III thrust him unprepared into his new position. With little to no training in court manoeuvres, he was likely not aware of the position's full power or influence.

The naïve young man was thus unable to manage the boisterous court environment he inherited from his late brother. Court politics had lately devolved into a feud between two chief advisors: Hermeias and Epigenes, two courtiers who understood that the stability of their own power was linked to the favour of the young and inexperienced king. While the two disagreed on certain substantive policy points, their conflict seems driven largely by intense and ultimately murderous personal rivalry.

Both Hermeias and Epigenes were leading figures under the rule of Antiochus' older brother. Hermeias had governed Seleuicia-on-the-Tigris while Seleucus III campaigned north against Attalus and his breakaway kingdom. Hermeias may have become Antiochus' most powerful advisor because he was the senior official closest to him when he was still a cadet prince resident in Babylon, and would have been able to ingratiate himself almost immediately when Antiochus was proclaimed king unexpectedly.[5] Hermeias dominated the physical court where the young King lived. Like all monarchs of the day, Antiochus depended utterly upon the loyalty of others to ensure his day-to-day survival. A myriad of courtiers, chamberlains, pages and slaves fulfilled every need: cooked for him, tasted his food to guard against poison, poured his wine, opened doors as he passed, emptied his chamber-pot, and ushered in mistresses. This array of staff was carefully controlled and orchestrated by Hermeias. In addition, Hermeias held the loyalty of the royal bodyguard, which gave him the power of coercion and resources for potential assassination should the need arise.

The second advisor, Epigenes, was a leading general who had accompanied Seleucus III on his final campaign. Following the assassination of the King, he regrouped the army and marched the militiamen in the phalanx back to their homes in the Syrian tetrapolis. Epigenes was popular within the army, making him a much needed ally. While his reputation as a capable military man earned him the young King's trust and respect, Epigenes lacked contacts within the inner court, strings that Hermeias pulled with ease.

A third figure in the young King's reign stood outside the court: Antiochus' elder cousin Achaeus, who had been assigned a command in Asia Minor. Achaeus, like Epigenes, had accompanied Seleucus III on campaign, but afterward he had remained in Asia Minor with a sizable force. Proving his loyalty to the new King by refusing the army's attempt to proclaim him king,[6] he was rewarded with an extraordinary command and tasked with recovering territory lost to the Attalids. Achaeus carried out his task with alacrity and soon backed Attalus I into his citadel of Pergamon. Achaeus' successes in Asia Minor would provide a bright spot of success in Antiochus III's grim first year as king.

The first matter of royal policy to decide was the location of Antiochus' first personal military campaign. Epigenes recommended that the King lead the army against Molon, in part because he hoped that the King's presence would convince the rebels to desert. Hermeias, concerned about the potential consequences of Antiochus' limited military experience, advocated an incursion against the softer target of Ptolemy IV in Koile Syria; for the King himself to march against Molon would lend dignity and legitimacy to a rebel and traitor, he argued. Experienced mercenary generals ought to deal with such a character. A king, he flattered Antiochus, should only fight against another king.

In support of his position, Hermeias produced a letter, possibly forged, claiming that it was intercepted correspondence between Achaeus and Ptolemy IV. In the letter, Ptolemy encouraged Achaeus to revolt against Antiochus and offered him material support. The letter (which despite Hermeias' unsavoury reputation was likely genuine, as Ptolemy IV would have had every reason to incite Achaeus to rebellion) would serve as a perfect pretext for going to war. Ultimately, Antiochus sided with Hermeias. Two generals, Xenon and Theodotus Hemiolios, were tasked with removing Molon, and preparations were made for a royal campaign into Koile Syria.

The royal campaign was delayed while an absolutely necessary dynastic task was accomplished: the young King must be married and produce an heir as soon as possible. These tasks were critical for two reasons: given the mortality rates in the ancient world, it was necessary to produce a son as soon as possible with the hope that he might be of age before his father's death. Second, since the time of Seleucus I and Antiochus I, an adult son served as co-king with his father: this had proven an effective way of managing succession (a similar scheme would later be adopted by the French Capetians). If the king fathered a son at nineteen, there was a good chance that he would have a co-king by the time he reached his late thirties. Given the problematic loyalty of generals like Molon, it would also be a tremendous boon to count on the absolute loyalty of adult sons as independent commanders. Indeed, the best way for the Seleucid king to produce faithful generals was to father them.

With respect to the mother of such an heir, it is unclear how much choice young Antiochus III was given when selecting his bride. He likely gave his uninformed consent to marry a girl he had never met, but the young King was likely unconcerned that the match be one of everlasting romance. Like traditional Macedonian kings, he had the option of contracting plural marriages in the future.[7] Furthermore, the young monarch's position and power allowed him a great deal of extramarital sexual freedom if he so chose.

The bride chosen was Laodice, the daughter of Mithradites II of Pontus. Pontus was a traditional Seleucid ally in the complex game of Antatolian diplomacy, and the Seleucids had a long tradition of intermarriage with the Pontic royal house. The bride herself was a granddaughter of Antiochus II, who had bequeathed his daughter (also named Laodice[8]) to the king of Pontus, and Laodice III and Antiochus were therefore first cousins. To confuse matters even further, Laodice had a sister also known as Laodice, who was married to Antiochus' cousin Achaeus around the same time.

The Seleucid fleet commander (*nauarchos*) Diognetus, who had connections in the Pontic court, escorted Laodice to Seleucia at the Bridge (Zeugma), on the Euphrates River, where Antiochus III had established a temporary residence. After their royal marriage, the couple then travelled to Antioch, where Laodice was formally proclaimed queen (*basilissa*).[9] Antiochus delayed his campaign long enough to father a child, and their first son, also named Antiochus ('the son' or 'the younger'), was probably born around 220 BC.

Preparations were not yet complete for the campaign into Koile Syria when news arrived of a serious setback in the war against Molon and Alexander. Theodotus Hemiolios and Xenon had marched their forces east but had declined to engage the rebels in battle. Polybius reports that they were 'panic-stricken'.[10] The reasons for the retreat are unclear, although it was likely that they became convinced that their forces were unprepared and unequal to the task. Theodotus Hemiolios continued in Seleucid service, which makes it likely that their refusal to fight was based upon the realities on the ground and not cowardice.[11] We lack general information about the size of Molon's forces and the nature of the army under the two generals, so judging his claim here is difficult. However, given that Molon controlled the best horse-breeding grounds in the empire, as well as levies of Medish and Persian tribesmen, it is likely that he managed to build a sizable force from local recruits available to him.

With this newfound confidence, Molon moved south. He came close to capturing Seleucia on the Tigris, but was prevented by a timely defence of the riverbank by a junior commander named Zeuxis. This show of military competence, at a time when Antiochus III was sorely in need of good generals, would eventually propel Zeuxis to increasingly important commands. Following this setback, Molon retired to Ctisiphon in central Mesopotamia, near modern-day Baghdad.[12] Hermeias, however, continued to advise the King not to abandon the planned designs against Koile Syria, and another general was sent east to contain the situation, an Achaean mercenary captain named Xenoitas.

Xenoitas was an aggressive commander, although critics soon murmured that the unexpected command and lofty title of 'general-in-chief' (*strategos autokrator*) had gone to his head. Deserters from Molon, perhaps planted agents, swam across the Tigris and brought intelligence that the rebel army was wavering in its loyalty. Hearing this, Xenoitas hoped that an immediate show of force might cause much of the rebel army to simply melt away. He crossed the Tigris River and marched directly against Molon's camp. In response, Molon attempted a cavalry raid against the vulnerable troops on the far side of the river, but the horses stumbled into an extensive marshland. A number of riders drowned, and the bogged-down counterattack was quickly aborted. Molon abandoned his camp and retreated. Xenoitas allowed his men, exhausted from the successful river crossing, to loot the camp and refresh themselves with captured provisions; their victory celebration quickly devolved into a riot of heavy drinking.

It is unclear whether Molon's retreat was a feint or a hasty withdrawal to reorganize his forces. Either way, he halted his retreat and countermarched back to his abandoned camp. Xenoitas had failed completely to establish an adequate security perimeter, and Molon caught the royal army utterly unprepared, butchering Xenoitas' soldiers in their drunken stupor. Xenoitas avoided disgrace by fighting to the death, leaving Zeuxis to rally the survivors into a long retreat.[13]

Molon then crossed the Tigris and captured the major prize of Seleucia on the Tigris, the most important Seleucid foundation in Mesopotamia. He maintained his relentless momentum, occupying Babylonia and then moving to attack east. The former Persian royal capital of Susa resisted, and Diogenes, the Seleucid governor of the city, withstood the siege in the citadel.[14] Leaving a small force behind to blockade the defenders, Molon returned to Seleucia-on-the-Tigris. He paused to allow his army to regain its strength, and then marched north, following the line of the Euphrates River, as far as the garrison town of Dura. He detached a force to besiege the town, and then returned south, effectively the master of Mesopotamia.

Meanwhile, Antiochus' personal campaign against Koile Syria was quickly becoming a failure. The parallel ranges of the Lebanon and Anti-Lebanon mountains created a series of choke points, which funnelled the attacker into narrow avenues of possible advance. Modest Ptolemaic garrisons held these points, and they were well positioned to defend the passes against numerically superior attacking forces. Antiochus attempted to force the pass of Marsylus at the mouth of the Biqua Valley, but his assaults were repelled by a talented Ptolemaic mercenary commander called Theodotus the Aetolian. The young King had suffered significant casualties while making little progress when messengers arrived bearing news of Xenoitas' humbling defeat.[15]

The startling setback in Mesopotamia forced Antiochus III to abandon his campaign against Koile Syria and prepare to confront Molon in the east. This decision tilted the court dynamics in favour of Epigenes, who had previously advocated for Antiochus' direct engagement with Molon. The military setback was therefore a dire political setback for Hermeias, and the failure of his advice jeopardized his standing in the court. He sensed that Epigenes was now set to displace him as the King's chief advisor. A meeting of the royal council exploded as Hermeias furiously abused Epigenes, leaving Antiochus alarmed by the fragmentation of his court. However, Hermeias realized that he had no choice but to support the decision of the young King, and he actively threw himself into preparations for the royal counterattack in Mesopotamia.[16]

An opportunity soon emerged for Hermeias to salvage his vulnerable position. The loss of Mesopotamia and the Upper Satrapies to Molon severely constrained Seleucid revenues, as some of the richest agricultural land in the empire was now in rebel hands. Antiochus III lacked cash to pay his armies, and a violent mutiny broke out due to arrears of pay. Since the campaign could not proceed until the soldiers were paid, Hermeias offered the King a bargain. He would pay the army from his personal fortune, on the condition that Epigenes retire permanently from political life. Antiochus was in a corner. If this campaign failed, it would prove disastrous for his nascent rule. He must have been aware, based on the experience of his late brother, how a dissatisfied army could prove lethal to a Seleucid king. Antiochus accepted the deal. Epigenes was popular with the army, but a long overdue payday was even more popular. The mutiny was thus quelled, save for a 6000-strong contingent that hailed from the city of Cyrrhus.[17] This splinter group was a dangerous development, as these men were not just disgruntled native auxiliaries, but part of the main phalanx, descendants of Greek and Macedonian settlers. The Cyrrhestians left their barracks and marched toward their home city, which erupted in revolt. Subordinate generals eventually contained the rebellion, but such an uprising in the centre of the empire indicates the delicate and tenuous condition of the Seleucid body politic.

Epigenes retired to his home city of Apamea, but Hermeias still sensed danger from his rival. To rid the scene of his political enemy, Hermeias conspired with Alexis, the commander of the citadel (*archophylax*) of

Apamea, to frame Epigenes for conspiring with Molon. Upon obtaining a forged letter indicating such cooperation, Alexis promptly executed Epigenes. Antiochus III was not informed of this judicial murder until after the fact and was carefully led to believe that Epigenes was indeed guilty.[18]

With his chief rival thus dispatched, Hermeias was now Antiochus' most trusted advisor. Through his manipulation of court-protocols, he continued to control access to the King, making Antiochus a virtual prisoner of his ministrations. Now that Queen Laodice had given birth to a son, the King had reason to worry that Hermeias might murder him in order to become regent to the infant son.

But Hermeias' position in the court was more tenuous than it appeared. A large portion of the royal council was becoming concerned with Hermeias' power and influence. While his habit of labelling opposing voices as traitors stifled open dissent, it steeled many toward more drastic furtive actions. The King himself was increasingly uncomfortable with Hermeias' high-handed ways.

As a result, the King found a new counterweight for Hermeias in Zeuxis, a military man of proven talents. A war council in Mesopotamia offered Zeuxis the opportunity to challenge Hermeias publicly on matters of strategy before the King. Hermeias advocated an advance along the Tigris that would use the banks of the river to cover the army's flank. This plan sounded good in theory but ignored significant logistical concerns. It would take the army through the largely deserted territory on the eastern bank of the Tigris, making the provisioning the army difficult.

Zeuxis recommended instead that the army cross the Tigris and advance perpendicularly to the river toward the agricultural region of Apollonia. There was good reason to think that the population would welcome the King; either way, the rich Mesopotamian farmland could feed the army as it marched through. Furthermore, this plan would cut off Molon's path of retreat back to his strongholds in Media and likely force a decisive battle. Antiochus formally backed Zeuxis' plan in open council, a clear repudiation of Hermeias and a sign that his influence was on the wane.[19]

After a swift march, Antiochus and his troops arrived at Apollonia, now north of Molon, blocking his road to Media. Molon left his base at Seleucia-on-the Tigris and marched north toward Apollonia, seeking confrontation. After Antiochus' pickets detected Molon's vanguard, both the royal and the rebel armies encamped and then deployed for battle.

We have no information about the strength of the armies. Molon likely enjoyed an advantage in cavalry, given that Persia and Media were a source of horsemen. Given that the Syrian tetrapolis was the prime recruitment ground for the phalanx, the King likely enjoyed a superiority of heavy infantry.

Antiochus placed his phalanx in the centre, and on his right a body of Greek mercenaries, who also fought as heavy hoplite infantry, as well as Galatian and Cretan mercenaries. The Galatians generally fought as light infantry, while Cretan mercenaries were valued for their skills as archers, although they may have simply been light troops. Antiochus commanded the right, with a large body of *xustophoroi* cavalry, armed with lances called *xustoi*. On his left flank, under the command of Zeuxis, he placed his elite companion (*hetairoi*) cavalry. He had ten war elephants with him, which he placed to the front of his troops.

Molon likewise positioned his phalanx in the centre along with his own contingent of Galatian mercenaries. He placed his cavalry on either wing. In an unusual tactic, he moved his light troops beyond his cavalry on either flank, a rare case in antiquity where infantry, rather than cavalry occupied the extreme flanks. This may have been due to the rugged terrain of the battlefield, which required Molon to position his cavalry on the limited level terrain adjacent to his infantry formations, while he placed his light infantry in the rugged terrain on his flanks, providing both elevation and enfilading fires for archers and slingers. To the front, Molon positioned a number of scythed chariots to counter the imposing presence of Antiochus' war-elephants. Molon commanded the right wing himself, while his brother Neolaus commanded the left.

Despite the careful tactical preparations on both sides, the battle itself proved anti-climatic. The appearance of Antiochus caused Molon's advancing left wing to desert en-masse. The rebel infantry in the centre subsequently collapsed as Antiochus rolled up the entire battle line. Molon committed suicide, ending the rebellion.[20]

After his death, Molon's corpse was subjected to a gruesome display, conspicuously crucified at the base of Mount Zagrus as a warning to future traitors and a symbol of the King's reasserted control. Molon's brother Neolaus escaped from the battle, and is said to have killed Molon's children and their mother, presumably acts of mercy to pre-empt expected royal retribution. Neolaus and Alexander subsequently committed suicide.[21]

The rebel soldiers were dealt with leniently. After issuing a stern rebuke, Antiochus 'gave his right hand', which probably meant a public pledge that they would not be subsequently punished.[22] The army was assigned to loyal officers and returned to Media, where most of the ex-rebels had served as garrison troops previously. Given that the same Persians, Medes and Iranians would serve with Antiochus in the Battle of Raphia in 217 BC, it does not seem that Molon's revolt had particularly deep roots. With the pretender gone, the native inhabitants of Media, Persia, and central Iran returned their full loyalty to Antiochus.[23]

In the wake of this victory, Hermeias was given authority over the city of Seleucia-on-Tigris, and according to Polybius, he governed in a brutal fashion, exiling a popular local magistrate named Adeiganes and executing many others. He imposed a shocking 1000 talent fine on the city, the equivalent of 30 tons of bullion. Antiochus, playing good-cop to Hermeias' bad-cop, reduced this fine to a more manageable 150 talents, which likely represented the city's normal tax bill that had gone unpaid during the revolt.[24] Antiochus then marched across Media with his army, proving to the rebel province that the King and his army were back in control. Diogenes, the governor of Susiana and defender of the citadel of Susa, was subsequently made the governor of Media.[25]

The fall of Hermeias

The episode in Seleucia-on-the-Tigris was another public rebuke to Hermeias, although the minister again lobbied for a royal attack against Egypt. But instead of resuming his campaign against Ptolemy IV, Antiochus marched into Media Atropatene, a former vassal state in the Caucasus whose loyalty to the Seleucid Empire had long since lapsed. Media Atropatene was ruled by a native dynasty descended from

Atropanes, a Persian aristocrat who collaborated with Alexander and his successors. The current dynast was an elderly man named Artabarzanes, and the old King quickly acknowledged Selecuid suzerainty after a brief display of force. Antiochus allowed Artabarzanes to maintain his kingdom with nominal independence in exchange for a symbolic act of submission, an important precedent for future deals with breakaway kingdoms.[26]

Hermeias had now been slighted three times. This made him all the more dangerous, as there was a great risk that he might attempt to eliminate the King in an act of calculated desperation. Antiochus' brother Seleucus III had suffered a similar fate at the hands of a disgruntled minister.

Sensing Hermeias' intentions, Antiochus struck first. Since court protocol generally required the presence of the minister during the King's meetings (hence the source of much of Hermeias' power), Antiochus feigned illness, which allowed him to confer privately with his court physician Apollophanes. The doctor could have also been a leading partner in the conspiracy against Hermeias: Polybius' account has him approach the King rather than vice versa. Either way, Apollophanes likely spoke for an anti-Hermeias faction in the court and was perhaps selected to broach the topic of a nascent conspiracy to the young king.

After his initial conversations with the doctor, Antiochus claimed to be suffering from a serious and prolonged illness. His normal cohort of bodyguards loyal to Hermeias was dismissed, replaced by physicians and attendants loyal to Apollophanes. While in this seclusion, the details of the plot were decided upon. One morning, when Hermeias joined the King on a rehabilitative walk in the cool of the dawn, he was surrounded and stabbed to death.

A gruesome, additional massacre was arranged in Antioch. Hermeias' wife and sons were stoned to death in ceremonial fashion: the elite women of Antioch targeted his wife, while elite boys pelted his sons with stones. Antiochus perhaps wished to portray Hermeias as grasping at royal power for himself, an inappropriate ambition that required the extermination of his entire line. Whatever the motive, it is clear that the murder of Hermeias' family was a typical but hideous act of royal spite.[27]

Polybius portrays Hermeias as the model of an 'evil advisor', with Epigenes cast in the role of the honest but doomed counsellor. However,

Polybius' narrative of this court schism has little nuance: wretched Hermeias is almost entirely evil and driven by ambition, noble Epigenes is the wronged innocent. One potential reason for these characterizations is Polybius' reliance on official Seleucid versions of events, which required an obvious villain to justify so treacherous a murder. The reality was no doubt far more complex.[28] We should doubt that Hermeias was a raging mad counsellor to the core, or that his advice was always bad or ill-timed. The allegation that he advised Antiochus to embark on dangerous wars after the birth of his son was mere gossip, although it may reflect the King's legitimate fear of assassination. Despite these caveats and potential source biases, the basic outlines of the saga of Hermeias and Epigenes reflect common dynamics of court life in a monarchal government. Ambitious men vied for influence with the monarch, and like Hermeias, some were able to monopolize the King's time and attention through manipulation of court protocol. In an age before gentlemanly letters of resignation or timed exits, murder was the only way for the King to rid himself of such a minister. The murder of excessively powerful advisors is a common feature of pre-modern monarchies across geographic areas: the court dynamic between Hermeias and Antiochus III was not terribly different from those between Sejanus and the emperor Tiberius or Thomas Cromwell and King Henry VIII.

The murder of Hermeias marks the point when Antiochus III matured as a ruler. Having discovered the power to control and thwart overreaching ministers when necessary, he would no longer be cowed by ambitious advisors. Also, Antiochus was no longer a teenager, but a twenty-two-year-old man: he had married, fathered a son, and gained his first significant military experience. With the revolt of Molon put down, he was now able to turn his attention to the more traditional dynastic rivalry with Ptolemy IV. Resources also seemed to be in greater abundance: the tax revenues and recruiting grounds of Mesopotamia and western Iran had returned to the empire, and he no longer had to devote tens of thousands of troops to containing the rebels. Yet these advantages and the defeat of Molon were tainted by the subsequent defection of Achaeus, his cousin and *strategos* in Asia Minor. Reunifying the troubled Seleucid Empire would be more difficult than he first envisioned.

The revolt of Achaeus (220 BC)

While Antiochus III was busy waging two wars simultaneously, his older cousin Achaeus, an experienced military commander who had served as viceroy in Asia Minor, rebelled and attacked south while the King was away in the east. Hoping to proceed into Syria through the Cilician Gates and proclaim himself king of the entire Seleucid Empire, Achaeus wished to join the remaining rebels in the north Syrian town of Cyrrhae. In a sense, Achaeus' rebellion was akin to the revolt of Antiochus Hierax and the so-called 'Brothers' War', in which a member of the royal family assigned as principal commander of Asia Minor launched a bid to rule the entire kingdom.

An army mutiny ended Achaeus' grand ambitions. His soldiers refused to advance past Cilicia, the border region between Anatolia and Syria. The soldiers' motives were likely two-fold. First, many of the troops with Greek or Macedonian descent retained residual loyalties to the Seleucid Crown. They would support Achaeus in his more local schemes of personal domination, but they were unwilling to venture into Syria to depose the royal family that had ruled legitimately for almost a century. Second, Achaeus' army likely consisted of many soldiers recruited from Asia Minor. These local contingents may have been willing to support the creation of another breakaway kingdom within their homeland, but were uninterested in initiating a larger Seleucid civil war.

With the army unwilling to follow him, Achaeus turned back. To appease his soldiers and save face as a commander, he allowed the troops to pillage the town of Pisidia, in southern Anatolia. Although the Seleucid Crown was now out of reach, Achaeus consoled himself by assuming the trappings of royal power as a regional king in Asia Minor. He wore the diadem, set up a royal court in Sardis, and minted coins with the appellation AXAIOU BASILEW – 'of Achaeus the King'.[29]

The mutiny in Cilicia eased Antiochus' mind and military position. He learned that Achaeus lacked offensive power, unlike Molon, whose aggressive and unchecked expansion had required immediate royal attention. Thus, even though his rebel cousin was situated dangerously near Syria, Antiochus could return to the unfinished war with Ptolemy IV over Koile Syria. With Achaeus with his unruly troops safely on the defensive beyond the Taurus Mountains, Antiochus had the luxury of delay in dealing with him. In the meantime, he sent outraged correspondence to Achaeus, protesting the usurpation of royal power. Such diplomatic protest might seem strange, given that once Achaeus had assumed the diadem any hope of a peaceful settlement was moot, yet the missive makes more sense when understood as an item for public consumption within the Seleucid court. Antiochus, about to march south against Koile Syria, had to demonstrate that he would not allow such misbehaviour by a former subordinate and kinsman to stand. Confident in this response and in the coming campaign, Antiochus dismissed his troops for the winter at the end of 220 BC with orders to muster in Apamea the following spring.

The capture of Seleucia Pieria (219 BC)

Before beginning the long-delayed campaign into Koile Syria, Antiochus III reignited the war with Ptolemy IV by attacking the city of Seleucia Pieria. Founded as the maritime capital of Seleucus Nicator, Seleucia Pieria had been captured by Ptolemy III during the Laodicean War (246–241) and held by a Ptolemaic garrison ever since. This Seleucid humiliation gave the Ptolemies control of the mouth of the Orontes River and deprived the dynasty of a major Mediterranean port.

It seems that Antiochus had initially planned to leave Seleucia Pieria in Ptolemaic hands, yet reconsidered after an impassioned plea from his newly empowered physician, Apollophanes. Apollophanes had private reasons for advocating an attack: he himself was from Seleucia Pieria, and had been living as an exile ever since the Ptolemaic capture of the town. The council of friends endorsed the physician's opinion, and so the attack on Koile Syria proper was briefly postponed so that Seleucia Pieria might be reclaimed.

Theodotus Hemiolios, evidently rehabilitated after his humiliating retreat before Molon, led a small force to block the northern pass of the Biqua valley in order to prevent potential Ptolemaic reinforcements from coming north to relieve the besieged city.

Before the assault was launched, Antiochus made every attempt to try to bribe the garrison into surrender. Sieges were expensive and often frustrating enterprises; subversion was the most effective way of reducing a walled population. The commander of the Ptolemaic garrison, Leontius, refused these Seleucid attempts, but his lieutenants proved more vulnerable. A secret deal was cut: as long as Antiochus could capture the suburb of the city and its attached port, the corrupted officers would use this setback to pressure Leontius to surrender. Diognetus and Ardys spearheaded the main assault: Diognetus was the Seleucid admiral who escorted princess Laodice from Pontus, and Ardys had recently earned his spurs commanding a cavalry wing in the battle against Molon.[30] Since most of the city was surrounded by steep, difficult terrain, the only plausible way to attack was from the sea. Diognetus' ships landed an amphibious force to seize the port, while Ardys secured the suburb. When these fell, the Ptolemaic officers did as promised, using the calamity to urge their commander to surrender the entire garrison.

With Seleucia Pieria captured, Antiochus made generous and unusual dispositions for the population. While civilians captured in a siege were normally sold into slavery as spoils of war, Antiochus III proclaimed that all free persons in the city, some 6000 inhabitants, would remain free and maintain their property. After all, many citizens were descendants of the original Seleucid settlers and had simply traded masters during the Third Syrian War. Antiochus also made arrangements for the return of those exiled by the Ptolemaic regime and the restoration of their property.[31]

The defection of Theodotus the Aetolian

While Polybius reports that Antiochus had previously decided to ignore Achaeus' revolt in favour of renewing the war with Ptolemy IV, it seems that he changed his mind, for Polybius later states that preparations were underway to confront Achaeus in Asia Minor.[32] While making these preparations, however, an extraordinary letter was brought to his attention, written by Theodotus the Aetolian, a Ptolemaic mercenary general and marshal (*tetagmenos*) entrusted with organizing the defence of the entire region. Theodotus had loyally served the Ptolomies, but had recently fallen out of favour, perhaps for his open condemnation of Ptolemy IV's excessive and debauched lifestyle. After successfully repelling the young Antiochus two years before, Theodotus was recalled to the Ptolemaic court and now felt he was in great danger of being assassinated by his political enemies. Although restored to his command in Koile Syria, Theodotus no longer trusted Ptolemy and his ministers and decided to defect to Antiochus.[33] Even before his letter reached the stunned Seleucid king, Theodotus raised the banner of rebellion by seizing the city Ptolemais in the Biqua valley and the Phoenician city of Tyre on the coast. After these initial acts of disloyalty, Theodotus immediately came under attack by Nicolaus, another Ptolemaic general.

Upon receipt of this fortunate letter and notice of the response by Nicolaus, Antiochus immediately cancelled his operations against Achaeus. Leaving behind phalangites to attack the positions held by the Ptolemies, the King took a force of light infantry and rushed into the Biqua Valley. Nicolaus withdrew, and Theodotus joined Antiochus' force. Together they now had control of the Biqua Valley and Tyre, although Ptolemiac mercenaries still controlled the northern Phoenician coast. At Tyre, Antiochus captured a squadron of the Ptolemaic fleet, some forty ships, which then joined the small Mediterranean fleet commanded by Diognetus.

Ptolemy IV was shocked by the rapid pace of Antiochus' campaign into Koile Syria. Rather than advance to challenge him, he ordered the irrigation canals in the Nile Delta flooded to halt any the Seleucids from entering Egypt itself. While Antiochus had hopes of marching to Pelusium and forcing a quick end to the war, he was soon occupied with the many tasks of managing the newly won territory, which included enforcing the submission and winning the loyalty of many small communities.

Unable to stop the Seleucid advance, Ptolemy's ministers offered a truce at the end of the campaign season in 219. Antiochus accepted this arrangement, hoping a negotiated settlement would give him a secure claim to the entirety of the region.[34]

Chapter Three

Seleucid Institutions

The Seleucid army

The most important royal institution was the Seleucid army; without it, the Seleucid Empire would simply cease to exist.[1] Seleucid soldiers and sailors provided the coercive force that was necessary, if not always sufficient, to hold the realm together. The Seleucid army consisted of four main components: 1) citizen soldiers, drawn from the cities of the Empire, 2) a professional cadre of elite infantry and cavalry units, 3) native levies of subject peoples and 4) mercenaries hired from across the Mediterranean.

The citizen phalanx

The core of the Seleucid army was the Macedonian-style phalanx: a dense and deep formation of heavy infantry. The phalangite's primary armament was an enormous pike called a *sarissa*, approximately 21 feet (6.3m) long.[2] A phalangite also carried a round shield, between 2 to 2½ feet (.66–.75m) in diameter, smaller than the shield carried by Classical Greek hoplites, which allowed him to grasp his *sarissa* with both hands.[3] As a secondary weapon he wore a short-sword (*xiphos*) or a small slashing machete called a *machaira*. The phalangite's armour varied, but non-metallic armour made of laminated linen (*kotthybos/linothorax*) seems to have predominated.[4] Since phalangites supplied their own equipment, there would have been reasonable variation, and metal cuirasses were likely also in use.

Phalangites fought in close formation, with each man occupying nearly three feet when on the offensive and closing tighter on the defensive in order to form a wall of interlocked shields (*synaspismos*). A phalanx was usually sixteen men deep, although it was common to make the formation even deeper (doubling to thirty-two) to provide extra defensive mass. Men in the front five ranks projected their pikes outward, although only the first few ranks would have a reasonably clear line of sight in front of them. Men in the rear would angle their pikes forward to provide a screen against arrows, javelins, and other projectiles raining down on the formation. The overall manoeuvrability of the phalanx was limited by these close-order intervals of the soldiers and the unwieldy nature of the lengthy *sarissa*. [5]

Phalangites were recruited primarily from a class of military settlers who were descendents of Macedonian soldiers of Alexander the Great or the mercenaries of the *diadochoi*. Discharged veterans received a plot of land (*kleros*), which obligated them to serve as either Macedonian-style infantrymen or cavalrymen. Recipients of such land grants were most commonly referred to as *katoikoi*. While most veterans with *kleroi* were of Greek or Macedonian descent, other ethnicities could also obtain land grants, most notably 2000 Jewish military settlers granted land in Phrygia by Antiochus III in the 200s. [6]

The citizen phalanx was drawn largely from the major cities of the Seleucid Empire. [7] Such recruitment was based on inheritable military obligation tied to land grants or through deeply rooted traditional patterns of military service. (The initial population of Greco-Macedonian settlers in cities founded by Seleucids may have been used to determine the rate of required conscription.) For example, Seleucus I had settled between 4000 and 6000 military settlers in each of the four cities of the tetrapolis, and the best attested Seleucid urban muster, from the city of Cyrrhus, produced a brigade of 6000 soldiers. Thus, from the urban centres in Syria and Mesopotamia (the tetrapoleis plus Seleucia on the Tigris and Cyrrhus), Antiochus could draw on 20–30,000 settlers with military obligations. This figure corresponds with the attested field strength of the Seleucid heavy phalanx, usually between 16,000 and 20,000 men. [8] It is important to remember that the men of the Seleucid phalanx were not professional soldiers, but citizen soldiers mobilized in times of military crisis, though some might serve longer stints during protracted periods of warfare.

Native levies

In addition to the 'Macedonian' heavy infantry, the bulk of the Seleucid army consisted of lightly armed troops, most of whom wore native arms and armour. Native archers, slingers, and skirmishers proved a tremendous addition to the heavy and relatively immobile phalanx, but they also posed problems of command and control. It proved difficult to coordinate the actions of many different contingents, each with their own language, tactics, and native aristocrat commanders. This need to incorporate large numbers of non–Hellenistic light troops may have led to some unfortunate developments in Seleucid tactics, including excessive depth of troop formations and an over-reliance on pre-established battle plans. Nonetheless, the sheer numbers provided by native light troops were eminently valuable for garrison operations, foraging, securing and extending supply lines, and general skirmishing.

Native equestrian traditions were critical to the recruitment of Seleucid cavalry. The vast Iranian plateau in particular supplied some of the best cavalry in the ancient world, and cavalry contingents from Persia, Media, and other parts of Iran are well attested. An important military development with potential Persian roots was the introduction of *cataphractoi*, a new type of heavy cavalry.[9]

Traditionally Mediterranean cavalry rode and fought lightly armed and armoured. Horsemen were admired for their agility in the saddle and valued for their manoeuvrability, not the shock of their charges. While light Mediterranean cavalry was highly manoeuvrable, it lacked the ability to clash directly with heavily armed massed infantry. Instead, they manoeuvred at the flanks and harassed formations with javelins, butchering fugitives in the pursuit.

Unfortunately, there is no good evidence on the exact nature of cataphracts during the Selecucid period. We do know that by the Roman period, the term 'cataphract' described heavy Iranian cavalry clad head to toe in scale armour, with a similarly armoured horse. These 'boiler boys' (*clibanarii*) were designed to shock. Their heavy armour gave them confidence to plunge their horses into the iron bristle of a heavy infantry formation, a manoeuvre that would have been suicidal for a lightly armoured cavalryman. We do not know if the Seleucid *cataphracti* were identical to the Parthian and Persian cataphracts attested during the Roman Empire or the late Roman units that mimicked them. However, there is reason to speculate that Seleucid cataphracts were far more heavily armed and armoured than most traditional Mediterranean cavalrymen, as they successfully defeated the Roman legionary infantry at the Battle of Magnesia.

The professional cadre: Silver Shields and royal cavalry

In addition to the standard phalanx, Seleucid kings also maintained a special unit of heavy infantry, the 'Silver Shields' (*argyaspides*). The Silver Shields had their origins in a special brigade of Hypaspists formed by Alexander the Great. Following Alexander's death, diadoch generals granted favoured brigades of soldiers special status by allowing them to gild their shields with various metals: gold, silver and bronze shields are attested in the sources.[10] By the reign of Antiochus, the Silver Shields were a professional brigade, with an attested strength of 10,000.[11] This number would also correspond to the 10,000 'Immortals', the full-time infantry brigade that accompanied the Persian king, whose strength was maintained at 10,000, and may represent an administrative survival from the Achaemenid military tradition.[12]

Seleucid kings maintained two professional cavalry regiments of 1000 men apiece. The first was known as the *hetaitroi* or 'companions' (sometimes referred to as *ile basilike*, or 'the king's company'). The second elite cavalry regiment was called the *agema*. Both of these units were composed of professional soldiers recruited from across the empire, and were thus polyethnic. The *agema* was said to be men primarily of 'Medes and a mixture of many peoples drawn from many regions', while the *hetairoi* were drawn from ' Syrians, mingled with Phrygians and Lydians.'[13] Professor Bar Kochba has hypothesized that these cavalrymen were drawn from the sons of military settlers living in Media, Syria, Phrygia and Lydia, but there is no proof of this assertion. Like the Roman emperor with a Germanic bodyguard, the Seleucid king may have preferred to draw his closest ranks from outside peoples, whose loyalty was ensured by their outsider status and subsequent dependence on the king's favour and goodwill for their position in society.

Mercenaries

Seleucid kings also employed mercenaries to supplement the field armies during major campaigns. Mercenaries remained the minority of

Seleucid soldiers, and the overall characterization of Hellenistic armies as mercenary hordes is incorrect. Mercenaries seldom comprised more than 20 per cent of any large army fielded by Antiochus III. The most prominent mercenaries were the ferocious Galatians, who consistently provided both light infantry and cavalry contingents to the Seleucid army; while the most notorious were perhaps the Cretans. Known for their skill in archery, Cretans were widely sought as specialist troops, although they could also fight as conventional light infantry. Other sources of mercenaries included the nomadic Dahae (a tribal group of the Eurasian steppes), Thracians from Europe, and, of course, Greeks. Greek mercenaries were particularly valuable, as they could integrate tactically and linguistically with the main phalanx. Mercenary officers were heavily employed throughout the Seleucid army and even commanded non-mercenary units. Nor were all mercenaries opportunistic killers; many spent long careers in the service of a particular power. Rewarded afterwards with a land grant, many saw mercenary service as a form of honourable immigration.

Elephants and chariots
Elephants were considered a crucial military asset. Antiochus III's herd peaked at 150 beasts, making it the largest in the world at that time (Carthage possessed perhaps 80 war-elephants in 202 BC). In this respect Seleucid kings benefited from the shared border with India. During the third century BC, two types of elephants were in use, the Indian elephant and the now extinct North African forest elephant (*Loxodonta africana pharaoensis*). The largest and most aggressive species of elephant, the African bush elephant (*Loxodonta africana*), was not used in Ancient Mediterranean warfare.[14]

Significantly larger than the North African forest elephant, the Indian elephant (*Elphas maximus indicus*) was considered superior for war purposes. Furthermore, an elephant was worthless without a specially trained mahout, and the best mahouts also came from India. Antiochus III therefore enjoyed the best elephants and the best elephant drivers.[15]

The rival Ptolemies were not so lucky in their access to the pachyderms. Ptolemy II had undertaken epic provisions to secure African bush elephants in the Sudan, establishing the garrison town of Ptolemais 'of the Elephant Hunts' and even digging a canal to transport the captured beasts. From these significant efforts, it is clear that Ptolemy II considered it vital to match the Seleucid war-herd. While some moderns have doubted the efficacy of war-elephants, ancient evidence suggests that they could prove a terrible and effective force on the battlefield. Trampling infantry and scattering cavalry, they could only be countered by heavy infantry formations with the highest levels of discipline and poise. The physical damage they inflicted was exceeded only by their psychological impact, as the size and appearance of such animals intimidated men unfamiliar with the animal. The smell of elephants was even believed to frighten cavalry horses. Despite these advantages, the deployment of elephants on the battlefield was problematic, as they could badly disrupt friendly formations if spooked.

A less-useful weapon in the Seleucid arsenal was the scythed chariot, a weapon employed by the Persians for several centuries and used in a failed charge against Alexander at Guagamela.[16] Molon used them with equal lack of effect against Antiochus. While these contraptions looked ferocious, and no doubt gave kings extravagant visions of easily mowing through enemy formations, they were difficult to employ effectively even on relatively level ground. Nonetheless, scythed chariots remained part of the Seleucid arsenal and were deployed against the Romans at the battle of Magnesia with little success. Their continued existence must be attributed almost entirely to their fearsome appearance.

The court of Antiochus III

Like any modern executive, the Seleucid king was obliged to delegate power in order to manage his kingdom.[17] Unfortunately, individuals entrusted with this power could prove dangerous to the king if not carefully managed. In many court settings, kings disperse social favours with the hope that competition for these will forge a culture of loyalty and cooperation among otherwise ambitious and aggressive noblemen.

It is important to note that the term 'court', a word derived from the European medieval and early modern experience, did not have a direct equivalent in Greek. Rather, Hellenistic courtiers described themselves using terms of friendship or kinship with the king. In the early

Macedonian court in the fourth century BC, high-ranking noblemen who enjoyed the king's favour were known as *hetairoi*, 'companions', a term that emphasized their personal relationship to the king and the rough equality they shared with the monarch, drinking, hunting, and fighting by his side.

Philip II radically altered the court culture in Macedonia, modelling it upon more absolutist Persian lines. He forced powerful noblemen to send their sons to serve as 'royal boys' (*bailikoi paides*), effectively holding them hostage in his court and indoctrinating them into the mindset of royal service as playmates and friends of the heir apparent.

The Macedonian royal page system survived in the Seleucid court, and we find former *basilikoi paides* holding important commands: Myiskos, for example, who later commanded a contingent of war elephants for Antiochus at the Battle of Raphia.[18] Other men are referred to as 'foster brothers' (*syntrophoi* – literally 'fellow nursling') of the king, pages raised alongside the young prince.

There was no established empire-wide aristocracy, although there were many local influential notables. Men earned high position in the king's court not through lineage but by winning the king's personal favour: the ability to drink, dance, and engage in witty conversation could lead to important political postings. Heavy drinking and banqueting was important in both the Macedonian and Persian court traditions. Persians were reported to consider courses of action at least twice: once sober and again drunk, while Alexander's binges may have substantially shortened his life.[19] According to the Roman author Athenaeus (c 200 AD?), whose literary cast of 'clever diners' (*deipnosophistai*) preserves scenes of courtly life, Antiochus drank heavily at banquets and danced wearing his armour and weapons, encouraging his entourage to do likewise. Dancing with weapons and armour echoed a very old Macedonian court custom called the *telesias,* attested as far back as the mid-fourth century BC.[20] In one instance, the poet Hegesianax reportedly declined the King's insistence to join the dance, but had a witty comment at the ready: 'Shall I dance badly, O king, or would you rather have me recite my poems well?' According to the story, Antiochus ordered an impromptu recitation, and was so pleased with the poem that he promoted Hegesianax to the rank of 'friend' (*philos*).[21]And as such a 'friend', he was subsequently given important diplomatic assignments, including missions to the Romans in 196 and 193 BC.[22]

Notable in this episode is Antiochus' leadership role, even in fun and feasting. It is he who decides that his 'friends' will dance, and he subsequently takes the lead in dancing himself. He is the one who calls out courtiers such as Hegesianax who decline to participate in the revels, and he alone judges the quality of the poetry recital. The king is not an equal in drinking and dancing but rather remains fully in charge: elites at the party are socially honoured or humiliated as they compete for his attention and approval.[23]

The social environment of the court maintained the fiction that courtiers were the friends or even relatives of the king. The senior soldier Zeuxis, it seems, enjoyed the title of 'father', and later Seleucid kings would refer to close advisors as 'brother'.[24] In 193, the general Minnio is described by Livy as the *princeps amicorum*.[25] This may be the Latinization of the Greek 'first friend' (*protos philos*), a title later attested in the book of Maccabees.[26] Other 'friends' enjoyed specific titles based on their occupation: one important courtier was the chamberlain who controlled the king's private bedroom. Nicanor was one such chamberlain (*koites*), whom Antiochus later appointed to the lucrative position of chief-priest of Asia Minor.

'Friends' in court also enjoyed special privileges, such as the wearing of purple garments, access to the royal stables, and physical proximity to the king and his family. One story even reports that Seleucus I granted a favoured courtier the privilege of dropping by while he was having sex with his wife.[27] Yet what the king could give, he could also easily take away. Antiochus III's murder of Hermeias and his family is perhaps the most dramatic example of royal retribution against a fallen and disgraced courtier.

A select group of friends constituted the king's council, the *boule* or *synedrion*, and here the king sought frank advice on various issues. The *boule* was likely relatively informal in its membership requirements and was based on the king's preference of advisors. For example, Apollophanes the physician seems to have joined after demonstrating his loyalty during the Hermeias affair, despite lacking other military or administrative experience. Indeed, military talent did not on its own ensure a coveted spot: Hannibal Barca would later be relegated to the outer circle of the court due to Antiochus' suspicion of his motives.

Not all titles were ceremonial indications of friendship or kinship. Some men within the Seleucid court held more generally defined offices. Chief among these was the *epi ton pragamaton*, the 'man of affairs,' or 'prime minister.' The *epi ton pragmaton* was a powerful figure, although his powers and duties were never entirely specified, and could therefore be abused or manipulated. Other titles include the *epi ton prosodon*, the 'finance minister', and the *epistolographos*, or royal secretary. Junior positions in the court include an archivist (*bibliophylax*) and the master of the elephants (*elephantarchos*).[28]

It comes as no surprise that doctors were also prominent players in the Seleucid court. We have already met Apollophanes, the 'chief doctor' (*archiatros*). Hailing from the island of Cos, the homeland of Hippocrates, Apollophanes was also the author of a treatise on cures for poisons, a field of research that likely made him even more useful in court.[29]

Finally, the court contained what Greeks dubbed 'parasites', men who flattered the wealthy and powerful in exchange for a dinner invitation. We know of several parasites in the Seleucid court, although none for the court of Antiochus III: Sostratus during the time of Antiochus I and Apollonios during the reign of Antiochus VIII.[30] Most of these men simply had the misfortune of being at the bottom of the court hierarchy.[31] Ironically, the most notorious parasites such as Sostratus and Apollonios were probably closer to real friendship with the king than most of his official *philoi*, as they provided him with companionship and good cheer untainted by manoeuvres for position and power.

In terms of the court's physical location, the king moved frequently, maintaining a peripatetic lifestyle that took him through multiple palaces in major cities throughout the empire. Unfortunately, only limited archaeological work has been done on Seleucid royal palaces, but we know that these were massive buildings with monumental architecture in the Greek style. Like traditional Macedonian palaces, a Seleucid royal palace was constructed around a large central courtyard surrounded by a series of smaller dining rooms. They also incorporated Persian elements, most notably the *paradision*, an expansive and luxurious park. The most impressive 'paradise' was likely located at the Seleucid court at Daphne, nourished by natural springs and spacious enough to accommodate enormous parades and feasts of more than 9000 people.[32] Paradise parks contained manicured orchards, opulent gardens and well-stocked hunting grounds,[33] following a long Near Eastern tradition of parks as both places of royal pleasure where groomed gardens and slaughtered animals symbolized the king's domination over nature. Palace complexes were large, imposing, and often removed from the general city: the palace at Antioch was located on an island in the Orontes river, and occupied over 25 hectares of land.[34]

The maintenance of these palaces and of a court that required such feasting and entertainment was tremendously expensive. Theopompus, writing in the fourth century, claimed that the Persian king spent between twenty and thirty silver talents a day maintaining his court.[35] Much of this went to support the Persian army, but G.G. Aphergis estimates that Seleucid kings still spent between 2000 and 3000 silver talents supporting the luxurious lifestyle of the king and his court.[36]

The arts and culture under Antiochus III

The Seleucids are generally not remembered for great patronage of Hellenic culture. The Ptolemies sponsored the Museion and Library in Alexandria, which became a great centre of scholarship and literary production in the ancient world.[37] The Attalids to the north also established a vast library, and commissioned some of the most famous pieces of Hellenistic art: the Dying Gaul series and the reliefs of the great altar at Pergamon.

While patronage of art, literature, and other displays of culture was not a top priority for the Seleucids, there is evidence that Antiochus tried to compete culturally with his rivals in Alexandria in Pergamon. Antiochus patronized poets in particular: the prominent role of the court poet and historian Hegesianax has already been mentioned, and he also hired a Greek poet named Euphorion to head the public library in Antioch.[38] The poet and historian Mnesiptolemos was active in the court of Antiochus III, so much so that Athenaeus claims that his presence 'was especially prominent'.[39] This is no doubt an exaggeration, or possibly an echo of the grumblings of rival courtiers, but it shows that men of letters claimed high standing in the Seleucid court as well as in Alexandria. Mnesiptolemos produced his histories in verse, including a poem about Seleucus II quaffing a potent draught of mead. Mnesiptolemos' son Seleucus, the author of 'cheerful songs', was also a courtly poet. Athenaeus preserves a fragment of his work that praises pederasty in a military context:

> Better to love the boys than take a wife
> A boy lends a hand in times of strife.[40]

The royal economy

Like most other states in the ancient world, the economy of the Seleucid Empire was rooted in agriculture. More than 90 per cent of the population was devoted to farming or pastoralism. Most small farmers strove for self-sufficiency, but in reality no family or community could hope to achieve this. Variations in climate, soil, and weather patterns meant that the chance of local crop failures was high in any one area, and the grim reality of starvation enforced connectivity and cooperation; people had to trade and redistribute food to compensate for regional shortages. There was a brisk if low-level trade in basic foodstuffs, yet agricultural production focused on foods that were easy to store and redistribute: grain, wine, figs, and olive oil.[41] The most important agricultural regions of the empire were Mesopotamia, the Amuk plain along the Orontes River, and following the capture of Koile Syria, the Gaza strip. Antiochus' campaigns in Asia Minor primarily focused on the rich agricultural lands in that region.

While perhaps less than 10 per cent of the population resided in cities, these were critical focal points of consumption, redistribution and craft production, although urban economies could also suffer from inefficient markets and local economic dislocation. The urban economy was driven in part by a phenomenon known as *euergetism*, or benefaction. Examples of *euergetism* might involve petty elites subsidizing grain and contributing to public works for a particular city. The most important benefactor was the king himself, with grants to individuals, cities, and peoples. Royal family members also engaged in the practice. For example, in 196 BC Antiochus' queen Laodice gifted the city of Iasus with an annual gift of

45 tons of grain. The grain was to be sold at a subsidized price, and the town authorities were to utilize the cash proceeds to provide dowries for local girls.[42] Such benefactions helped towns suffering from economic problems, and validated royal authority.

Seleucid kings generated most of their revenues through the control of agricultural land. In theory, Seleucus I and his successors claimed ownership of all the land under his control as 'spear-won'. Despite such rhetoric, much of the king's territory was either administratively controlled by tributary cities, subject peoples (*ethne*), or temples. Land not granted to communities or individuals was then directly administered as the kings' personal property. A major form of royal benefaction was the granting of land, parcelled out as *kleroi* to veterans and others.

As discussed above, the recipients of *kleroi* were obliged to pay rent and provide military service in exchange for their land. *Kleroi* could take the form of vast seigniorial estates, complete with villages of serfs (*laoi*) who owed cash payments to the estate owner. In the third century BC, for example, a man named Mnesimachos was granted the right to exploit lands belonging to the Temple of Artemis, provided he paid tax to both temple and king. Estate holders and *kleroi* helped collect taxes from villages under their control, and forwarded these revenues to royal officials.[43]

The king also established local monopolies over important salt flats and created royal forests to control timber resources, his 'private domain'(*idios logos*). Although we do not have a clear picture of the Seleucid tax system, excises were extensive and varied, consisting of land taxes, guild taxes, taxes on cattle, poll taxes, road tolls, and excise taxes.[44] Our best depiction of the procedures of tax collection comes from Judea in the Book of Maccabees. Here, the hard work of tax collection was farmed out to the High Priests, who extracted the revenue from their people and then paid a lump sum of 300 silver talents to the Seleucid treasury. The Judean arrangement is an example of a relatively common type of delegation that flowed to local officials and even to native leaders.

No ancient source lists the exact revenues of the Seleucid king. According to Herodotus (3.90–96), Persian kings collected around 9000 (Attic) talents from the region controlled by Antiochus III, although significant economic development in Syria and Mesopotamia would have increased the revenues of these regions since the time of Darius

I. Antigonus One-Eyed, whose reign in the 300s roughly overlapped that of Antiochus III, collected revenues of 11,000 talents.[45] From both these textual references, there is reason to think that the minimum royal revenues of Antiochus consisted of approximately 10,000 talents, although Aphergis has estimated that they might have been close to double this.

While Antiochus enjoyed revenues of 10–20,000 talents, he also had enormous expenses. An active army of 100,000 soldiers could cost over 6000 talents per year.[46] Benefactions to cities, often through tax breaks, but also in the form of gifts of food or oil, dowries for the daughters of the local elite, and monumental building projects cost the king a great deal of money, even if the exact amount is impossible to reconstruct. Maintenance of the court was another large if poorly attested expense, as the king was expected to feed and entertain his friends and companions in high style, and also to lavish gifts and money upon favourites. Thus, while the king was rich, he was also continually strapped for cash.

The Seleucid king had none of the sophisticated financial mechanisms available to modern governments. He did not issue government bonds or engage in deficit spending. There was no central bank. Private banks existed, but in very rudimentary form and not on a scale to assist state finance. In some cases, wealthy individuals might offer the state private loans for particular causes or initiatives: Hermeias loaned Antiochus cash to fund his army in 219 BC.

As in most ancient economies, war loot played a critical role in Seleucid finances. Success or failure in war reinforced itself through a vicious cycle: military success provided large sums of cash, which could be used to cover the immense cost of waging war (including the expense of hiring thousands of mercenaries) and fund subsequent campaigns. Defeat in battle left the loser saddled with tremendous debt and looted cities and resources. If not quickly reversed by energetic leadership and compensating victories elsewhere, a serious military setback could lead to long-term state decline.[47]

Seleucid religions and the royal cult

The Selecucid Empire was characterized by sweeping cultural and religious diversity. The official attitude of the Seleucids toward this religious variation swung between two poles: tolerance on one side to full-blown participation in native religious rituals on the other. Seleucus I, for example, patronized the temple of Atargatis, a native goddess whose cult centred on Bambyke in Northern Syria,[48] and Antiochus I rebuilt the temple to Nabu in Borsippa, a suburb of Babylon, claiming to shape the bricks with his own hands.[49]

The Seleucid policy of toleration is best illustrated by Antiochus III's policy toward the Jews, as he recognized the power of the Jewish priestly elite to enforce religious taboos with necessary force. After his capture of Jerusalem, he also would directly subsidize religious rituals performed at the Temple.

Yet royal toleration had its limits: at the end of the day, Seleucid kings needed cash to pay their armies. Native temples doubled as repositories of dedicatory treasures, and these stockpiles of wealth often proved irresistible. Seleucus I despoiled temples in Ecbatana and Babylon to help finance his campaigns against Antigonus One-Eyed, and Antiochus III would also find the riches locked within native temples a temptation too difficult to resist.[50]

With respect to the traditional Greek pantheon, Apollo stood out as a Seleucid favourite. Seleucus I Nicator claimed that he was, in fact, the natural son of Apollo, who had stamped him with an anchor birthmark as a sign of divine parentage.[51] In many ways, this story mimicked earlier legends that claimed Alexander the Great was the natural son of Zeus Ammon.

Antiochus I assiduously patronized the temple of Apollo at Miletus, and the Seleucids turned the springs of Daphne near Antioch into a major shrine of Apollo and his sister Artemis.[52] The native Babylonian deity Nabu, a frequent recipient of royal patronage, was syncretised with Apollo: the polytheistic Seleucids were capable of interactions with nearly all the gods they came across.[53] Antiochus III sacrificed to Athena at Ilium prior to his invasion of Europe, and his son Antiochus IV would later claim a special relationship with Zeus Olympios, helping to finance construction of the temple of Zeus in Athens.[54]

In addition to Greek and native deities, Seleucid kings were themselves gods. Greeks had been honouring powerful persons as gods since the Classical era, most notably the Spartan admiral Lysander who received altars and sacrifices following a dramatic victory in the Peloponnesian War.[55] Alexander the Great claimed divine honours for his companion Haephestion, and toward the end of his life seems to have demanded such a status for himself.[56] In the age of the successors, successful warlords were the objects of voluntary worship by local communities: Antigonus One-Eyed and Demetrius Poliorcetes were welcomed as gods in Athens.[57] As warlords transitioned into kings, many Greek cities bestowed them with divine honours, establishing cults for deceased kings as well as living monarchs and their families. These cults were for the most part voluntary and were initiated by the civic leadership of individual *poleis*.

Greeks active in the royal cult did not necessarily believe that the kings they honoured with libation and sacrifice were equivalent to the Olympian gods. Rather, such divine honours acknowledged the kings' exceptional worldly power, their ability to mete out punishment and bestow material favours: tasks far more present and real, it seemed at times, than the immortal gods ever were.

A major change in the Seleucid royal cult took place under Antiochus III, who established the royal cult as an imperial institution, chiefly regulating its quality and content, and personally appointing high priests to oversee the cult at the satrapal level. In 193 BC, for example, Antiochus stated that his wife Laodice was to be honoured as a goddess, and he sent instructions throughout the empire to this effect.[58]

Chapter Four

The Battle of Raphia

Ptolemaic preparations

At the end of the campaign season of 219, Antiochus accepted the truce offer from Ptolemy IV. Leaving behind a strong garrison in Koile Syria under Theodotus the Aetolian, he retired to Seleucia Pieria with the remainder of his army. He dismissed his troops to winter quarters, sending many of his military settlers back to their homes in Syrian tetrapolis, and dispatched envoys to Sosibus, who was then stationed in Memphis, the old capital of the pharaohs. Seleucid envoys returned claiming a friendly reception, giving Antiochus further confidence that a negotiated settlement was at hand.

Yet Sosibus was in Memphis for a reason: he did not want Seleucid envoys to see what was happening in the capital city of Alexandria. Sosibus and Agathocles had decided on a bold course of action: they would raise a new, massive army and seek a final showdown over Koile Syria. To this end, they enlisted a host of mercenary generals: Echecrates of Thessaly, Phoxidas of Melita, Eurylochos of Magnesia and Socrates the Boeotian. All these men had a long history of service with the Macedonian army.

The Ptolemaic army, like its Seleucid counterpart, was based around a phalanx manned by the descendents of Greco–Macedonian military settlers. Some 25,000 were mustered from across Egypt, an impressive levy, but one that fell somewhat short of the 20,000 strong phalanx and 10,000 Silver Shields then deployed by Antiochus.[1]

Sosibus and his aides therefore scrambled to bulk up the Ptolemaic army with mercenary hires. Some 8000 Greek mercenaries were trained to fight as heavy phalangite infantry, along with a squadron of Greek mercenary horsemen. Some 3000 Cretans were hired to provide the light infantry, and they were reinforced by another 1000 'neo-Cretans' who fought with Cretan equipment and tactics.[2] A total of 2000 Thracians were recruited from abroad, and these joined a brigade of 4000 Thracian military settlers, descendants of previous mercenary hires rewarded with land grants.

The audacious Ptolemaic build-up required more than mercenary hires. Indeed, 218/17 BC was a difficult year to increase military strength, as the mercenary labour market was saturated with demand. To the north, Macedon and its Achaean allies were at war with the Aetolian League. Rome and Carthage had just renewed their epic hostilities in the west. While the mercenary market in the Mediterranean was bifurcated between east and west, Carthage's demand for soldiers to fill her enormous armies likely further reduced the mercenaries available to Ptolemy IV.

Sosibus and his fellow ministers therefore undertook an unprecedented step: they recruited and trained 20,000 native Egyptians to fight as heavy infantry. Previously, the Ptolemies did not employ native Egyptians in their armies, aside from a small internal police force.[3] This was a major difference between the Ptolemaic and Seleucid regimes: the Seleucids had always been willing to deploy armed subjects in large native contingents in order to exploit the manpower of their more warlike peoples. Traditionally, however, the Ptolemies had exploited their Egyptian subjects economically, maintaining them as heavily taxed and unarmed peasants in order to fund armies manned by Graeco–Macedonian settlers and Greek mercenaries.

In addition to the Egyptians, another 3000 Libyans from Ptolemy's western realm were trained as heavy phalangites, and 2300 Libyans and Egyptians were recruited into the cavalry. The total Ptolemaic force came to 70,000 infantry and 5000 cavalry, a triumph of diplomatic obfuscation and hasty military mobilization.[4]

While the green Ptolemaic army drilled in Alexandria, wearisome peace talks were taking place in Seleucia Pieria. When the four-month truce expired in the spring of 218 BC, it became apparent that Ptolemy IV and Sosibus were not interested in negotiation but were simply buying time. Antiochus collected his royal army of 58,000 men and proceeded to hook around the Lebanon mountains and attack up the Phoenician coast, still defended by the trustworthy Ptolemaic general Nicolaus the Aetolian.

Nicolaus based his defence of the Phoenician seaboard on the Porphyrion pass, where the Lebanon mountains and the coastline formed a natural chokepoint, aiming to prevent Antiochus from pivoting north out of the Biqua Valley up the coast toward the Phoenician city-state of Sidon.

Antiochus prepared a three-pronged assault of this pass, with three specially formed battalions of light troops. One force would attack the pass directly and pin the blockading force. Another unit would attempt to infiltrate through the Lebanon mountains, as a distraction to the defenders in the pass. The main effort, led by Theodotus the Aetolian, would storm the slope just above the pass, and then turn the Ptolemaic blocking position. The plan worked perfectly. Antiochus' men killed 2000 of the defenders and captured 2000 more. One of the prisoners was likely Nicolaus the Aetolian himself, for by the next time we hear of him he is fighting as a mercenary general in Seleucid service. Antiochus' forces quickly surged north, where he detached units to capture Sidon. The King, however, turned south and cut across the Jordan River Valley to target Ptolemaic outposts on the Arabian frontier. More Ptolemaic officers soon defected, including the governor (*hyparchos*) Keraias and the Thessalian mercenary captain Hippolochus, who brought with him a contingent of 400 cavalrymen. Antiochus rewarded both defectors lavishly, hoping to turn more Ptolemaic commanders.[5]

These military successes led to a further diplomatic victory. Various Arab tribes living in the arid lands at the edge of Ptolemaic territory sensed the tide shifting in favour of the Seleucids and came over to Antiochus in quick succession. His new allies provided roughly 10,000 light infantry to supplement his forces.[6]

Antiochus' blitz during 218 BC had been extraordinarily successful. He occupied virtually the entirety of Koile Syria and chased Ptolemy's forces to the border of Egypt. Now he was on the defensive, fighting more to cement his territorial gains than to obtain further conquests: there is no evidence that he wished to conquer the whole of Egypt. As the fighting season ended, Antiochus put his army into winter quarters.

The Battle of Raphia

In the early spring of 217 BC, the King learned that Ptolemy IV was finally marching from Alexandria with an army of 70,000 infantry and

5000 cavalry, the impressive new army his advisors had worked for over a year to raise and train. Antiochus assembled his forces, 68,000 men with his newfound Arab allies, and moved south to confront the Ptolemaic counterattack. He marched down the Gaza coast, narrowed by coastal highlands near the town of Raphia. (Indeed, modern-day Rafa serves as a border checkpoint between Palestinian Gaza and Egypt.) Here, geography funnelled the two armies into one other and towards a decisive conclusion to the conflict.

Yet as the armies closed, both sides hesitated. The stakes in a set-piece battle were high, and neither had reason to hasten to a confrontation immediately. Antiochus may have hoped Ptolemy might lose his nerve and retreat back to Egypt, ceding the region to him. The two kings were roughly the same age, but Antiochus now had several years of successful campaigning under his belt, while Ptolemy IV was taking to the field for the first time. His troops were inexperienced and newly trained, the enormous Egyptian phalanx of 20,000 men was unproven.

The two armies initially encamped from each other at a distance of two kilometres (ten stades). After several days, Antiochus moved his camp forward to within one kilometre of enemy lines. Both sides lingered across from each other for five days, skirmishing all the while over control of watering holes.

Meanwhile, Theodotus the Aetolian, still nursing a private grudge against the King of Egypt, carried out a daring private mission. In the middle of the night, he entered the Ptolemaic camp, sneaked past the guards, and located the King's tent. Ptolemy IV, however, had taken the precaution of sleeping in a separate tent, and Theodotus merely wounded two men asleep in the royal headquarters and killed the King's hapless personal physician. Foiled in his plot to assassinate the King, he quickly returned to the Seleucid camp.[7]

It is unclear if this brazen assault jolted Ptolemy into action, but shortly afterwards he formed his army for battle. Antiochus immediately followed suit.[8]

Both sides arranged themselves in a relatively conventional fashion. Heavy infantry held the centre of each battleline. Antiochus' heavy units consisted of his phalanx of reservists, 20,000 strong along with his 10,000 strong Silver Shields. These were supplemented by 5000 Greek mercenaries fighting as heavy infantry, commanded by Hipparchus, the Thessalian mercenary who had recently deserted to Antiochus. This gave the King 30,000 heavy infantry altogether. Ptolemy's heavy units were his phalanx of 25,000 military settlers, his phalanx of Egyptian infantry, 20,000 strong, 8000 Greek mercenaries who fought as phalangites, and 3000 Libyan's armed in the Macedonian fashion. This gave Ptolemy 56,000 heavy infantry, an overwhelming advantage over Antiochus in terms of sheer numbers – even if the quality of these hastily trained troops was still to be tested. Nonetheless, Antiochus was forced to face part of the Ptolemaic heavy infantry with light or medium contingents, either native troops or his recently acquired Arab allies, a fact that put him at a distinct disadvantage in the infantry fight.

Yet Antiochus enjoyed a slight edge in cavalry: 6000 horsemen to Ptolemy's 5000. His greatest advantage was undoubtedly his 102 Indian elephants. Sixty elephants on his right wing were commanded by an officer named Philip who Polybius is described as Antiochus' 'foster brother' (*syntrophos*) – presumably a man who had grown with Antiochus while serving as a royal page in the court of Seleucus II. The forty-two elephants on his left wing fell under the command of Myiscus, a former page now graduated into a military command. The presence of both these ex-pages in important commands suggests that Antiochus held full control of his court and could promote favourites to positions of honour and responsibility.

Ptolemy IV only had seventy-three elephants, forty on his left flank and thirty-three on his right. But Ptolemy's elephants were African elephants, smaller and less aggressive than the Indian breed employed by Antiochus.[9] These 'African' elephants were not the species of elephant that today lives in sub-Saharan Africa, and which are decidedly bigger and more aggressive than Indian elephants. Rather, Ptolemy employed a species of now-extinct bush elephant that lived in North Africa, and Antiochus had a distinct edge in both the quantity and aggressiveness of his elephant corps.

The quality of the troops also tilted in Antiochus' favour. His army consisted of battle-hardened veterans victorious in the campaign against Molon, who had also performed well in the recent fighting in Koile Syria. Antiochus made only limited use of foreign mercenaries, who composed less than 10 per cent of his total force; mercenaries made up over 20 per cent of Ptolemy's soldiers. Also, Antiochus planned to lead the cavalry charge on the right wing himself, and it seems he hoped Ptolemy would be present to counter him. He may have entertained hopes of personally challenging the rival king to a duel.[10]

The battle began with a clash of titans. According to Polybius, the elephants on both sides crashed into each other and grappled directly with their tusks, channelling their instinctual mating season duels for the purpose of human violence. The size and numbers of Antiochus' two elephant battalions quickly scattered the Ptolemaic herd, and many of these were subsequently captured by Seleucid forces. Antiochus' victorious elephants did not play a large role in the battle to come; only three were killed and two were mortally wounded.

Antiochus' personal presence proved decisive on the Seleucid right flank, and his charging horsemen shattered the cavalry on Ptolemaic left. The young king, however, now made a critical tactical error. The correct action would have been to turn his horse and begin to roll up the Ptolemaic infantry formations on their exposed left flank. This was, admittedly, as Professor El'azar Galili has noted, easier said than done. Antiochus would have had to judge the disarray of the opposing cavalry to time his turning manoeuvre, and the collapsing Ptolemaic left may have been protected by the fortifications around its camp.

Antiochus, however, was not in a position to make calm or collected tactical decisions. Rather, he was on the front line of his cavalry charge, surrounded by the dust and gore. Carried away by the adrenaline rush of battle and perhaps his own lust for glory, he instead indulged in a full on pursuit of the fleeing Ptolemaic cavalry, perhaps hoping to catch Ptolemy IV among the fugitives.

Meanwhile, things were going badly on the Seleucid left. Ptolemy's Greek mercenaries, 8000 heavy infantry, smashed through Antiochus' Arab allies, leading to a complete collapse of the Seleucid left flank. The Ptolemaic commander in this sector, a mercenary captain named Echecrates, failed to turn and flank the Seleucid centre. At this point, each side had its left flank badly mauled. The heavy infantry on both sides, however, remained in the centre out of contact, and the clash of the two infantry lines would therefore decide the battle.

But Ptolemy IV had not fled to the rear with his scattered cavalry. Instead, he had drifted towards the centre of his main phalanx. Despite the setback suffered on his left flank, he was present at the centre of action just as the two heavy infantry formations collided together. He rallied his phalanx as it shoved its way forward, step by step. The superior mass of the Ptolemaic heavy infantry soon overwhelmed the Seleucid centre, and the entire Seleucid infantry line collapsed. Antiochus called off the pursuit too late to salvage the situation, and he had no choice but to retreat ingloriously with his men.

According to Polybius, Antiochus was 'convinced that in his own share of the battle he was victorious, but that he had been altogether ruined by the sorry cowardice of others'.[11] This view was unfair to his men, for Antiochus had failed them as a commander. He lost the battle of Raphia largely because he was trapped in the command philosophy of Alexander the Great, who practised what military historian John Keegan has called 'heroic leadership'.[12] Alexander sought action always at the front line, thus validating his claim to lead the warrior aristocracy of Macedonia. Yet this was a leadership strategy that was inherently risky, and Alexander was nearly killed in battle on multiple occasions. Both Alexander and Antiochus' tendency to place themselves in the blood and chaos of the fray was dangerous in another respect: it greatly limited the ability to control the tactical evolution of a battle. In this case, it was the fleeing Ptolemy IV who found himself in the position to lead his army to victory, whereas the momentarily triumphant Antiochus sacrificed his control in order to run amok.

Antiochus lost some 10,000 infantry and 300 cavalry in the defeat, and another 4000 were captured; this represented nearly 20 per cent of his combat power. Ptolemy's losses were light in comparison: 1500 infantry and 700 cavalry, although most of his elephant corps was captured.

After the conclusion of battle, Antiochus retreated with his army back into Syria and evacuated his garrisons in Koile Syria, which were quickly reoccupied by Ptolemaic forces. The defeated King worked energetically to establish a firm defence of southern Syria, concerned that Ptolemy IV might capitalize on their victory by entering the Seleucid homeland while his army was still in disarray. To his relief, ambassadors arrived offering peace terms. The proposed peace agreement reaffirmed the Ptolemaic claim to Koile Syria, but allowed Antiochus to maintain Seleucia Pieria.

Thus, despite the humbling defeat at Raphia, Antiochus could still claim partial territorial gain in the war, although these gains essentially re-established the status quo that existed from before the Laodicean War.

Ptolemy IV had performed well at Raphia and was able to bask briefly in his victory. The Egyptian priests issued a decree to commemorate his victory, known today as the Raphia stele. In a symbol of unity, copies of the text were posted in Greek, demotic (Egyptian written with the Greek alphabet), and hieroglyphics. The best-preserved copy depicts Ptolemy as an Egyptian pharaoh, though mounted upon a horse in Macedonian manner, rather than atop the chariot Egyptian pharaohs traditionally rode. Grovelling beneath Ptolemy is the miserable Antiochus, depicted as a bound captive begging for mercy. The scene recalls the Egyptian myth in which the pharaoh god Horus defeats, captures and castrates Seth, the god of chaos, in an epic cosmic battle. The inscription celebrated Ptolemy's victory, although it was not particularly interested in capturing the historical details. Like traditional Egyptian battle narratives, it sought to represent the defeat as effortlessly inflicted upon a miserable and unworthy enemy by a pharaoh engaged in personal combat:

> On the first day of the month of Pachon, in the fifth year [of his reign] he marched out from Pelusium and fought with King Antiochus at a town called Raphia near the frontier of Egypt…On the tenth day of the same month he defeated him in a great and splendid manner. Those of his enemies who in the course of this fight drew close to him he slew himself, even as in the past Horus, the son of Isis, had done with his foes. He pressed Antiochus so closely that he was obliged to throw away his diadem and his royal cloak. He fled with his bodyguard and only a few stayed with him after his defeat in a miserable and sad manner. The greater number of his soldiers suffered severe want. He saw the best of his friends perish in a miserable fashion. They suffered hunger and thirst. Everything that he left behind him was seized as booty. Only with the greatest exertion was he able to reach his home, and he suffered bitter grief.[13]

After four months' campaign, Ptolemy dismissed his troops, paying them a generous donative of 300,000 gold pieces, and soon drifted back into alcoholism, leaving an able cadre of advisors led by Sosibus to run the government. Antiochus, by contrast, emerged from the defeat with his energy and drive undiminished. With the war with Ptolemy finally at an end, he now was ready to focus upon another pressing matter: the rebellion and separatist kingdom of his cousin Achaeus in Asia Minor.

Chapter Five

The Defeat of Achaeus

The next three years of Seleucid history, from 217 to 214, are largely undocumented, as Polybius becomes distracted by the centrepiece of his history, the epic confrontation between Rome and Carthage. Nonetheless, it is clear that Antiochus spent these 'lost' years slowing grinding away at Achaeus' realm.

The rebel still controlled much of Asia Minor. With Antiochus distracted fighting Ptolemy IV, Achaeus had further expanded his domain with a successful campaign against an Anatolian people known as the Selgians.[1] The size of the rebel army is uncertain. At one point Achaeus was able to detach a force of 6000 infantry and 500 cavalry under a subordinate,[2] but his overall force was likely several times this. This strength would still have been no match for Antiochus' royal army, although the King probably campaigned with far fewer than the 68,000 troops he commanded at Raphia. There is no record of any set piece battle. Instead, Achaeus waged a defensive campaign, and it took Antiochus two full years (from 216 to 214) to fight his way up the old Persian royal highway and finally besiege Achaeus in the capital of Sardis.

Sardis was an old city, first the royal seat of the dynast Croesus' mid-sixth century Lydian empire and then the regional capital of the Persian Empire. It was well fortified and dominated by an imposing acropolis. Once Achaeus and his remaining forces drew behind Sardis' walls, the war reached a stalemate, as reported by Polybius:

Around Sardis were endless skirmishes and combats, both by night and day, as the soldiers devised every manner of ambush, retaliation and assault against each other. To write about these things one after the other would be not only profitless, but altogether time-consuming. (Polybius 7.15.1)

The siege had lasted for over a year when one of Antiochus' frustrated mercenary officers sought to infiltrate the city.

This officer, named Lagoras, was a Cretan mercenary with considerable combat experience. He had fought under Ptolemy IV during the recent war and suffered defeat at the hands of Antiochus in Beruit.[3] The end of the Syrian war closed off his opportunities with the Ptolemies, and he now turned to Antiochus, as did many other Ptolemaic mercenary officers. On his own initiative, Lagoras observed Sardis' defensive walls, looking for areas of weakness. He knew from experience that sections of the wall overlooking rough terrain were often times inadequately guarded, and he observed a cliff where the besieged inhabitants dumped refuse: human corpses as well as the entrails of dead horses and mules (the defenders were by now hungry enough to eat dead animals, but not so hungry as to feel compelled to eat the tripe!). Vultures flocked to this area, and the fact that these birds did not abandon the cliff after they had eaten their fill suggested to Lagoras that no guards were regularly posted in this spots. Acting on his own initiative, Lagoras sneaked up to the cliff at night and confirmed that it was unguarded and could be scaled with ladders.

Lagoras took this scheme to the King, who approved it instantly and gave him permission to lead the attack. Perhaps fearful of blame in the event of failure, Lagoras asked that two of the King's favourites join the assault, Theodotus the Aetolian and Dionysius, the commander of the hypaspists, an elite subset of the Silver Shields.[4]

Three special units were organized. The first consisted of fifteen men, selected for their strength, which would carry the ladders to the cliff, scale the wall, and enter the city, along with Lagoras, Theodotus, and Dionysius. They would then proceed to the nearest gate, where they would pull out the pins and remove the bar.

A second platoon of thirty soldiers would rush to the gate from the outside and assist in the demolition. Once opened, a special battalion of two thousand men (possibly the hypaspists themselves) would rush to take position at the top of the city's theatre, seizing key urban terrain that would allow follow-on forces to overrun the remainder of the city.

The plan required a moonless night to cover the movement to the cliff face. After waiting for the moon to wane, the operation was set into motion: the three units took their position at the base of the cliff and waited for daybreak to scale the wall. As expected, the steep cliffs shielded the attackers from Achaeus' sentries. However, the soldiers in Antiochus' main army, many of whom had front-row seats to the dramatic operation from their siege lines, caused an unforeseen and unfortunate commotion. The King feared that these undisciplined cheers might betray the assault force as it scrambled up the ladders, and to divert the defenders' attention, he launched an impromptu diversionary assault at one of the other gates into town, known traditionally as the Persian Gate. Unaware of the larger strategy, Achaeus' garrison commander, Aribazus, dispatched a force to repel Antiochus' attack; he even opened the gate to facilitate a counter-attack against Antiochus' diversionary force. Achaeus himself ordered the opposite gate to be reinforced as a precaution, but the reinforcements did not arrive in time.

Lagoras and his special force quickly tore down the gate from the inside, permitting the 2000 men stationed outside to rush into the city and seize the theatre. Aribazus sought to recall his troops to deal with this new threat, but opening the Persian gate was a grave mistake. The rebel soldiers withdrew back into the Persian gate, but failed to close it. Antiochus' men followed in close pursuit, and secured this second gate after a brisk struggle. The King led his assembled forces into the city, and Seleucid units burst through gate after gate. Aribazus, realizing the situation was hopeless, withdrew his troops to the inner defences of the city's imposing citadel, where Achaeus and his family were already secured, and watched as Antiochus and his men inflicted the traditional punishment upon a besieged city. On this scene, Polybius nonchalantly reports:

> Some murdered anyone they happened to encounter, while others burned down the dwellings and others prowled about in search of spoils and loot. The destruction and sack of the city was total. In this way, Antiochus became lord of Sardis. (7.18.9–10)

Now in control of the city, Antiochus needed to access the steep citadel in order to capture Achaeus and end the rebellion once and for all. Back in Egypt, Ptolemy IV's minister Sosibus was eager to ensure that Achaeus escaped alive from Sardis. While Ptolemy IV was technically at peace with Antiochus, the energetic minister knew that active war had merely been replaced by a cold war of subterfuge and containment. Any Seleucid loss would be a Ptolemaic gain. Sosibus also knew the narrow margins of Ptolemaic victory in the previous war. It would be advantageous to the fragile Ptolemaic state if Sosibus could sabotage Antiochus by smuggling Achaeus out of Sardis: the rebellion's persistence would continue to compromise the Seleucid position in Asia Minor.

With this in mind, Sosibus commissioned Bolis, a Cretan mercenary captain, to facilitate a dangerous rescue mission. Bolis had previously visited Sardis and was familiar with the terrain of the citadel. Even more significant, Bolis was friends with another high-ranking Cretan mercenary commander then in the service of Antiochus, a man by the name of Cambylus, whose unit of Cretans secured a forward outpost in rough terrain near the citadel. Sosibus provided Bolis with encoded letters of recommendation, as well as ten talents of silver to cover travel expenses and the cost of bribing Cambylus to agree to the plan.

Bolis made his way to Sardis via Rhodes and Ephesus, meeting with Ptolemaic agents and confidants of Achaeus along the way. He finally met with his friend and relative Cambylus, and the two men engaged in a plot that seems to confirm ancient stereotypes that portray Cretans as untrustworthy and treacherous. The two men agreed to split the ten talents between them, and then betrayed the entire plot to Antiochus in the hopes of receiving an additional reward. Antiochus was thrilled when the double agents presented themselves and immediately endorsed their plan. Bolis would cross enemy lines and offer to slip Achaeus to a friendly Ptolemy, only to treacherously deliver him directly to Antiochus.

Bolis sent letters, supposedly smuggled through Seleucid lines, urging Achaeus to accept his offer of rescue, and Achaeus decided the proposal was his best chance of escaping a hopeless military situation. But he decided to hedge his bets. When Bolis arrived, Achaeus dressed himself as an attendant and instructed a friend to impersonate him. To prevent betrayal, he told no one of his plans to depart, save for his loyal wife Laodice.

Achaeus and his followers linked up with Bolis in the middle of the night, and sneaked down the crags surrounding the citadel. As they moved over the steep terrain, Bolis noticed that the seemingly lowly attendant was receiving excessive deference from the better-dressed members of the party, especially when he required assistance down steep sections of the path. Having uncovered the switch and identified his target, Bolis gave a whistle that initiated the prearranged ambush. Bolis tackled Achaeus, overpowering him and preventing him from attempting suicide with a hidden blade; the King wanted his quarry alive. Polybius describes the scene that follows, emphasizing the irony of Achaeus' suddenly degraded position:

> The king, for a long while waiting the outcome in suspense, dismissed his courtiers and remained awake in his tent with only two or three bodyguards. When Cambylus and his men arrived and deposited Achaeus upon the floor bound hand and foot, Antiochus was utterly speechless at this incredible sight and remained silent for some time. Finally, full of sympathy, he wept and was deeply affected and burst into tears, affected, it seems to me, by seeing how difficult it was to withstand or anticipate such a turn of fortune (*tyche*). For Achaeus was the son of Andromachus, the brother of the Laodice who married Seleucus. He married Laodice the daughter of King Mithridates, and was lord of the whole of Asia this side of the Taurus. At that moment, it was believed by both his own troops and those of the enemy that his was in the safest spot in the whole world, but in fact he sat bound upon the ground, in the hands of his enemies, no one knowing what had just happened except those who carried it out. (Polybius 8.20.8–12)

For all the King's tears, he would have no mercy upon the rebel. The King's friends were summoned to witness the unhappy Achaeus and debate the proper punishment. They crafted a grisly execution protocol: Achaeus' genitals were cut off, and his misery ended shortly afterward with decapitation. His head was sewn into the skin of a donkey, while his headless body was crucified for display by the army. While this punishment was the ad hoc product of the more sadistic urges of Antiochus and his council, the habit of mutilating pretenders had Persian precedent and recalled the grim treatment of Molon's corpse almost nine years previously.

In the citadel, Laodice despaired at the joyous commotion in the Seleucid camp and realized that her husband's escape attempt had failed.[5] Shortly afterwards a royal herald arrived at the citadel to announce the gruesome execution and demand an immediate surrender. Despite this, the rebels maintained position, but there was no clear notion of who might succeed Achaeus. Both Laodice and the citadel commander Aribazus claimed to be in charge, and their quarrelling divided the garrison, prompting an eventual surrender. Eight years after the initial revolt, the rebellion of Achaeus and Laodice was over.[6]

The city of Sardis faced harsh punishment in the aftermath of the revolt. An additional 5 per cent tax was levied upon the inhabitants. Half the houses in the city were appropriated to quarter royal troops, and the city gymnasium converted to use for military purposes.[7] Soon, however, a more conciliatory policy emerged that focused on reconstructing the war-ravaged city, as evidenced by an inscribed royal letter:

> ....and immediately to cut the wood for the reconstruction of the city and to take it from the forests of Taranza, as Zeuxis may decide. We also exempt you from the on-twentieth tax that had been added to the city tax, and have ordered that the gymnasium you used previously be restored for you.[8]

In this respect, Antiochus III appears not as a mindless conqueror but rather a pragmatic imperialist. His wars caused significant destruction, but he also took measures to help affected communities rebuild. Yet this was not done out of compassion for individual or collective suffering: all of his conquests were designed for tributary exploitation. Antiochus and his administrators seemed particularly aware of the need to 'prime the pump', to jumpstart war-torn economies so that they might quickly return to reliable sources of tax revenue. Other royal benefactions to Sardis followed that pushed the city forward economically. The number of houses occupied by royal troops was reduced from half the houses to one third. A generous gift of 200 measures of oil was granted for use by the young men in the gymnasium, although this also supported the physical training necessary to provide future recruits for the Seleucid army.[9] When Sardis proved its loyalty by celebrating the Laodician festival in honour of the King's wife, Antiochus exempted the city from taxation for the three days of the festival.[10] John Ma has used a series of inscriptions around Sardis to illustrate the ongoing process of negotiation between subject communities and the royal administration. The King, of course, negotiated from a position of military strength, but the King and his army could not possibly be everywhere at once. In order to achieve desired ends, he was obliged to employ incentives as well as military coercion. Benefactions, even to a formerly disloyal city such as Sardis, provided additional glue that bound the empire together after troops departed. And indeed, Antiochus would soon depart Asia Minor with his royal army. He left behind Zeuxis, who would loyally serve as governor of the region for the next twenty-three years.[11]

Chapter Six

The Anabasis

In 212 BC, Antiochus embarked on an ambitious campaign east to restore Seleucid power and influence in the Upper Satrapies and the breakaway regions of Parthia and Bactria in particular. An eastern campaign was filled with historical significance: the obvious point of comparison was the epic march of Alexander the Great from the Hellespont to the Hydaspes River in India. Seleucus I Nicator had undertaken a similar march to secure the upper satrapies that ended in the Indus River valley. Yet victory in the East was not guaranteed. Antiochus' own father, Seleucus II, had launched a fruitless campaign against the Parthians in the 230s.

We do not know the exact size of Antiochus' army in this undertaking. Justin states that he brought with him 100,000 infantry and another 20,000 cavalry, but these numbers are undoubtedly exaggerated.[1] A more reasonable estimate would be an army under 70,000 soldiers, based on the figures attested for his armies on other major campaigns (68,000 at Raphia and 72,000 at Magnesia). Familiar components are attested: mercenaries (including Cretans), archers and slingers, roughly 10,000 peltasts (most likely the elite Silver Shields fighting as light troops), miscellaneous light infantry, the heavy infantry phalanx, and the cavalry. The sheer size of the army was an argument marching in cadence, reminding peripheral regions of the enormous coercive force that backed Seleucid claims to dominion.

Prior to his departure, Antiochus III proclaimed his son (also named Antiochus) co-king.[2] This continued the long Seleucid tradition of naming a son as co-regent, although in the past co-kings were adult men who were capable of undertaking kingly duties. Antiochus, the son of the King (as he was commonly referred to differentiate himself from the King himself), was likely only eight or nine years old at this time, and did not accompany his father on the campaign. Instead, the son remained in

Antioch as a figurehead, though one who received a practical education in the day-to-day administration of the empire.

The Armenian campaign

The first recalcitrant vassal in Antiochus' path east was Xerxes, the king of Greater Armenia. The Armenian landscape was mountainous and treacherous terrain for an army but of vital strategic importance, as it linked Anatolia and Mesopotamia to the Caspian Sea through mountain highways well trod by both traders and armies. The Armenians had stopped paying tribute in the time of Xerxes' father, taking advantage of the severe instability that shook the Seleucid realm in the 230s BC.

The campaign was largely uneventful. Antiochus besieged the Armenian royal city of Arsamosata, located between the uppermost reaches of the Tigris and Euphrates rivers. Xerxes himself abandoned Arsamosata and withdrew his armies to the interior. The ease with which the Seleucid army occupied his territories and besieged his capital undermined Xerxes' political position, and rather than trying to fight, Xerxes sent messages to Antiochus proposing a peace conference.

According to Polybius, Antiochus' closest advisors ('the most trusted of his friends') then dispensed a piece of Machiavellian advice: under the banner of truce, the King should seize Xerxes, execute him, and then install his own nephew Mithradites on the throne. But Antiochus decided against this course of action.[3] As he was about to embark on a lengthy campaign that would necessitate both diplomacy and force, it would not look good to acquire an early reputation for such acts of bad faith.

With respect to the peace, Antiochus and Xerxes hammered out a compromise. Xerxes remained the king of Armenia and would pay most of the back-taxes owed by his father. The initial payment would be most useful for the ongoing campaign: 300 talents of silver destined for Antiochus' war chest, along with 1000 horses and 1000 mules: Armenia was famous for its excellent horses. Xerxes also received in marriage Antiochus' sister Antiochis, at once a wife and Seleucid agent in a foreign court.[4]

The operation in Armenia was a propagandistic victory. The King had easily proven his military supremacy over the despot Xerxes, but the generous settlement allowed him to portray himself in the best of light, as a ruler who 'acted in a great-hearted and kingly fashion'.[5] In a postscript to this saga, his sister Antiochis had the hapless Xerxes murdered several years later, but it is unclear whether she did this on her own accord, or in collusion with her brother.[6]

The temple at Ecbatana: 211 BC

From Greater Armenia, Antiochus marched into Media, pausing at the capital of Ecbatana to muster his forces. He pillaged the temple to the Iranian goddess Anaitit located within the city. The loot from this despoilage was approximately 4000 silver talents or 140 tons of bullion. Seleucid policy toward native deities was generally one of respect and accommodation, but as he set out on his great campaign, Antiochus needed the cash to cover his expenses and pay his soldiers.

Military pay is uncertain, but the standard rate seems to have been a base pay of 5–6 obols a day, plus rations.[7] An army of 50,000 paid at this rate would cost around 3000 talents a year in pay alone, not counting the considerable expenses associated with provisioning such a large force. Thus, Antiochus needed the money and took it. While the looted bullion would serve as a down payment for the cost of the campaign, Antiochus need continual access to money to keep his troops paid, either through the expensive transport of specie east from his mints, or from funds acquired from the sale of loot or extorted from native populations along the way.

The temple in question had been pillaged before: both by Alexander the Great and Seleucus Nicator.[8] Here perhaps we might find a justification, or at least one that likely resonated with the Greco-Macedonian subjects of the empire: Antiochus wished to present himself as an equal and successor to both of these godlike kings. If they had removed wealth from the temple at Ecbatana to fund their Eastern campaigns, Antiochus' own expropriation was therefore defensible.

The Parthian campaign: 210–208 BC (Polybius 10. 27–31)

From Ecbatana, Antiochus prepared to cross the long Madayan desert to the city of Hecatompylos. The city was the largest in the region, and had recently come under Parthian control. Polybius calls Hecatompylos the 'centre of Parthia', but this is somewhat misleading. At that time, Hecatompylos lay on the periphery of Parthia; the administrative centre at the time was located in Nisa (now in modern-day Turkmenistan). Still, Hecatompylos was an important Parthian possession. It name literally means '100 gates', an exaggeration of course, but one that points to its importance as a major node on the desert road network.

A march of nearly 350 miles from Ecbatana to Hecatompylos took over a month. It is unlikely that an army of that size could cover more than ten miles in a day, usually much less. Antiochus' army would likely have been quite spread out, with cavalry and light skirmishers in the vanguard, ahead of the plodding heavy infantry, who transported their sixteen foot long pikes on wagons or mules. Behind them followed the long baggage train necessary to supply the men in such an arid environment. Indeed, Antiochus' logistical network must have been impressive.[9] A total of 50,000 men could easily eat thirty-five tons of grain a day, all of which had to be shipped east from grain growing districts, foraged, or purchased from locals.[10]

While arid, the desert territory was not a wasteland, but was rather dotted with wells and the remnants of Persian reclamation schemes. The Parthian king Arsaces deployed mounted troops to destroy wellheads along the route, but Antiochus sent an officer named Nicomedes and a thousand cavalrymen ahead of his main body to secure the water supply before each day's march. Sharp skirmishing ensured that Antiochus controlled a string of wells to water his thirsty troops and pack animals.

The King finally arrived at Hecatompylos, where he rested his exhausted army. Aside from small groups of skirmishers, he had no contact with anything that could be described as a Parthian army. However, he realized that his force was even more vulnerable in the arid territory beyond Hecatompylos, and he suspected that Arsaces was retreating with the very purpose of drawing him deeper in order to strain his logistics and demoralize his troops.

It was probably for logistical reasons that Antiochus therefore decided to turn north and advance into Hyrcania, on the eastern bank of the Caspian Sea. By pillaging the relatively fertile lowlands on the bank of the sea he would be able to replenish the army's supplies. Furthermore, he would deny Parthian access to this land, where they already controlled at least one city. It would have been a 60-mile march from Hecatompylos through the Harborz (Elburz) mountain range, and in crossing with his army, Antiochus and his forces would have to crest the ridge at about 7000 feet.

Antiochus' scouting intelligence seems to have been quite good in this portion of the campaign, for he knew that the army needed to pass through a narrow defile created by winter snowmelt. Furthermore, he expected ambush from local 'barbarians', whose determined resistance suggests affiliation with the Parthian army. The enemy fighters effectively blocked the defile, the most feasible route for the heavy infantry and the animals of the baggage train. Yet reconnaissance revealed that the enemy forces had focused too much on blocking the pass itself and were vulnerable to attacks by light troops who could scramble across the boulders and crags to challenge their position from the flank and rear.

Antiochus prepared three elements to assault the Parthian roadblock. The first was a specially assembled contingent of archers, slingers, and javelin throwers, drawn from men from mountainous regions and commanded by a lieutenant named Diodotus. A second contingent comprised 2000 Cretan mercenaries commanded by the mercenary captain Polyxenidas of Rhodes, the third was two companies of light troops commanded by the mercenary commanders Nicomedes of Cos and Nicolaus the Aetolian.

Antiochus ordered the missile troops to move in loose formation outside the main defile. Their task was to launch a hail of stones, arrows, and darts down upon the enemy forces manning the roadblock. Simultaneously, the Cretans and other light troops would charge the defile directly. Once a section had been secured in this manner, the light troops would clear obstacles and debris to allow heavier components to move through; the process was to be repeated continuously for eight days until Antiochus and his forces reached the main pass.

Here, a high altitude battle developed, as a concentrated mass of enemy fighters attempted to block the army. For the first time in this alpine fighting, Antiochus deployed his heavy infantry phalanx. Unbeknownst to the enemy fighters blocking the pass, Antiochus had that night dispatched a flying column of light troops (probably the same ad-hoc task force) to flank the pass. As Antiochus' heavy infantry fixed the enemy in the defile, his light troops materialized in the rear, yet the enemy fighters managed to flee before the trap closed hard upon them. Fearing that elements of his army might become lost in the mountains, Antiochus had the trumpeters call off further pursuit. With the collapse of enemy resistance, the King regrouped his forces and crossed the pass into the plain of Hyrcania. He camped near the un-walled city of Tambrax (Zadrakarta), and was informed that resistance was hardening nearby in the walled city of Sirynx. In a short, aggressive siege Antiochus filled the city's moat and tunnelled under the walls. Enemy soldiers massacred a number of Greek citizens in the city (who were probably sympathetic to the Seleucid crown) and attempted to evacuate their position, only to be driven back within the walls by Antiochus' mercenary forces. His peltasts finally forced their way into the gap in the breached wall and captured the city.

Unfortunately, with the fall of Sirynx, we enter a narrative black hole that engulfs the rest of Antiochus' eastern anabasis, yet geography provides some clue to the end of the campaign against the Parthians. The next time we hear of Antiochus' location, he is near the Arius river. The most direct route from Hyrcania to the River Arius would have taken him through the Astuauene valley, between the modern day Kopet Dagh and Binaḻud mountain ranges. This was the Parthian heartland, where Parni nomads had first settled as they wandered in off the European steppes, a fact that suggests his victory over the nascent Parthian state was almost total.

The Parthians were vanquished but not exterminated. The Parthian king Arsaces II was humbled, but Antiochus allowed him to maintain local authority after reducing his realm to the Astauene Valley and the northern steppeland around the capital city of Nisa. Historians often forget that Antiochus reclaimed significant territory from Parthia, in particular the crossroads city of Hectambylos and the fertile flatlands of Hyrcania. Indeed, he reincorporated the Parthians' most arable land into direct Seleucid rule, leaving local autonomy over mountainous terrain on the edge of the empire. Allowing local 'client kings' to manage their own affairs was a consistent policy of ancient empires, one practised previously by Achaemenid Persia and later by Rome. The later growth of the Parthian empire in the 150s, a rise that occurred at the expense of

Seleucid power, has led many historians to suggest that Antiochus was too mild in his settlement with the Parthians. The most ruthless course would have been a brutal campaign of ethnic cleansing to root out the Parni entirely, but Antiochus lacked the military capacity to wage such a war, and thus settled for a conditional victory. Nonetheless, Antiochus checked Parthian expansion, expelled the Parthians from Hecatompylos and Hyrcania, and reduced them to the status of fringe vassals, setting back the course of Parthian state development by twenty-five years.

Administrative business

During the war in Parthia, Antiochus maintained long-distance correspondence with Zeuxis, who had been left in charge of Asia Minor. Through these letters, which travelled more than 1700 miles to reach him, Antiochus appointed Nicanor, his chamberlain and a close confidant in court, to the High Priesthood (*archireos*) of the entire region north of the Taurus Mountains – nearly all of Asia Minor then under Seleucid control. It is not clear what Nicanor was going to be the high priest of. It is quite possible that by this date Antiochus was already taking control of the royal cult, so that Nicanor's job would be overseeing and possibly standardizing the royal cult in the region.[11]

Antiochus' letter worked its way down the Seleucid chain of command: to Zeuxis, the overall commander in Asia Minor, then to a subaltern named Philotas, and then to a regional official names Bithys.[12] The letter is evidence that despite the distance, Antiochus still concerned himself with important domestic policy decisions. The King did not simply vanish into the east, leaving viceroys to function independently in his absence; rather, the Seleucid Empire remained a centralized state. While men like Zeuxis obviously retained a local initiative in their spheres of responsibility, many decisions were reserved for the King alone. The ability to govern over such distances implies certain governmental infrastructure and a form of organized post-rider system in particular. Even if a post rider managed to cover 50 miles a day (the top speed of the Roman imperial post), well over a month would have elapsed before Antiochus' letter from Parthia reached Zeuxis in Mysia.[13]

Plate 1. Antiochus III: portrait bust, Louvre Museum, Paris. (*Courtesy of the Wikimedia Foundation*)

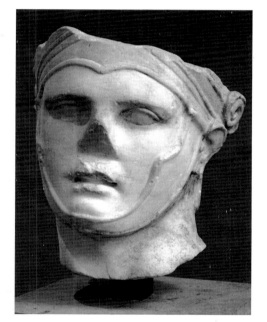

Plate 2. Seleucus Nicator (r. 312–281 BC), portrait bust, Louvre Museum, Paris. (*Courtesy of the Wikimedia Foundation*)

Plate 3. Antiochus IV (r. 175–164 BC), portrait bust. (*Courtesy of the Wikimedia Foundation*)

Plate 4. Attalus I: Portait bust of Attalus I. Openly proclaiming himself king in the 240s BC, he ruled a shifting territory in Asia Minor until his death in 197 BC. During his low-water mark after Antiochus III's vigorous campaigns, Attalus controlled only his citadel at Pergamon and its environs. (*Courtesy of the Wikimedia Foundation*)

Plate 5. Eumenes II (r. 197–159 BC): Portrait of Eumenes II, son of Attalus I, who led the decisive cavalry charge at Magnesia, and obtained major territorial concessions in the Peace of Apamea. Now on display in the Hierapolis Museum. (*Courtesy of the Wikimedia Foundation*)

Plate 6. Arsaces II: The king of the Parthians, defeated but not overthrown during Antiochus III's anabasis. He contented himself as a Seleucid vassal, with the official title of 'autokrator'. (*Courtesy of the Wikimedia Foundation*)

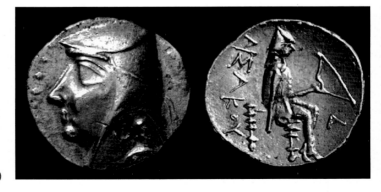

Plate 7. Euthydemus: Coin of the Bactrian king Euthydemus, who defended his realm from Antiochus' attacks from 210 to 208 BC, ultimately accepting the status of a subordinate but still largely independent client king. (*Courtesy of the Wikimedia Foundation*)

Plate 8. Demetrius I: Son of Euthydemus. Antiochus III ceremoniously approved him as a successor to the Bactrian throne in 208 BC, paving the way for peace between a semi-independent Bactrian dynasty and the Great King. He ruled from c. 200 to 180 BC. (*Courtesy of the Wikimedia Foundation*)

Plate 9. Gilded metalwork from Ai Khanoum in Bactria, showing a mix of Hellenic and Eastern motifs. The piece is widely held to embody the intercultural fusion facilitated by the geographic scope of the Seleucid Empire. (*Courtesy of the Wikimedia Foundation*)

Plate 10. Ptolemy IV (r. 221–205 BC): Despite a reputation of sloth and debauchery, his personal heroism at Raphia led to a resounding victory over Antiochus III. (*Courtesy of the Wikimedia Foundation*)

Plate 11. Ptolemy V (r. 205–81 BC): He succeeded his father as a mere boy overseen by a tumultuous regency government. As a condition to peace after the Battle of Panion, he married Antiochus III's daughter Cleopatra 'the Syrian'. (*Courtesy of the Wikimedia Foundation*)

Plate 12. Rafah (ancient Raphia). Modern day border crossing between Egypt and the Gaza strip, situated at the natural choke point, near to where almost 150,000 Ptolemaic and Seleucid troops clashed in 217 BC. (*Courtesy of the Wikimedia Foundation*)

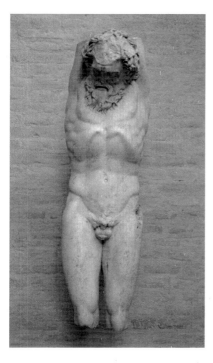

Plate 13. Marsyas: Statue of the satyr Marsyas, who in myth was flayed to death by the god Apollo in Asia Minor. The legend may have resonated with Antiochus' brutal torture and execution of his older cousin Achaeus outside Sardis, given the close association between the Seleucid dynasty and Apollo. (*Courtesy of the Wikimedia Foundation*)

Plate 14. Sardis Citadel: Commanding position held by Achaeus and his wife after Antiochus III captured the main city. (*Photo courtesy of Randall Souza*)

Plate 15. Demetrias (modern-day Volos): One of the fetters of Greece, Antiochus landed in 192 BC, commencing his invasion of Greece. (*Photo by author*)

Plate 16. Thermopylae: The cliffs of Mount Callidromos loom above the narrow pass at Thermopylae. Marcus Porcius Cato was able to find a path through the mountains to flank the Seleucid position, imitating the Persian manoeuvre against the Spartans almost three centuries earlier. (*Photo by author*)

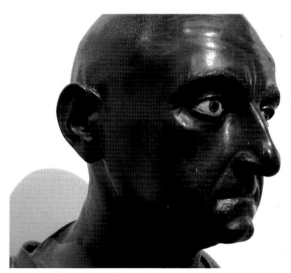

Plate 17. Scipio Africanus (consul 205, 194 BC): Vanquisher of Hannibal and one of the greatest Roman generals of all time, he was a strong advocate for war with Antiochus III. While serving as a legate with his brother, Lucius Scipio, he took ill and was therefore absent from the Battle of Magnesia. (*Courtesy of the Wikimedia Foundation*)

Plate 18. Pen and ink drawing of a bronze plate found during German excavations around Pergamon. While initially believed to depict a battle between Hellenistic forces and Galatian warriors, it most likely depicts the Battle of Magnesia, with Roman infantry and Attalid cavalry assailing the beleaguered Seleucid phalanx. (Illustration from Alexander Conze, *Die Altertümer von Pergamon, Vol I.ii*, Berlin: W. Spemann, 1913)

Plate 19. Trireme: The *Olympias*, a modern reconstruction of the ancient warship and a commissioned vessel in the Greek navy. While the heyday of the trireme was the 5th and 4th centuries BC, Antiochus III still had many of these un-decked vessels in his new blue-water fleet. (*Photo by author*)

Plate 20. Galatian: Terracotta of a Galatian warrior, now in the Louvre Museum. Galatian mercenaries were an important supplement to Seleucid armies. (*Courtesy of the Wikimedia Foundation*)

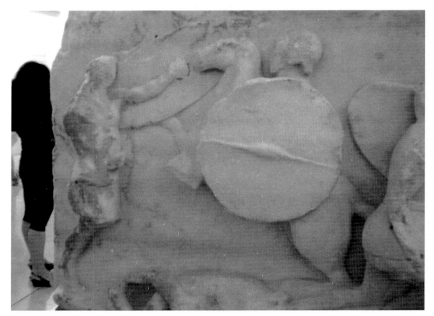

Plate 21. Roman infantryman and Macedonian cavalrymen: A dramatic scene from the Pydna monument of Aemilius Paullus (c. 165 BC). It could equally portray the clash between Antiochus III's heavy cavalry and L. Scipio's legions at Magnesia. Now on display at the Delphi museum. (*Photo by author*)

Plate 22. Another scene from the Pydna monument, featuring a fallen Macedonian heavy infantry phalangite with characteristic shield. Antiochus' phalanx would have been equipped very similarly. A Roman cavalryman rides over him and a Roman infantryman rushes up with his long shield. (*Photo by author*)

While he was in Anatolia, Antiochus was notified of revolts in both Phrygia and Lydia, yet these do not seem to have been serious. We do not know how it was repressed; though presumably Zeuxis proved capable and the King did not learn of the unrest until after the rebellion was crushed. From a distance, Antiochus III ordered additional measures to contain future problems in the region: the establishment of military colonies of 2000 Jewish military settlers, recruited from the large Jewish populations in Babylon and Mesopotamia and settled in strategic locations in Anatolia.

Antiochus also ordered that the unique religious identity of the colonists be preserved, guaranteeing the integrity of Jewish law by royal decree. It is likely that Antiochus specifically ordered the recruitment of Jewish settlers as desired custodians who were outsiders to the region. Perhaps the original revolt involved military settlers who had mixed too closely with the native population (this had certainly been the case with the troops who had previously supported Achaeus). While other polytheist military settlers might mingle and socialize with locals in pagan temples and religious festivals, the monotheism of the Jews would keep them necessarily separate. Unusual dietary practices would also stand in the way of assimilation, and the Jewish practice of circumcision and other social customs would keep them out of the baths and gymnasia. In short, Jewish identity was a military asset. Unlikely to sympathize with the local native population, they could prove loyal guardians for the King's interests in the area.

To ensure the success of this military colonization, Antiochus issued a number of specific orders, and his letter provides the best evidence of the considerable logistics involved in founding a Seleucid military colony. The settlers were to be moved with their families, cattle, slaves, and other personal property. Rather than one location, they were to be scattered around military strongholds designated by the King in a previous letter to Zeuxis. Each man was allotted land for a home, as well as land for growing crops and vineyards, though Zeuxis was to provide grain rations until families were able to harvest a first crop. Settlers' crops were exempted from taxes for ten years.[14]

The Bactrian campaign: 208–206 BC (Polybius 10.49/11.34)

Polybius' narrative picks up in Bactria, with Antiochus besieging a city three days' march from the Arius River. The Bactrian king Euthydemos arrived on the scene with a large army spearheaded by 10,000 cavalrymen and proceeded to block the ford over the Arius, a three-day march from Antiochus' position. We do not know the total size of Bactrian forces, but 10,000 cavalry is an enormous mounted force by ancient standards. Cavalry usually comprised 10–25 per cent of ancient armies. However, the Bactrian army seemed to have been dominated by cavalry, unsurprising given its location on the edge of the Eurasian steppe.

Alerted to the presence of Bactrian troops, Antiochus abandoned his siege and marched his army at a steady pace for two days. Again, his human intelligence networks were excellent, reflecting the residual loyalty toward the Seleucid crown among the native population. He learned from locals that the Bactrian guard at the Arius River ford was posted only during the day; at night, the Bactrian soldiers retired to a town twenty stades (four kilometres) away. Thus Antiochus waited until nightfall to forward a group of 10,000 peltasts (quite possibly the Silver Shield brigade) along with 2000 horsemen of the royal guard (the *agema* and *basilikoi*) and additional light infantry.

The next morning, the main body of Bactrian cavalry was alerted to the Seleucid presence and counterattacked. Fierce fighting ensued, with Antiochus in the middle of battle. A spear struck his horse, killing it out from under him, and he took a wound in the mouth that knocked several teeth loose. The royal squadron had successfully repulsed the first wave of Bactrian cavalry, but as more and more Bactrians counterattacked, the King and his horsemen found in a tenuous position. Commanded by an officer named Panaetolus, the 10,000 peltasts charged, rescuing the King and thus turning the tide of the battle. According to Polybius, Antiochus 'earned at this time a special reputation for courage'.

The defeat shook the confidence of Euthydemos, the Bactrian king. Caught unprepared, his absence at the battle against the Seleucid king was a source of royal shame. Furthermore, he now knew the size of the Seleucid force. Even if the Bactrian had possessed a modest infantry force, it would have been no match for Antiochus' army. Humbled by a cavalry skirmish, a set-piece battle was now out of the question, and Euthydemos withdrew his remaining forces east to the administrative capital at Bactra–Zariaspa.

While events for the next two years are almost entirely lost, we know that Antiochus besieged the capital city Bactra for part of the period, as

Polybius later lists the siege as one of notable significance.[15] The final fragment of his narrative gives an account of the negotiations that ended the siege, yet we can assume that the war was now stalemated.

After two years of siege, an envoy named Teleas arrived from the Bactrian camp to initiate negotiations. Through this herald, Euthydemos emphasized his Magnesian origins and Greek identity, presenting himself as a potential ally who never openly rebelled against Seleucid authority.[16] Rather, he overthrew Diodotus II, the son of the rebel satrap Diodotus I, an act that could be construed as a favour to the Seleucid king. Furthermore, Euthydemos claimed that he provided a worthy service to Antiochus by repelling nomadic peoples sweeping off the Eurasian plain. If Antiochus were to overthrow his dynasty and destroy his military forces, he argued, these nomads would overrun the Seleucid Empire. This risk from Steppe nomads was not exaggerated: in the 140s BC, the Bactrian kingdom would implode after a wave of uncontrolled migration from the north.

A compromise was soon achieved after Antiochus met privately with Euthydemos' son Demetrius. Euthydemos was an old man by this time, and Antiochus wished to ensure that his successor would also prove a loyal and effective client king. Antiochus was impressed by Demetrius' 'appearance, conversation, and dignity of bearing worthy of royal rank'. This 'inspection' may have taken place publicly in the Seleucid camp before the assembled court, an act that would establish Antiochus' position of supremacy as he adjudged young Demetrius a worthy vassal king. Polybius reports that Antiochus promised Demetrius one of his daughters, although there is no evidence that the marriage took place.

Euthydemos was now a king, but the manner in which the kingship was bestowed emphasized his subordination. His royal power was a direct gift from Antiochus, and gifts could be easily revoked. In addition, Euthydemos was tasked with the expensive duty of providing rations for Antiochus' army and compelled to surrender his elephants. Euthydemos advertised his new position by minting coins with an anchor stamped upon them – the anchor a Seleucid symbol since the reign of Seleucus I Nicator.[17]

As mentioned previously, many modern historians have criticized Antiochus for not asserting a more direct control over Bactria – it seems they would be satisfied only by Euthydemos' head on a pike. The mutilations of Molon and Achaeus certainly prove that Antiochus was capable of ruthless savagery when necessary, yet his dealings with Euthydemos reveal a decidedly pragmatist streak. In this case, there were sound reasons to acknowlege Bactria's *de facto* independence. Operations in Bactria had consumed two years with few concrete results. The tumultuous frontier of Bactria meant that a total victory would also come with the expensive task of frontier defence, and Euthydemos was probably correct when he claimed that he could better serve Antiochus as a client king buffering the Seleucid frontier. And given that Antiochus was able to maintain control by personally approving of Demetrius, Bactria's *de facto* independence was not a severe political blow. The King had already acquired a good deal of political capital for his personal valour at the River Arius, and the fact that he ended the Bactrian war with a negotiated settlement did not diminish his standing in the eyes of ancient contemporaries.

After the Bactrian affair, Antiochus marched south, perhaps reaching the Indus River in modern day Pakistan. Seleucus I Nicator had previously ceded his claims to this region to Chandragupta, the founder of the powerful Mauryan Empire. The Mauryan king Asoka enjoyed some degree of suzerainty in the far eastern satrapies in the 240s, a time period that coincided with the near collapse of Seleucid power during the third Syrian War, judging from the survival of a number of rock cut inscriptions in Afghanistan testifying to Asoka and his newfound Buddhist faith.[18] Both Seleucid and Mayaran empires had since fallen out of contact with each other. While the Seleucid Empire had recovered from its troubles of the previous generation, the Mauryan dynasty seems to have virtually collapsed by this point, and Antiochus III was likely aware of the Mayaran troubles. His march to the Indus River was probably to see if there were any scraps for the taking.

Yet in the interim the Indus river region had been secured by a local potentate named Sophagesenus, who was naturally quite alarmed by the sudden appearance of an enormous army at his border. Antiochus was not interested in bloody conquest, but he was not above a hasty shakedown. Sophagesenus agreed to pay Antiochus a substantial sum to leave, and he provided rations for Antiochus' army and a new herd of elephants. By now Antiochus had over 150 war war-elephants, the largest herd attested in the ancient world since Seleucus I Nicator. The King left behind an officer named Androsthenes the Cyzician to collect the promised 'protection money', and then departed with his army for the return trip west.[19]

The return route took him north across the Erymandros river (the modern Helmand river valley in Southern Afghanistan) into Dragiana (central Afghanistan), and then south-east into Carmania. This was a circuitous route, suggesting that Antiochus was more interested in 'showing the flag' through his upper satrapies than in making a speedy return to the heart of Seleucid territory. There is no evidence that he engaged in any active military operations, nor that there was even active revolt to quash. Nonetheless, in regions that rarely received direct royal attention, the presence of king and army would not be without effect.

Wintering in Carmania, Antiochus next travelled to Antioch-in-Persis, where he received ambassadors from the Greek city of Magnesia on the Maeander, a free Ionian city within the Seleucid sphere of influence in coastal Asia Minor. The citizens of Magnesia had recently established elaborate games in honour of Artemis and were now engaged in a furious diplomatic campaign to have these games recognized as 'isopythian', or equal in prestige to the games held in honour of Apollo at the Greek sanctuary at Delphi. Antiochus was not the only king the Magnesians approached for assistance – they wanted their games acknowledged by all the major Hellenistic powers, including Ptolemy IV and Attalus I. Antiochus spoke with diplomatic language: he acknowledged the games as isopythian, a designation that included the right to issue victors a crown (*stephanos*) made of laurel leaves, as was the custom as the Pythian games in Delphi. However, Antiochus, unlike Ptolemy IV, did not proclaim the city of Magnesia 'holy and inviolate' (*hiera kai asylos*). He therefore reserved the right to campaign against Magnesia in the future, despite his protested friendship. This was perhaps a sign that he already was considering a campaign in Asia Minor after he returned from his eastern *anabasis*.[20]

While the ambassadors from Magnesia-on-the-Maeander were in Antioch-in-Persis, they took the opportunity to affirm their city-to-city relationship in the presence of the King. Antiochus I Soter had settled the original colony of Antioch-in-Persis with Thessalian veterans drawn from Magnesia-on-the-Maeander. The civic leadership of Antioch-in-Persis passed a decree recognizing Magnesia's games as 'isopythian' and voted that envoys should be equipped to travel the distance to Magnesia proper (in Thessaly) to sacrifice to Artemis-Leucophyrene.[21] Such diplomatic contacts across the vast distances – between a Macedonian dominated city in Thessaly and a Seleucid city in Persia – are illustrative of the scope of the Hellenistic experience.

On their return trip back to Magnesia, the ambassadors visited Antiochus, the son of the king, who by now was probably fifteen years old. The Magnesians, well aware of their delicate relationship with their Seleucid overlords, were clearly looking to the future. The meeting was not particularly substantive, but shows that the adolescent prince gained diplomatic experience from an early age.[22] By the April of 205 BC Antiochus III was back in Babylon, where he participated in the celebration of the Babylonian new year; the people of the city made 'sacrifices for Ishtar of Babylon and the life of King Antiochus'.[23]

But the anabasis was not yet over. In the spring of 205 BC, Antiochus marched his army south along the eastern shore of the Persian Gulf. This region was controlled by the Gerrhae, Arab farmers and traders, although the Seleucids had traditionally maintained a presence on the Persian Gulf through a garrison on the island of Ikaros (now Failaka). The Gerrhae begged Antiochus 'not to abolish the gifts the gods had bestowed upon them, namely perpetual peace and freedom' (Polybius 13.9.4). In exchange for 'peace and freedom', the Gerrhae paid Antiochus 500 talents of silver, 30 tons of frankincense, and six tons of '*stakte*', oil of either cinnamon or myrrh.

From the Persian Gulf, Antiochus moved north across Syria and into Asia Minor. By 204 BC the King was in Teos, a Greek city on the coast formerly controlled by Attalus I. Although a military contingent came with him, the goal in Teos seems to have been one of well-armed goodwill. Using standard Hellenistic diplomatic language, Antiochus declared that Teos was to remain 'holy, inviolate and tax-exempt'.[24] This was a sign that he did not have any immediate designs of the city and would respect its autonomy.[25] The large army camped outside Teos did not necessarily contradict this pronouncement: benevolent rhetoric and coercive force were rather two sides of the same imperial coin.

The city responded with a series of gracious gestures, stock actions of Hellensitic diplomacy, including the installation of statues of Antiochus and his queen Laodice.

In 203 BC, Antiochus paraded his army through the city of Amyzon. After a show of force, he proclaimed the Temple of Apollo and Artemis in the city inviolate (*asylon*), another show of royal goodwill to a city recently subjected to military actions under Zeuxis.[26] Such royal pledges often conflicted with the baser instincts of soldiers, and shortly afterward Antiochus formally rebuked his troops for depredations against shrine of Apollo and Artemis.[27]

How should we judge the *anabasis* of Antiochus III? A tremendous disparity exists between the pointed criticism of modern historians and the unqualified praise of ancient authors. Professor Peter Green reflects the line of modern scepticism, suggesting that 'if the propaganda was good, the actual achievement was insubstantial'.[28]

Yet other historians have been more optimistic about the concrete benefits of Antiochus' campaign. Most notably, Michael Rostovtzeff believed the *anabasis* critical to solidifying Seleucid control over the long-range caravan routes with India and China, making the campaign an economic as well as military and diplomatic boon.[29]

It is true that Antiochus did not crush all of his opponents unconditionally. But the campaign made Seleucid royal power explicit. Subjects along the line of march saw such power materialize in the forms of infantry and cavalry, endless streams of men embodying an impressive argument in cadence. Aside from the actual fighting in Parthia and Bactria, the procession of troops throughout the Upper Satrapies presented a potent and unambiguous message to any would-be separatist. Such display was a reminder that the King could muster overwhelming force and deploy as far east as the Indus River. Antiochus' *anabasis* was not merely symbolic, but rather a physical exercise of coercive power over native people and their rulers.

We can rely on Polybius to offer a more effusive commentary on the success of the expedition (11.34.15–16):

All in all, he secured his kingdom, stunning all his subjects with his audacity and tenacity. Through this campaign, he proved himself worthy of the kingship, not only to the inhabitants of Asia, but to also those living in Europe.

Antiochus' celebrated the success of his anabasis with a new and aptly chosen royal title: 'the Great' (*megas*), in deliberate imitation of Alexander.[30]

Chapter Seven

Brave New World

The pact between the kings

In 205 BC, as Antiochus was returning from his Eastern Anabasis, Ptolemy IV died in Alexandria. Since his victory over Antiochus III at Raphia some twelve years earlier, he had gained a reputation as a voluptuary and drunk. As heir, he left behind a five-year-old child, clearly no match for his ferocious counterparts in Antioch and Pella. Both Antiochus III and Philip V were now battle-hardened commanders, secure in their reigns and in the prime of life. The pharaoh's death was initially kept a secret. According to Polybius, this was so that his *epi ton pragmaton* Sosibus and the inner circle might solidify their grasp over the hapless young boy, and the regency established for young Ptolemy V quickly degenerated into dysfunctional court strife.

Internal violence wracked Egypt. In 207 BC, a rebellion had erupted in the Thebaid region of southern Egypt. Leading the revolt were the 20,000 native Egyptian hoplites that had been hastily mustered into service ten years before to meet the Seleucid invasion at Raphia. Newly confident in their martial prowess, they mobilized against the dynasty that they now considered foreign occupiers. The rebellious Egyptians nominated their own pharaoh and established him in the traditional royal capital at Memphis.

To make matters worse, the skilled administrator Sosibus died shortly after Ptolemy IV. The regency then devolved to his chief assistant, Agathokles. Agathokles had played the role of the 'enforcer' during the regency government, and his sister Agathokleia had entered the women's quarters of the palace to murder Ptolemy V's mother when she proved too meddlesome. But Agathokles quickly proved unpopular once he became regent. Mob violence erupted in Alexandria, and both Agathokles and his sister were lynched by the crowd in the city's hippodrome.

The combination of a contested regency and uncontained insurrection showed that the Ptolemaic kingdom was effectively a failed state. Up to this point, the international system of the Eastern Mediterranean had been 'tri-polar'. The rough equality of Macedonia, Egypt, and the Seleucid Empire maintained a general stability. This system did involve plenty of border disputes (i.e. the Syrian wars) and wars fought through proxies (such as Ptolemaic support for Achaeus), but the basic resource parity of the three ensured that no single one could achieve total domination. When all three dynasties were healthy, a general balance of power prevailed in the Eastern Mediterranean.[1]

With the death of Ptolemy IV, the third leg of the stool was disrupted. His untimely passing brought about a chain of violence that would ultimately result in Roman intervention and reshape the power dynamics of the Mediterranean world.[2]

At first, however, the death of Ptolemy IV produced friendship and cooperation between the enemies of the vulnerable Egyptian realm. The Antigonid and Seleucid monarchies already had a long history of such friendly alliance, and Philip V and Antiochus quickly made a secret pact, probably in the year 203. Some modern historians have doubted the validity of this 'pact between the kings', arguing that it was the invention of Roman writers seeking to justify their interventions in the Greek world. Despite this, the testimony of Polybius and epigraphic sources provide strong evidence that such a covert pact was authentic.[3]

We do not know the specific details of this secret agreement, but the gist as reported by Polybius was the following: Antiochus III and Philip V agreed to split the Ptolemaic possessions that each had long coveted. Ptolemaic enclaves in Thrace, the Hellespont and Western Asia Minor would go to Philip V, who hoped to become master of a new empire in the Aegean Sea. Antiochus III would claim a prize long sought by his dynasty, and one almost within his reach before the fiasco at Raphia: Koile Syria. While the agreement lacked a mutual defence clause, the two powers agreed to aid one another as they took possession of their conquests. It is likely that the agreement contained a clause protecting Egypt proper from the hands of either power.

John Grainger has raised the intriguing hypothesis that Ptolemy IV's death abrogated the peace treaty that ended the fourth Syrian War, arguing that peace treaties between Seleucid and Ptolemaic kings ought to be viewed as applicable between individual, signatory monarchs and not between states. Under this model, Antiochus pledged his personal honour to keep the peace with Ptolemy IV. With the King dead, however, the peace was abrogated.[4]

The fifth Syrian War and Battle of Panium

In 202 BC, Antiochus launched a renewed attack against Koile Syria. He selected the route through the desert expanse east of the Anti-Lebanon mountains, which allowed him to circumvent Ptolemaic forces at the northern entrance to the Biqua Valley. Logistically, this could only be accomplished by a swift march to the desert oasis of Damascus. Captured quickly, Damascus might serve as a supply base and allow Antiochus to march south and then hook westwards by skirting the Anti-Lebanon and entering Palestine. Now the capital of the modern Republic of Syria, Damascus was not then a major strategic site, although it was an important caravan city. While garrisoned, it remained largely unfortified.

The desolate nature of the country would not support a long-term siege. Antiochus equipped a force of cavalry with four-day rations and timed the assault to coincide with a local festival that would hopefully distract the garrison. Antiochus' horsemen swooped into town after the ride through the desert and captured the city.[5]

From Damascus, Antiochus quickly assaulted into Palestine, likely cutting a direct line for Gaza, as the Gaza strip was an excellent place to block an Egyptian counterattack. The siege against a group of determined defenders lasted well into the spring of 201 BC.[6] The final capture of Gaza was considered a major success, but Antiochus still did not control the whole of Koile Syria. Most of the Ptolemaic fortifications in the Biqua Valley held, as did cities in Palestine, including Jerusalem. Much of the Seleucid army returned to quarters in Apamea during the winter of 201/200, and the anaemic Egyptian response perhaps lulled Antiochus into a sense of complacency.

The regents of young Ptolemy V had not yet given up all hope: the regency government in Egypt mustered a large army to launch a counterattack against the Seleucid garrisons left behind. The exact size of the Ptolemaic army is not mentioned by any ancient source. It was certainly far smaller than the 75,000 man force that previously faced Antiochus III at Raphia. A rough estimate based on our knowledge of Ptolemaic manpower capabilities might be as follows. There is reason to believe that the Ptolemaic army had a maximum strength of around 80–90,000 in 217 BC, counting the Raphia field army (75,000) and a reasonable estimate of garrison requirements (5000–15,000).

There were now no Egyptian hoplites in the ranks, due to the ongoing native insurrection, so the 20,000 Egyptians present at Raphia in 217 must be subtracted from any total. The number of troops needed for operations against the insurrection in the Thebaid was substantial; at a minimum we would expect 20,000 Ptolemaic soldiers to counter the rebels. Yet with stripped-down garrisons, it is unlikely that the regency government for Ptolemy V deployed a field army of more than 40,000 troops to defend Koile Syria. Meanwhile, Antiochus was free to operate with his entire force. While we do not know the exact numbers of Antiochus' army, it probably consisted of around 70,000 troops, a strength similar to his invasion force in 217 BC, badly outnumbering the Ptolemies. Still, in 201, a large proportion of Antiochus' troops occupied the newly conquered territory, reducing the size of his field army.[7]

With no king fit for command, a mercenary general named Scopas the Aetolian took lead of the Ptolemaic army. Scopas was a high-ranking Aetolian politician who had served as league general (*strategos*) on numerous occasions and fought against Philip V during the wars between Aetolia and Macedonia from 220 to 206. After failing to reform the Aetolian constitution in his favour, Scopas exiled himself to Egypt, where his competent military leadership might prove an advantage. He was especially attractive to the regency government on account of his high-level connections in Aetolia, a prime recruiting ground for Greek mercenaries. In 202, he took a seemingly bottomless chest of silver with him on a recruiting mission and returned with 6000 Aetolian infantry and 500 cavalry for mercenary service in Egypt.[8] As a reward for his efforts, Scopas was placed in command of the Ptolemaic army rebuilt largely around his own mercenary cadre.

Scopas launched an ambitious counter-attack. He drove deep into Koile Syria and recaptured Judea, punishing the region's inhabitants for going over to Antiochus.[9] In response, Antiochus hastened his army out of winter quarters and marched south to halt Scopas' advance. Scopas set up a blocking position at Panium (the modern-day Golan Heights), named after a local Hellenistic shrine to the god Pan and site of an older shrine to Ba'al.

The account of the Battle of Panium is highly problematic. Polybius' discussion reads mostly as a pointed critique of Zeno of Rhodes' description of the battle. It is possible that Polybius lacked an alternative source for the encounter, and was thus reduced to critiquing the implausibilities in his one available source. However, Polybius was also a relentless and self-serving critic. Hoping to become the definitive historian of his era, he took delight in smearing perceived competitors. It is very likely that Zeno of Rhodes' narrative was reasonably accurate and at least reliable enough to provide a basic outline of combat. Based on the location of the Jordan River that would have split the battlefield into two topographical areas, Professor Bar Kochba argues that many of Zeno's statements were indeed reasonable.[10]

Compensating for his reduced numbers, Scopas attempted to anchor his right flank against Mt Panium. Antiochus the Younger led a vanguard action, crossing the Jordan River with a large army of cataphracts. Antiochus III followed with the main body, two wings of cavalry and the main infantry phalanx. To his front, he positioned a powerful line of elephants, with Tarantine Greek mercenaries, archers, and slingers stationed in between.

After this, the tactical details are lost, save for Antiochus the Younger's decisive cavalry charge upon the light horse of his enemy. It is unclear whether the main infantry phalanxes engaged one another. Polybius believed they did not, noting that Zeno reports that Antiochus positioned skirmishers, elephants and even his royal cavalry in front of his main phalanx. However, a lull in the fighting could have provided time to move elephants and skirmishers to the flanks, or the ranks of the phalanx could have been maintained in an open order to allow light troops to fall back to the rear. Still, Polybius was an experienced military man, so his opinion is not to be dismissed lightly. It is also possible that Antiochus III stacked his troops so deep that they were not in a position to engage the enemy.

The defeated Ptolemaic army then returned to Egypt, its casualties unknown but significant. Scopas the Aetolian rallied 10,000 survivors (including his cadre of Aetolian mercenaries) and stationed them in the city of Sidon on the Phoenician coast.

Shortly after the Battle of Panium, in the summer or early fall of 200 BC, Roman envoys arrived in Antioch. Antiochus had returned to the city after his victory, allowing subordinates to clean up from the most recent battle. The Romans had administered a stern warning to Philip V to call off his attacks in the Aegean, and now they issued a similar warning to Antiochus III: he was to 'abstain from the realm of Egypt'.[11]

Had Antiochus harboured serious intentions against Egypt at this point, a message from the Romans would not have been sufficient to stop him. As we will later see, Antiochus would completely ignore future Roman embassies ordering him to refrain from other territorial ambitions. The only conclusion that can be drawn here is that Antiochus did not have designs on Egypt. Why would he want to occupy a country torn by urban riot and rural rebellion? Yet Antiochus cannily used the demands to score some easy diplomatic points with the Roman delegation. He indicated that he had no territorial designs against Egypt, and in exchange for this, he was declared a 'friend and ally of the Roman people' (*amicus sociusque Populi Romani*).

Besides, Antiochus still had clean-up operations that would take the next two years to complete. He turned his attentions first to Scopas the Aetoliean and his 10,000 defenders in Sidon.[12] This force endured a siege of several months and finally surrendered under generous terms that allowed the mercenaries to return to Egypt or home to Aetolia. At this point, Antiochus felt assured of victory and did not need to exterminate this sliver of Ptolemaic manpower.

Despite the fall of Sidon, the Phoenician city of Gaza continued to hold out. Destroyed by Alexander the Great in an epic siege that transformed their island into a peninsula, the Gazans' resistance was motivated by this history as they again withstood Antiochus' siege. The city finally fell in 198 and the conquest of Koile Syria was complete.[13] Finally, Antiochus III realized an ambition over a hundred years in the making, as Seleucid kings had claimed Koile Syria for nearly a century after the battle of Ipsus in 301 BC. He had gained control of the agricultural resources of the Gaza strip and Jordan River valley, the wealthy mercantile cities of Tyre, Gaza, Sidon, and Beruit, themselves connected to Arabian caravan routes that stretched as far as China and India.

The organization of Koile Syria

The central figure in the new administration of Seleucid Koile Syria was also the central figure from in the old administration of Ptolemaic Koile Syria. His name was Ptolemaios, son of Thraseas, and his family had a long tradition of Ptolemaic service: both his father Thraseas and grandfather Aetus had been high-ranking Ptolemaic officials.[14] The family had over two generations of roots in the region and had acquired property, clients and relatives who were not to be left behind lightly. Rather than retreat with the Ptolemaic armies, Ptolemaios son of Thraseas switched sides. For this he was richly rewarded and named the *strategos* (general) of Koile Syria, as well as the high priest of the entire region, presumably of the royal cult. In exchange for his swapped loyalty, Ptolemaios son of Thraseas provided Antiochus with administrative continuity in the new province, and was able to advise the King on the standard operating procedure already in place in the province. For example, he explained to the King that large landowners were accustomed to settling any minor disputes that arose between their own peasants. In the event that peasants from two different villages got into a dispute, this should be settled by a local official called the *oikonomos*. Ptolemaios advised that he himself as the *strategos* should have jurisdiction over any murder charges or significant civil cases, while he emphasized that garrison commanders and regional commanders should also be responsive to civilian appeals.

In the aftermath of the campaign, however, it was clear that many Seleucid officials and soldiers were exploiting the locals, forcefully billeting troops in houses, illegally requisitioning goods, and even kidnapping local peasants to sell into slavery. As a leading local landowner who saw his own serfs victimized by such actions, Ptolemaios wrote a sharp letter of complaint to the King:

Memorandum to the Great King Antiochus from Ptolemaios the strategos and high priest. I request, if it appears good to you, o king, that you send written instructions to Kleon and Heliodoros, the *dioketai*, so that no one should have the authority, under any pretext, to billet in the villages that I own with the right of inheritance and in those that you ordered be transferred to me, no bring others there, nor requisition any possessions, nor carry off the peasants (*laoi*)...

Antiochus was not pleased. He fired off a letter to a subordinate, ordering the end to such abuses:

King Antiochus to Marsyas, greetings. Ptolemaios, *strategos* and high priest has informed us that many of those passing by take billets by force in his villages and commit not a few other crimes, paying not attention to the orders we have sent about these matters. So make it your duty not only to prevent them, but also fine them ten times the cost of the damage they do....[15]

These letters were part of a long string of correspondence, involving both the King, his general and a slew of low-level administrators, providing a picture of the complex local bureaucracy of the empire.

The Jews and Jerusaelm
With the conquest of Koile Syria, Antiochus III inherited the problem of Jerusalem. Certainly he was not unfamiliar with the Jewish religion, as Babylon was home to a sizable Jewish population, and he had previously settled a large body of Jewish military settlers in Asia Minor. However, as the former seat of the Davidic kings and the site of the second temple, Jerusalem was a vortex of potentially destabilizing religious politics. Any conqueror would be wise to tread lightly.

For their part the inhabitants of Jerusalem took the initiative by sending delegates to Antiochus arranging for a swift and tidy surrender. According to the Jewish historian Flavius Josephus, writing in Rome nearly 300 years later, Antiochus accepted the surrender with generous terms. Josephus appears to be transcribing an inscription that he had seen personally. As the language he preserves is not the usual stilted form common to official inscriptions, there is reason to think that Josephus polished the text and embellished the style. Still, despite the doubts of a few historians, most hold that Josephus provides accurate information about the settlement of Jerusalem. In the inscription, Antiochus writes to Ptolemaios son of Thraseas:

> King Antiochus to Ptolemaios, Greetings. Since the Jews, when we entered their country, at once displayed their enthusiasm for us, and when we arrived in their city received us magnificently and came to meet us with their *gerousia*, and have provided abundant supplies to our soldiers and elephants, and assisted us in expelling the Egyptian garrison in the citadel, we thought it right on our part to repay them for these services and to restore their city which had been destroyed by the accidents of war and to re-people it by bringing back to it those who had been scattered about.
>
> In the first place, we have decided because of their piety to provide them with an allowance for sacrifices consisting of sacrificial animals, wine, olive oil and frankincense, to the value of 20,000 silver pieces,[16] and sacred artabas of the finest flour in accordance with their native law, and 1460 medimnoi of wheat and 375 medimni of salt.[17] I wish these grants to be made to them in accordance with my instructions, and the work on the temple to be completed together with the stoas and anything else which needs to be build. The timber required for the woodwork shall be brought to Judea itself, from other nations and from Lebanon, and no one shall charge a duty on it. Similarly, for the other materials needed for repairing the Temple in a more splendid way.
>
> All the people of the nation shall govern themselves in accordance to their ancestral laws, and the *gerousia*,[18] the priests, the scribes of the Temple and the Temple singers shall be exempted from the poll tax, the crown tax and the salt tax.
>
> To hasten the re-peopling of the city, I grant to the present inhabitants and to those who come back before the month of Hyperberetaeus (around October) freedom from taxes for three years.
>
> We also remit for the future one third of their taxes to make good the injuries they have sustained. As for all those who were carried away from the city and are now slaves, I grant their freedom to them

and to their children, and order the restitution of their property to them.[19]

Many of the features described here were common in Seleucid relations with captured cities. In exchange for loyalty, the king offers negotiated local autonomy. As a show of regal goodwill, he makes specific benefactions. To account for the damage inflicted by Scopas' garrison, he remits taxes to allow the community to recover. These policies helped ensure excellent relations between the Seleucid king and his Jewish subjects for the next forty years.

The Roman wars of Philip V

Antiochus was not alone in his assault against Ptolemaic possessions. Philip V embarked on his own rapacious campaign in the Aegean. In 202 he swooped down on the Ptolemaic naval base at Samos, although a costly naval battle near Chios against the combined fleets of Athens, Rhodes, and Pergamon curbed his hopes of conquering the entire Aegean.[20] Philip then landed in Asia Minor to begin a land campaign and marauded through Caria. He ran into severe logistical difficulties there, and his army risked starvation. He appealed to Zeuxis for help, perhaps citing a concrete provision within the secret pact, but the provided supplies proved insufficient. It is possible that Zeuxis helped Philip reluctantly, but it is more likely that he simply lacked the on-hand supplies to feed all of Philip's expeditionary force. The Macedonian king was reduced to handing the captured town of Myous to the city of Magnesia-on-the-Maeander in exchange for rations of dried figs.[21]

By now, news of the secret pact between the kings had spread through diplomatic channels. Attalus of Pergamon was particularly worried about defending himself against Philip V on one side and Antiochus III on the other. In the old world of the three major powers, it was possible for modest kingdoms to retain their independence by pluck and craft, literally by triangulating in between the three major powers. It would be far more dangerous to live in a world divided by the two allies Philip V and Antiochus III. Thus, a coalition of Pergamon, Athens, and Rhodes (all of which traditionally received support from Ptolemaic Egypt) looked to the West for assistance.

Of these newly allied kingdoms, Attalus I had recently established friendly relations with Rome. In 205 BC, the Romans expressed interest in a certain religious artefact under his control: the black navel stone of the Magna Mater ('Great Mother'), a cult centred in eastern Antatolia.[22] The Romans claimed descent from the city of Ilium (Troy) located in that region, giving an otherwise strange foreign cult special significance. Attalus I arranged the transfer of the black stone to Rome and thus strengthened diplomatic ties.

In 202 BC, Rome defeated Carthage after sixteen years of brutal warfare. The resulting peace treaty eliminated Carthage as a major power; she was stripped of her recruiting grounds in Spain and Numidia and deprived of her fleets and elephant herds. An indemnity of 200 talents per year for the next fifty years was imposed, designed to impoverish a state already out of nearly all sources of revenue. With Carthage crippled by this draconian peace treaty, Rome reigned supreme in the western Mediterranean.

When Attalus I arrived in Rome in 202, the Romans had much to fear from the secret pact between Philip V and Antiochus III. The war with Carthage had nearly ended in Roman defeat. Over 200,000 Roman and Italian soldiers had died in battle, including some 120,000 between 218 and 216 BC, a period of unprecedented military catastrophe. The war made the Romans sense the fragility of their own state: they appreciated afresh the vulnerability that came with sustained conflict. These feelings led to more than a hint of paranoia in matters of foreign relations. Now that the 'balance of power' was shattered in the eastern Mediterranean, Rome feared that Philip V or Antiochus III might grow too powerful with the addition of Ptolemaic resources and territories.[23]

For Rome, however, the most immediate enemy was Philip V. During the war with Hannibal, Philip V had made a logical decision. In 216, Hannibal enveloped and massacred a Roman army at Cannae. It was the third straight loss Rome had suffered in as many years. As many as 50,000 Roman soldiers were encircled and killed in a single horrifying day. To an outsider observer, it seemed that Carthage had won the war. Philip V sent envoys and signed a peace treaty with Carthage, promising aid and cooperation. Philip V was not obliged to join the war with Rome, nor was Carthage committed to any of Philip's adventures.

A copy of the peace treaty was intercepted by Roman troops in 215, and the furious senate declared war upon Macedon. But with Roman armies engaged in Italy and Spain, Rome relegated the so-called 'First Macedonian War' to a mere sideshow. While Roman fleets chased Philip off the Adriatic Sea and a small Roman army operated in Illyria, Rome used the Aetolian League to fight a war by proxy. Without firm Roman support, the Aetolians made a separate peace with Philip V in 206, and the Romans concluded a separate peace with Philip the next year, called the Peace of Phoinike. The proxy war had done little but create bad blood between the two powers, and when the final battle with Hannibal took place at Zama, rumours circulated that 4000 Macedonians joined the side of Carthage.[24] This was a total falsehood, although a few Macedonian mercenaries among the prisoners may have given credence to the tall tale. Nonetheless, if Rome were going to act against one of the two kings, there was reason to target Philip V first.

In 201 BC, after some reluctance, the Roman citizen assembly declared war on Macedonia. Modern historians refer to it as the 'Second Macedonian War'. In 197 BC, a Roman army led by T. Quinctius Flamininus destroyed Philip V's army at Cynoscephalae ('the Dog's Head'). Philip was allowed to keep his kingdom but was stripped of his external territories. He was also forced to surrender his eldest son, Demetrius, as a hostage to Rome and pay a hefty indemnity.

The Greeks, who by now had endured over 150 years of Macedonian subjugation, expected the Romans to set up permanent garrisons, in particular in the 'fetters' of Greece: strategic points at Corinth (Acrocorinth), the Athenian harbour at Piraeus, Demetrias, and Chalcis.

The Roman commander Flamininus was well aware of the diplomatic language of the Hellenistic world. Since the age of the successors, warlords and kings sought to position themselves as liberators of the Greek city, and liberty (*eleutheria*) was the operative word. While such liberty proved a very flexible concept, it was generally understood to reference autonomy in the realm of domestic policy, indeed the ability to remain under 'one's own laws' (*autonomos*). The most desirable kind of *eleutheria* involved the absence of tribute (*aphoros*) and garrisons (*aphylakes*).

In 195 BC Flamininus attended the Pan-Hellenic Ishmean games near Corinth. Before the representatives of the assembled cities, he made a dramatic announcement, spoken in Latin and translated through Greek heralds: the Greek cities were to be free. The Romans would level no tribute nor install garrisons.[25] The crowd went wild. If it had been a cynical announcement, it was certainly not received as such. Flamininus' handlers feared he might be injured in the joyous rush to shake hands that followed.

Lysias and Hegesianax, two of the men who met with the pro-consul at Corinth, were not part of the general rejoicing. Antiochus had dispatched them as envoys to make contact with the victorious Romans and assess the situation in Greece and Macedonia.[26] They met with the senatorial commissioners who had been sent over to help supervise Flamininus as he settled Greek and Macedonian affairs. The commissioners received the Seleucid envoys imperiously and gave them stark instructions as if they were the representatives from a defeated nation and not a waxing Mediterranean power:

> They admonished the envoys of Antiochus to stay away from the autonomous cities of Asia and not to wage war against any of them, and to withdraw from whatever cities previously subject to Philip or Ptolemy he had just captured. They likewise forbade crossing into Europe with an armed force, for now none of the Greeks were to be warred upon or enslaved by anyone. They indicated, without going into details, that some of the commissioners would come to meet with Antiochus (Polybius 18.47.1–5).

Such blunt speech was not uniquely Roman, but rather common in ancient diplomacy. Today, modern diplomats speak in a measured and nuanced language that has been developed over the centuries. Such speech allows discussion without the type of frankness that might prompt outbursts of anger. Ancient diplomacy, on the other hand, frequently resembled schoolyard 'trash-talking'.

The end of the fifth Syrian War

As Macedonian and Roman armies skirmished in Thessaly prior to the final showdown at Cynoscephalae, Antiochus continued his operations against Ptolemy V. With Koile Syria firmly in Seleucid hands and Philip occupied with the Roman war, Antiochus looked north to Asia Minor and Thrace. Philip V had claimed some of this territory, but at this time it seems the pact between kings was broken. With Philip fully distracted by his war with Rome, Antiochus prepared to seize some easy spoils.

In 197 BC, an army under the command of Mithradites and Ardys marched toward Sardis along the old Persian royal road. Mithradites was the younger son of Antiochus who had received his first important military command. Ardys was a senior soldier, who had served against Molon over twenty years before and taken part in the capture of Seleucia Pieria. His role was to advise and assist the young prince in his first military command.[27]

Meanwhile, Antiochus fit out a modest armada off the coast of southern Asia Minor, the first major Seleucid fleet to sail upon Mediterranean waters. Fleet and army now moved westwards in parallel thrusts, and Antiochus stopped his ships to force the submission of coastal towns along the way.

After a series of successes and submissions, a Rhodian delegation confronted Antiochus' fleet. The Rhodians had joined the Roman coalition against Philip V, but they were alarmed about Antiochus' naval incursions. The delegates from Rhodes demanded Antiochus halt his campaign until further negotiations take place between the two states. Even though Antiochus was a Great King and Rhodes a small island *polis*, he was obliged to halt and negotiate. Rhodes had a well-established navy, one far superior to his experimental fleet. The negotiations concluded to both parties' mutual satisfaction, and Antiochus agreed to bypass the region of Halicarnassus in Caria, an old Ptolemaic possession that would fall under Rhode's sphere of influence. Antiochus also agreed not to establish a naval base at Samos, a position that would threaten Rhodes' Aegean thalassocracy.

With the Rhodian negotiations complete, Antiochus continued to attack up the Ionian coast. He bypassed a number of cities still in Macedonian possession: Bargylia, Iasos and Euromos, but then captured a string of Ptolemaic cities, finally arriving at Ephesus, a strategically located city with a strong citadel, which if captured would allow domination of the western coast of Asia Minor and access to the

Hellespont.[28] He occupied Ephesus without fanfare, and as expected, the city would become his capital in Ionia and an important base for further operations in the west.

While in Ephesus, Antiochus heard of the death of Attalus I, who had reigned at Pergamon for forty-three years, and of the accession of his son Eumenes II.[29] Although Attalus' defection in 241 had made him an enemy to the Seleucid dynasty, he had allied with Antiochus in the fight against Achaeus, and the two powers had maintained a tenuous peace ever since. Yet Attalus I had most recently been alarmed by Antiochus' new campaign into Asia Minor, fearing that the capture of Ptolemaic territories would not satisfy the King's ambition for more territory.

Yet Antiochus' campaign season of 196 would be focused not against Pergamon but rather toward ensuring Seleucid dominance of the Hellespont. In the spring of 196 BC, a Seleucid garrison was installed in Abydos. This city had been a flash point in the Romano–Macedonian War, as Philip had captured it after a brutal siege in 201. Control of Abydos ensured Macedonian hegemony over the Hellespont and had prompted immediate Roman military intervention. However, Antiochus now occupied Abydos with little fanfare. Ilium, on the site of Homeric Troy, was also brought within the Seleucid sphere of influence at this time, at least according to an inscription from King Antiochus to the citizens of Ilium. Antiochus had his eyes also on the Ionian cities of Smyrna, Lampsacus, and Aeolis, and he sent detachments to the first two communities. But he was not willing to invest the military resources to besiege both cities, preferring to concentrate resources in order to secure the far side of the Hellespont. Still, Lampsacus was sufficiently alarmed by the display to appoint an envoy to travel to Greece and contact the Romans. Its envoy Hegesias met with Lucius Flamininus, the brother of the Roman commander.[30] Antiochus was also represented before the Romans, having previously dispatched Lysias and Hegesianax to advocate in front of the victorious Romans. Meanwhile, Antiochus crossed over to the European side with an armed force and occupied the Chersonesos (modern-day Gallipoli), and after a short siege of the city of Madytos, the remaining communities submitted.

The Ptolemies had previously controlled the Chersonesos, but relinquished this authority after the cascade of dynastic misfortunes.

Thracian war-bands took advantage of this power vacuum and ravaged the area, destroying the city of Lysimacheia. Antiochus secured the area, counter-raiding against the Thracians tribes on the borders. He sought to rebuild and repopulate Lysimacheia by ransoming captives sold into slavery and importing new settlers who were provided with cattle and agricultural tools.[31] The rebuilt city provided Antiochus with a base to control the vital passage between the Mediterranean and Black Seas.

While Antiochus was in Lysimacheia, a Roman delegation arrived to confront the Seleucid king. It consisted of four commissioners sent by the senate to supervise Flamininus' settlement. Led by Lucius Cornelius Lentulus, the group had been instructed by the senate to urge an immediate conclusion of the war with Ptolemy, but the overall purpose of the delegation was to discern Antiochus' intentions and to intensify diplomatic engagement.

The diplomatic meeting had both public and private aspects. The public aspect consisted of contentious posturing: Lucius Cornelius demanded that Antiochus relinquish all cities captured from Ptolemy and refrain from attacking the free Greek cities of Asia Minor. He concluded by questioning Antiochus' military operations in the Chersonesos, a campaign the Romans viewed as impinging on their settlement of Greece. Antiochus protested and argued the Romans' overreach: just as he had no right to the affairs of the Italian peninsula, they had no right to dictate policy in Asia. He also defended his right to intervene in Lysimacheia. The Roman ambassadors responded by calling in representatives from Lampascus and Smyrna to protest Seleucid depredations. Caught in this Roman diplomatic ambush, Antiochus stormed out of the room and insisted that Rhodes mediate the dispute as a mutual ally. With this exit, he left behind a festering diplomatic conflict, 'a study in Cold War' as Ernest Badian famously called the situation in 1959.[32] While some have criticized Badian for this analogy, a comparison of the Romans and Seleucids in the mid-190s BC to the cold war between the US and USSR may prove instructive. In both instances, unprecedented warfare had reduced a divided international system to two powers. The two victors saw each other across a 'contested periphery', territory that both sides claimed as spheres of influence: Greece in the case of Rome and Antiochus, Central Europe in the case of the US and Stalin. In both instances, diplomacy was terse and generally ineffective. Only the terror of nuclear annihilation prevented the US–USSR Cold War from turning hot.

Even as conflict festered between Rome and Antiochus, peace negotiations were underway with the Ptolemaic government, then controlled by the regents Aristomenes and Polykrates overseeing the boy king. By the time the Roman delegation arrived, the basic outline for peace had been decided. Ptolemy V recognized Antiochus' right to Koile Syria, Asia Minor, and Thrace, and Antiochus' daughter Cleopatra would marry young Ptolemy V.[33] This was in keeping with Antiochus' strategy of using female relatives to watch over vanquished kings. Cleopatra, born circa 215, was likely ten years older than her prepubescent husband. The only concession on the Seleucid side seems to have been that part of the revenue from Koile Syria would come with Cleopatra as a dowry (although this money was probably intended for her personal maintenance, rather than for the benefit of the Ptolemaic state treasury).[34] Antiochus could thus confidently tell the concerned Roman delegation that he viewed the boy king not as an enemy but rather a son-in-law. He was also gaining an important ally and agent in the Ptolemaic court. The book of Daniel (c. 100 BC) prophesized retrospectively that 'in order to destroy the kingdom, he (Antiochus III) shall give him (Ptolemy V) a woman in marriage'.

As the Roman envoys lingered in Lysimacheia, news arrived that Ptolemy V had died. If true, this threatened to upend the international structure of the Mediterranean once again, for the eleven-year-old Ptolemy V did not have an heir. The end of a major Hellenistic dynasty changed political and military calculations: it is possible that Antiochus now considered invading Egypt proper. He rushed to Ephesus and from there to Antioch, trying to confirm the report and make contingency plans to prepare his fleet for action.

The reports were false; Ptolemy V was still very much alive. Antiochus' hasty response confirmed the Romans' suspicions that he harboured continued territorial ambitions against Egypt. The issue of Smyrna and Lampsacus remained unresolved, a continued point of contention in Romano-Seleucid relations.

Having prepared his fleet to sail to Egypt, Antiochus made an assault on the island of Cyprus, a Ptolemaic possession important for its strategic location and substantial agricultural and mineral resources. The hastily conceived expedition was a complete failure. Worried about an expedition so late in the sailing season, the sailors briefly mutinied, and then a violent storm wrecked much of the fleet, killing many sailors and even some high-ranking 'friends'. The fleet limped back to Seleucia Pieria, and the King proceeded up the Orontes River to Antioch.[35] Frustrated in this endeavour as well and increasingly worried about tensions with the Romans, Antiochus prepared himself to sign the negotiated peace treaty with Ptolemy V.

Royal weddings

With the formal end of the fifth Syrian War and the diplomatic marriage between Cleopatra and Ptolemy V, Antiochus now sought to marry his remaining eligible children and return to the dynastic business neglected during the past five years of campaigning.

Antiochus' attempted to betroth his middle daughter, Antiochis, to Eumenes II of Pergamon. Eumenes had a consequential diplomatic choice: he could accept the alliance and marry the daughter of a traditional enemy. But he had little reason to pursue this course of action: by refusing to marry Antiochus' daughter, he gambled that the Roman Republic would prove a more reliable ally than the Great King. Antiochis was betrothed instead to Ariarathes, the king of Cappadocia.

The most notable marriage of 196, however, took place between Antiochus the Younger and his sister Laodice. For the first time, the Seleucid dynasty committed itself to incestuous marriage, mimicking Ptolemaic practice. The ultimate goal of this decision was the glorification of the dynasty, as incest rarefies royal bloodlines. While Antiochus forged marriage alliances with petty kings such as Ariarathes, the desire for purity of his own royal line reveals the rising status of the Seleucid monarchy. With Macedonia and the Ptolemies humbled, the Seleucid king saw no equal, and Antiochus therefore decided his heir ought not to interbreed with lesser kings. The recourse to incest may also imply a more assertive claim to divine status, as the phenomenon of royal incest is closely linked with claims of divine ancestry or actual divinity.

There is also evidence from this time that Antiochus established a state sponsored royal cult for himself and his wife Laodice. While the worship of Hellenistic kings dated to the era of Alexander and the successors, such cults were always organized on the initiative of subject communities as a gesture of loyalty and submission. Antiochus began to administer the royal cult through his own prerogative, yet another sign of an increasing sense of power and importance.

A refugee arrives in court

In 194, the Carthaginian general Hannibal Barca arrived in Ephesus and presented himself before Antiochus.[36]Although defeated at Zama in 202 BC, Hannibal remained an important fixture in Carthaginian politics for the next decade. In 195, he was elected *suffet* ('judge,' one of the two senior magistrates of the Carthaginian Republic) and he backed a number of reforms that strengthened democratic aspects of the Carthaginian constitution. Despite this involvement, Hannibal's political opponents arranged for his exile in 195 and spread rumours in Rome that he was plotting to renew hostilities.[37] Hannibal fled to Seleucid-controlled Tyre, the mythical homeland of the Carthaginians, where he was received with much fanfare. He then proceeded to the court at Ephesus. The Seleucid court was a logical destination for a political refugee of Hannibal's calibre. Perhaps he hoped to obtain employment as a senior mercenary captain, but despite his polite reception he was not granted any significant command. The Romans, however, took notice of this movement: Hannibal's presence in the Seleucid court was profoundly unnerving to them and strengthened their suspicions of Antiochus III.

Yet Hannibal was not necessarily an entirely welcome presence in the Seleucid court. His past outsized military and political achievements were viewed with suspicion by Antiochus, who likely resented Hannibal's claims of military pre-eminence.

Hannibal's position in court was complicated by the arrival of a new Roman delegation in 193. Hoping to sow discord, the Romans paid a great deal of attention to Hannibal's presence. Sensing that he was falling out of favour with the king, Hannibal responded by telling Antiochus a famous story from his youth: how as a young boy his father, Hamilcar, compelled him to swear an oath of eternal enmity against Rome. According to Polybius, this story convinced Antiochus of Hannibal's loyalty as an ally in his ongoing tensions against Rome, and the Carthaginian's standing within the Seleucid court improved.[38]

The view from Rome

The government in Rome was run by a small set of aristocratic families. Politically ambitious nobles ran for office in elections determined by popular vote; the consulship was the most important office. Two consuls were elected annually with a one-year term, although consular commands might be extended (prorogation) so that ex-consuls might serve as 'pro-consuls' in order to conclude an assigned task. Four to six junior magistrates called praetors held subordinate commands. The electoral predilection of the populace was relentlessly conservative and preferred a small number of well-established families. The same assembly of voters (the *comitia centuriata*) also declared war and ratified peace. Ex-magistrates formed a separate body known as the senate, literally a 'body of old men' (*senes*). While technically the senate was merely an advisory body to the consuls, it had claimed several important powers by this time: the right to assign elected magistrates to a particular province and control over the money stored in the Roman treasury.

Rome lacked formal political parties, although factions around powerful politicians and successful generals defined the political process. By 196 two powerful generals were in ascendance: Quinctius Flamininus, who conquered Philip V and settled the affairs in Greece, and Scipio Africanus, who had defeated Hannibal and the Carthaginians.

Flamininus had one primary objective: to preserve his influence over Greek policy. Having publically committed himself to the 'freedom of the Greeks', and the quick withdrawal of Rome's armies from Macedonia and Greece, it was in his political interest to avoid immediate military actions to confront Antiochus in Thrace and Ionia. At the same time, Flamininus was not naïve. While he hoped for a diplomatic solution to Antiochus' incursions in the area, he realized that force might become necessary as Seleucid aggressions moved toward the Greek mainland.

Finding his military pre-eminence upstaged by Flamininus' victory at Cynoscephalae, Scipio Africanus was eager to obtain a fresh military command. Custom prevented him from holding two consulships without a ten-year interval, and his first consulship had been in 205 BC. In the interim period, he served as censor: counting Roman citizens, revising the senate rolls, and awarding public contracts. In 195 he ran for consul again and easily won. He hoped to obtain a command in Macedonia for the consular year 194 so that he might confront Antiochus directly, but Flamininus still hoped that diplomacy might preserve his own settlement in Greece and his allies in the senate prevailed. The senate sent one consul to continue an ongoing war against the Gauls of Northern Italy, and Scipio Africanus was assigned the province of Italy, where he established a chain of maritime colonies on the Adriatic coast. Flamininus achieved his goal of the complete evacuation of Greece, fulfilling the dramatic promise even as his misgivings over Seleucid intentions began to grow.

The factions of Scipio and Flamininus meanwhile enjoyed alternating electoral successes. The election of 194 (for the consular year of 193) brought two Scipionic supporters to power: Cornelius Merula, from the same *gens* as Scipio himself, and Minicius Thermus. Thermus had served under Scipio in Africa, and as tribune of the plebs in 201 fought to protect Scipio's peace settlement against Hannibal. The senate, however, refused to assign Macedonia as a consular command, and both consuls fought in northern Italy, Merula against the Gauls and Thermus against the Ligurians. The next year, however, saw Flaminius' brother Lucius elected consul along with Domitius Ahenobarbus, defeating the Scipionic candidate Scipio Nasica. Thus, in 192, the consuls in power were close to Flamininus, who had until now personally opposed military intervention in Greece. Furthermore, the Romans had ongoing wars in Northern Italy to occupy their armies and provide commands for ambitious consuls. Despite the claims of William V. Harris, who argued that the Romans were a 'pathologically aggressive' people who actively sought war on the flimsiest of pretext, there is little evidence that the Romans plunged headfirst into the war with Antiochus.[39]

In many ways, however, Scipio Africanus' plan to dispatch an army to Greece or Macedonia in order to demonstrate against Seleucid ambitions in Europe would have been the best policy. It would have made clear to Antiochus that Greece was off limits, and would have perhaps prevented any miscalculation on his part that an invasion of Greece would bring war with Rome. The senate did not do this for two reasons. Firstly,

Flamininus had committed himself to the idea of 'freedom', and was therefore trapped by his own rhetoric. Aside from Flamininus' own immense prestige, many senators resented Scipio's preeminent military glory, and were hesitant to give him yet another command.

Ongoing negotiations

In 194 (or possibly early 193), Antiochus sent another delegation to Rome. It consisted of the two veterans of the conference at Lysimacheia, Hegesianax and Lysias, as well as Menippos, a rising star in the Seleucid court. Flamininus, fresh from Greece, was present in the senate to confront the Seleucid delegation. Hegesianax, who wrote history as well as poetry, offered the senate a history lesson, noting that the contested regions of Thrace and north-western Asia Minor had once belonged to the successor king Lysimachus. When Seleucus defeated Lysimachus, the territory became Seleucid by right of conquest. Other cities in Thrace, Hegesianax argued, belonged to Antiochus, his due for wresting them away from the Thracians. He argued that Lysimacheia had long been abandoned, so Antiochus wronged no one by appropriating and repopulating it. His history lesson complete, Hegesianax requested a treaty of friendship and equality with Rome that would acknowledge the rights over Thrace and Asia Minor.

Flamininus was less than impressed at this 'history lesson'.[40] In a counterpoint lesson, he pointed out that while Seleucus I had taken Thrace and Asia Minor from Lysimachus, Antiochus' own father and grandfather had failed to control these regions effectively. Thus, the Great King could make no claim to regions so long removed from Seleucid dominion. Flamininus then adamantly insisted that the cities of Ionia and Aeolis were to be free as well, if Antiochus wanted to maintain peace with Rome.

Menippos begged the senators to soften their line, lest 'by their decision the whole world fall into chaos'.[41] Realizing that the heated rhetoric might push both sides into an undesirable war, Menippos begged both sides to reconsider, and the Romans agreed to send to Syria the Roman delegates who had previously met with the King at Lysimacheia: Publius Sulpicius, Publius Villius and Publius Aelius.[42]

The Seleucid delegate Menippos, however, did not represent only Antiochus. He also had been charged by the city of Teos to negotiate a pact of *asylia* with Rome; such a pact would protect the city from piracy and violence. Teos had already negotiated these pacts with a number of other foreign powers, and the Roman praetor Marcus Valerius Messala granted Menippos' request, forwarding to Teos a letter acknowledging the city as sacred and inviolate. Sensing the winds of war, Teos hoped to guard itself against the possibility of a Roman sack.[43]

The Roman delegation arrived in the Seleucid court the next year, travelling first to Ephesus and subsequently on to meet with the king in Apamea. There they found troubling signs. Hannibal was still present in the court at Ephesus, and a delegation of visiting Aetolians was in Apamea to court Seleucid intervention in Greece.

The negotiations of 193 were cut short by the sudden death of Antiochus the Younger. The cause of death is not certain. Livy implies that Antiochus III had his son poisoned by court eunuchs, 'the father thinking the crown prince as a hazard to his old-age'.[44] Such court gossip cannot be substantiated, and it is highly unlikely that Antiochus III murdered his son. First, Antiochus was only forty-seven at this time, not an elderly man. He had carefully groomed Antiochus the Younger for succession: the son was already holding court in Ephesus and receiving ambassadors and dignitaries. He had earned his spurs through an important military command at Panium. Three years previously he had been married to his sister, and the royal incest marked him as the favoured son.

Livy suggests that when Antiochus III granted his middle son Seleucus (who eventually succeeded him in 187 BC) the territory of Lysimacheia, he intended to elevate him above the doomed Antiochus the Younger. But the grant to Seleucus is better understood as provision for a son who would *not* become king. Livy makes this false accusation against Antiochus in order to craft a tidy historical parallel between Antiochus III and Philip V, who without question murdered his elder son in the 170s. Historical inventions aside, there is no reason to believe that young Antiochus was murdered, and certainly not by his father.[45] Upon the death of the young Antiochus, the entire Seleucid court went into mourning, and the Roman embassy that had recently arrived politely withdrew to Pergamon.

One result of young Antiochus' death was a curious name swap. Antiochus III had named his youngest son Mithradites, the traditional dynastic name used by the allied Pontic Kingdom, used in part because the third boy was born to an exhausted supply of traditional dynastic names. But the death of young Antiochus had created a void: it would not be appropriate to use a Pontic dynastic name when there were no living sons named Antiochus. Young Mithradites, probably only ten years old, now assumed the name Antiochus.[46] He would eventually assume the diadem, known by modern scholars as Antiochus IV.

The Aetolian invitation

In 192 BC, neither Rome nor Antiochus actively wanted a war. Both powers had spent four years posturing and negotiating, trying to define a periphery that neither side wished to fight for more aggressively. Yet as frequently occurs in such situations, the actions of a minor power finally spurred the two reluctant giants to engage. In 192, the Aetolian League, acting on its own volition, invited Antiochus to liberate Greece.

Two major federal leagues (*koina*) dominated Greece, the Aetolian and the Achaean. Although they were occasionally allies, they had a longer tradition of hostility. During the Social War beginning in 221 BC, the Achaean League allied itself with Philip V of Macedon against Aetolia. A peace treaty was signed at Naupactus in 217, but the Aetolians were convinced to join Rome against Philip in 211. While this war was a sideshow for Rome, it also reflected the traditional Aetolian hostility toward the menacing power of Macedonia. As long as Macedon and Achaea were allies, Aetolia was cornered, and the alliance with Rome provided them the opportunity to alter the balance of power.

After the Battle of Cynoscephalae and the curbing of Macedonian power, the two federal leagues became the two most important military powers in Greece. Despite a twenty-year history of cooperation with Philip V, the Achaean League sided with Rome in 198 BC and received significant rewards. Corinth, the site of Flamininus' dramatic declaration of Greek freedom, became an Achaean stronghold. Under the aggressive leadership of the general Philopoemon, the Achaeans grew even more powerful, counting a string of military victories throughout the 200s and 190s. The

Achaean success alarmed the Aetolians, who felt that the Roman-backed era of Greek freedom favoured the Achaeans and made them a potential target. Seeking new alliances, the Aetolians looked east to Antiochus with the hope that Seleucid aid might rebalance the situation.

In 193, the Aetolians sent an embassy to Antiochus to enquire whether the Great King was interested in an alliance. Antiochus gave no response, likely in part because he was still mourning the death of his son.[47] The next year, the *strategos* of the Aetolian League, Thoas, led a second Aetolian delegation to the Seleucid court. This time, Antiochus expressed interest in increasing cooperation with the Aetolians and sent his experienced diplomat Menippos back to Aetolia.

The Romans closely watched the Aetolian assembly.[48] Flamininus felt obliged to leave Athens to deliver a warning to the Aetolians in person, yet he had no troops to back up the strong words. Meanwhile, Menippos presented a declaration of Seleucid support and friendship. In private, it seems that Menippos stressed to Aetolian delegates the vast military resources of the Great King and hinted at his willingness to use them. The Aetolians, in full view of Menippos and the Romans envoys, then passed a public resolution 'in which he [Antiochus] was invited to liberate Greece and settle affairs between the Aetolians and Romans'.[49]

Once Menippos relayed this message, Antiochus was trapped by the dramatic request made by the Aetolian assembly, as it was difficult to refuse the offer without losing face. How could a Great King turn down the opportunity to liberate Greece? To decline would suggest a fatal lack of confidence in his own martial prowess.

After almost five years of tense diplomacy, Antiochus III knew that moving an army into Greece to 'settle affairs between the Aetolians and Romans' would lead to war with Rome. Antiochus had not sought such a war willingly, but he was no pacifist. With most of his royal career dominated by military operations, there was little reason for him to flinch from this new challenge.

The King was also led to believe that the Aetolians would contribute a substantial contingent of troops, and that other Greek cities would contribute additional forces. These contributions were important, as the only troops at his immediate disposal for operations in Greece were the 10,000 infantry and 500 cavalry occupying the Chersonesos. And these would not be enough to stop a standard Roman field army, usually composed (as Hannibal could certainly tell him) of two legions of 4000–5000 foot soldiers, and an equal complement of Italian allies, around 20,000 infantry altogether. An Aetolian levy of at least 6000 infantry and 400 cavalry would be necessary to even the odds.[50]

During Antiochus' deliberations, Roman sources depict Hannibal as playing the role of evil counsellor, goading Antiochus into war in order to renew his personal vendetta against Rome.[51] This is no doubt a caricature, although Hannibal did become a well-regarded member of Antiochus III's court and eventually assumed command of Antiochus' Phoenician fleet. Still, Hannibal never rose high enough to lead a sizable land force, despite his brilliant record as a ground tactician. Perhaps such a charge was out of the question, given the risk that he might use these resources to act independently.[52] Yet in this situation, we do not know how Hannibal advised Antiochus III. At best, he offered valuable information concerning Roman military capabilities, facts that Antiochus needed to know. However, Hannibal remained in Syria during the initial outbreak of war and thus was not in a position to advise the King personally during the course of the campaign.

The facts that Hannibal relayed were likely encouraging: the Roman army was an amateur militia commanded by amateur aristocrats. It had no standing units, but rather each year fresh recruits were distributed into legions. Half of the army was composed of 'allied' wings; these soldiers lacked citizenship. As Hannibal had proved, the Roman army had suffered stunning defeats, due mostly to the combination of poorly trained levies and inexperienced or even incompetent generals. At best, a Roman consul had one or two years of provincial command as a praetor or pro-praetor; Antiochus III had commanded armies for thirty years. While the Seleucid army also contained citizen militiamen in the phalanx, it also had a splendid professional corps, the 10,000 Silver Shields, and the two regiments of royal cavalry. Thus, despite recent Roman successes against Carthage and Macedonia, Antiochus entered the war confident of victory.

The Aetolian first strike

With Antiochus' promised support, the Aetolians launched their own campaign in Greece. They targeted two key Greek cities: Demetrias and Sparta. Demetrias, a city in Thessaly on the modern-day Bay of Volos, was one of the most important harbours in northern Greece. Founded by Demetrius Poliorcetes, it was also one of the aforementioned strategic 'fetters' of Greece. The Aetolians conspired with disgruntled local politicians to plan a coup. Eurylochus, one such local worthy, had recently obtained permission to return from exile and was escorted into the city by a troop of Aetolian cavalrymen. The plan was for a few select troopers to gain control of the city gates as Eurylochus made his return, which would allow the main body of Aetolian horse to occupy the town. A few of Eurylochus' political enemies were executed, but the coup overall proved reasonably popular. The Aetolians now controlled Demetrias and the harbour that would accommodate Antiochus' landing.

Control of Sparta would also be particularly favourable to the Aetolians, as control of Spartan territory in Laconia would challenge the Achaean domination of the Peloponnese. The Aetolians had a long tradition of alliance with Sparta, and to this end a small contingent of 1000 infantry and 300 cavalry was sent to support the tyrant-king Nabis in his war against the Achaeans. However, the Aetolians sensed that Nabis was increasingly unpopular with the Spartan elite: he indulged in policies that redistributed land from wealthy oligarchs to his mercenary soldiers. The primary goal of this policy was to expand the number of arms-bearing Spartans, a number well below 1000 by the second century BC. Nor did Nabis rule as a traditional Spartan king, but rather he abolished the Spartan 'diarchy' of two kings. These unpopular reforms led many traditional Spartans to see him as a petty tyrant backed by a mercenary force. While Nabis' previous military successes had made him popular, recent defeats suffered at the hands of the Achaeans cost him much of his remaining political capital.

Despite the history of friendship between the Aetolian League and the city, the Aetolians considered Nabis too much of a loose cannon to be a reliable ally moving forward. Feigning a diplomatic mission, a small contingent of Aetolian troops murdered him while he reviewed the army outside the gates of Sparta. With the eccentric Nabis dead, the Aetolians hoped that Sparta might fall into line behind them.

For a brief moment, it seemed that the Aetolian contingent would be welcomed as liberators in Sparta. However, the Aetolians quickly sacked the royal treasure-house and carried out a general orgy of looting. The Spartans regrouped and attacked the outnumbered Aetolian force, killing its leader and selling the captives into slavery. Sparta was now an official enemy. Without the aggressive leadership of Nabis, however, the once vaunted city-state quickly faded into political obscurity.[53]

Chapter Eight

The Roman War

Chalcis

After the resolution of the Aetolian council, Antiochus III gathered a small army of approximately 10,000 infantry and 500 cavalry. His fleet was modest: only 40 quinqueremes and 60 triremes, and he had 200 additional transports for grain and horses (by contrast, Scipio Africanus invaded Africa in 202 BC with 800 transports). The availability of shipping necessarily limited the size of his expeditionary force.

The King then took a symbolic detour to Ilium where he sacrificed to Athena. For the Greeks, the Homeric legend of Troy represented the Hellenic victory over the barbarian, and the choice of Athena honoured the goddess who aided Achilles against Hector. Athena was also the patron goddess of the Athenians, who were then debating whether to join the Aetolian-Seleucid coalition.

Alexander the Great also sacrificed at Troy prior to his storied invasion of Asia, yet the Great King was now advancing the other way, inverting the invasion paths of Agamemnon and Alexander, attacking from Asia into Greece. The most pressing symbolism of the act, however, came from the fact that the Romans claimed direct descent from the Trojans and the refugee Aeneas, a survivor of the sack of Troy.[1] Antiochus' sacrifice at Ilium petitioned the goddess to aid the Greeks rather than the Trojans in the coming war.

Returning from the detour in the Troad, the King collected his fleet at the island of Imbros and proceeded to the Bay of Volos, disembarking at the recently secured port of Demetrias. The King then moved inland to Lamia, another strategic city on the coast of Thessaly, where he received news of an invitation to the Aetolian assembly. The announcement of the invitation before the King was politically staged for the approval of the crowd, and the citizens' cheers reassured Antiochus (and the sceptics in the audience) of the welcome he might receive in Greece as a liberating hero.

Boisterous cheers also met the King as he entered the council of the Aetolians, yet there were underlying tensions: the Aetolians were disappointed with the small force that the King brought with him. Having suffered from limited Roman aid in their war with Macedonia from 211 to 206, the Aetolians had a long history of disappointment with external allies, and Antiochus tried to assuage the fear that his commitment would be similarly lukewarm. He explained that the winter weather of the Mediterranean had prevented him from assembling a larger body of troops but promised to bring reinforcements once the sailing season began. In return, Antiochus asked the Aetolians to commit troops and to sell grain to his army (presumably at discount prices). Despite their reservations, the Aetolians elected Antiochus the *strategos autokrator* of the Aetolian League, thus affirming the military alliance and giving the Great King authority to command the Aetolian levy.[2] The newly minted *strategos autokrator* dispatched a brigade of 1000 troops and advanced south against Chalcis. Located on the west side of the island of Euboea and facing the Attic mainland, Chalcis was another 'fetter', a military stronghold that gave access to important sea-lanes and strategic proximity to Attica and Boeotia. Antiochus did not have enough troops to storm Chalcis directly, so he engaged in armed diplomacy, showing the flag and hoping that the pro-Roman Chalcidians would embrace his cause. They did not.

Joined by Aetolians ambassadors, Antiochus met with Chalcidian leaders outside the gates. Together, they urged Chalcis to unite with Antiochus. An Achaean League representative named Micythio was also present and urged the Chalcidians to remain aloof in the conflict. Micythio criticized the Aetolian proposition that Rome was oppressing the Greeks, citing as evidence the fact that Rome, true to Flamininus' Ishmian declaration, had neither installed garrisons nor mandated tribute. (The Chalcidians had long been home to an oppressive Macedonian garrison, and they were grateful for the new Roman peace.) Micythio convinced them, and the Chalcidians bid Antiochus to prove his aims of friendship by withdrawing his small army from the island of Euboea. Lacking troops to capture the town, the King returned to Demetrias.

The cool reception at Chalcis was a warning sign to Antiochus that the Greeks might be less than enthusiastic about his intervention. However, he gained more success in securing the aid of Amyander, the king of the Athamanians. The Athamanians were a tribe (*ethnos*) that lived in the rugged highlands of north-eastern Greece. Their history of alliance with the Aetolian League made them amenable to collaboration, but Antiochus courted King Amyander further. Amyander had married the daughter of an Arcadian nobleman named Alexander of Megalopolis. In grand fashion, this Alexander claimed lineage from Alexander the Great, and consequentially gave his children Macedonian royal names: Apamea, Philip, and yet another Alexander. Antiochus hinted to Amyander that in exchange for support, his brother-in-law Philip could be a serious contender for the Macedonian throne (Philip VI!). It was an idle promise, of course. Antiochus III was already sending feelers to the actual king of Macedonia, Philip V, to ensure his cooperation. Such casual lies were necessary to obtain support, troops and supplies.

The city of Athens was violently split about whether to support Antiochus or Rome, and was teetering toward what the Greeks called *stasis*, or civil strife. A coalition of wealthy Athenians favoured the Romans, while the populist faction supported Antiochus III.[3] As a rule, the Romans supported oligarchs in allied communities over populist impulses. Flamininus arranged for Achaean troops to enter the city, secure the key urban terrain of the port at the Pireaus, and silence democratic dissent.[4] After a series of violent street clashes, the democrats were defeated, and Athens remained on the side of Rome.

The Romans, meanwhile, did not declare war just yet, but effected their first forward deployment of troops. The praetor Marcus Baebius, previously stationed in Bruttium, crossed the Adriatic Sea from the south Italian port of Brundisium to Apollonia, on the coast of Epirus. He brought two legions with him, complemented by 15,000 allied Italian infantry and 500 allied horse.[5] In all, this was an army of roughly 25,000 men. However, Baebius' mission was not to secure Greece, but rather to watch over Macedonia, as the senate worried that Philip V might take advantage of the unstable diplomatic situation. Nonetheless, the arrival of Roman troops was a critical step toward open hostilities. While the bulk would be positioned against Macedonia, a small detachment was sent to intervene in Greece. 500 Romans (probably an *ad hoc* unit known as a cohort) were sent to Chalcis, joining Achaean and Attalid contingents that already reinforced the city.

The presence of the Roman, Achaean and Attalid soldiers at Chalcis gave Antiochus a clear choice. Further operations against Chalcis would involve Roman casualties and prove a convenient *causus belli* for the Roman senate. While the Romans were often aggressors, for religious reasons they were still committed to the pretence that all formal wars be defensive in nature.

By now Antiochus was ready to move against Chalcis in force. He ordered his lieutenant Polyxenidas to take the fleet and 3000 men and launch an assault against the city; he would follow with the main body of 6000 troops and a small contingent of Aetolian reinforcements. This force was no match for the 500 Achaeans and the handful of Attalid troops sent by Eumenes II to reinforce the city. The Romans' detachment had not yet crossed to the island of Euboea, but stood paused en route at Delium. Antiochus' troops fell upon the Roman cohort and inflicted heavy losses on the isolated detachment. The Achaean and Attalid soldiers within the city were permitted to depart under a truce. Antiochus now took possession of Chalcis, and of the entire island of Euboea: he now controlled two of the three fetters of Greece.[6]

His next target was Thessaly itself, a vast plain in Northern Greece famous for its horses. The Thessalians had been subject to Philip V of Macedon, but had been liberated by the Romans. A few Thessalian cities subsequently joined the Aetoliean League, but most formed their own federal league: a new and tenuous polity. Antiochus engaged in negotiations to arrange for his own 'liberation' of Thessaly, but when Thessalian communities used the negotiations as cover for military preparations, Antiochus struck. He captured Pherai, a leading Thessalian city, and massacred a number of the defenders. Other Thessalian cities fell like dominoes, except Larissa, the largest city, which continued to hold despite the Great King's siege.[7]

A funeral

In central Thessaly there lay a terrible sight: nearly 8000 sun-whitened skeletons. These were the remains of Macedonian soldiers killed in battle against the Romans nearly six years earlier. Philip V, in his hasty retreat from Cynoscephalae, had been unable to bury them, and the victorious Romans left them to rot as a potent reminder of their newly established power. With due diligence, Antiochus III sent a 2000-man detachment to collect the bleached bones and bury them with the proper funerary rites.

Antiochus' intention here was unclear, and piety alone probably does not explain the act. Certainly it was a gesture to the Greeks, as Greek mercenaries of Philip V numbered among the dead. It gave him an opportunity to contrast a fundamental Hellenic decency against a particularly brutal episode of Roman barbarism. Unfortunately, Antiochus permitted Philip of Megalopolis to accompany the burial party. This Philip, who harboured oversized ambitions against the Macedonian throne, could now claim that he had accomplished this act of royal piety, and Philip V took the mass funeral as an insult to his standing as king. His loyalty already wavering, he now set himself against Antiochus and formally declared his allegiance to Rome.[8]

In Apollonia, the praetor Marcus Baeblius was concerned about the easy success of Antiochus' Thessalian campaign and desired to relieve Larissa. He dispatched a detachment of 2000 men commanded by Appius Claudius, arranging with Philip V for the Romans to march across Macedonia and demonstrate before Larissa. The arrival of the Roman detachment, who took pains to exaggerate their strength by lighting extra campfires and building a larger camp, convinced Antiochus to withdraw his small force. Antiochus abandoned his siege of Larissa and returned to Chalcis. Both sides waited until spring to launch more ambitious operations.[9]

The Romans prepare for war

In November 192, the Roman consuls Scipio Nasica and Manius Acilius Glabrio took office (it was 15 March by the Roman count, four months off from the solar calendar). Both consuls had strong ties to Scipio Africanus: Scipio Nasica, as his name implies, was a cousin, and Acilius Glabrio was a 'new man' who rose through politics with Scipionic patronage. In 201 he had been one of several tribunes of the plebs to defend Scipio's African command.[10]

The voters of the *comitia centuriata* considered a formal proposal for war with Antiochus, and it easily passed, since Roman soldiers were already engaged in active fighting. Following the *populus'* declaration of war, the consuls' provinces were assigned by lot.[11] Italy and the seething violence in Cisalpine Gaul, Liguria, and Bruttium, went to the consul Scipio Nasica, and Manius Acilius Glabrio received the province of Greece. Thus, he would command the first phase of the war against Antiochus the Great.

Glabrio selected a command team that created a fine show of political unity and brought with him two senior military tribunes, Marcus Porcius Cato and Valerius Flaccus. Both men were ex-consuls: Marcus Cato, like Glabrio, was also a *novus homo*, the first member of his family from the village of Tusculanum to serve in the Roman senate.[12] Cato had risen with the support of politicians strongly opposed to the Scipionic faction, most notably Fabius Maximus.[13] Throughout his life, Cato displayed an almost pathological hatred of the Scipio brothers. Glabrio's invitation to Cato to serve under him acknowledged his proven military skills. He had enjoyed significant successes while campaigning as a pro-consul in Spain in 194 BC.

Serving as a fellow military tribune was Valerius Flaccus, a patrician who patronized Cato's early career, and subsequently shared the consulship with him in 195 BC (the lifelong political allies would later share a censorship together in 184 BC). Flaccus ('Skinny') had also been a veteran supporter of Fabius Maximus. Their inclusion in Glabrio's command team was a kind of olive branch from the Scipionic faction to its political enemies. The presence of two ex-consuls serving as subordinates also underlined the seriousness of the Roman war effort. The post of military tribune was a relatively junior office, usually held by young aristocrats at the start of their military and political career.[14] Nonetheless, one of the great weaknesses of the Republican Roman military system was that command fell to amateur aristocrats, who led armies by virtue of election rather than experience. Thus, Glabrio, who had never commanded a field army, had two veteran lieutenants by his side. In the spring of 191 BC Glabrio crossed the Adriatic to Apollonia with an army of 20,000 infantry, 2000 cavalry, and 15 war-elephants.[15]

A wedding

In Chalcis, Antiochus III celebrated his wedding to a young girl, the daughter of a local Chalcidian noble. He proclaimed her queen and gave her the grand name of Euboea, after the island on which Chalcis was located (unfortunately for young Euboea, her new nickname translates roughly to 'Happy Cow-land'). It is unclear whether Queen Laodice had died or if Antiochus was beginning to practise Macedonian royal polygamy.[16]

Antiochus made a grand show of politely wooing young Euboea. Hers was a social group that provided many Hellenistic kings with their mistresses, girls from families who would benefit by sending their daughters to court, but who were generally not politically powerful enough to warrant a formal marriage alliance.[17] Antiochus diligently courted Euboea and obtained the permission of her father to marry, both respectful gestures targeted toward the parochial aristocrats who controlled most Greek *poleis*. The subsequent marriage was a political spectacle calculated to show Antiochus' respect for Greek freedom and autonomy. Just as Euboea was a wife rather than a concubine, Antiochus would be an ally rather than a master to the Greek *poleis*. And by binding himself to a wife from Chalcis, he also signalled a determination to defend Greece from the impending Roman counterattack.[18]

Unfortunately, Antiochus badly miscalculated the message that his marriage sent to his Greek allies. To those already questioning the King's commitment to the Greek cause, the marriage read as one more unnecessary distraction. The Greeks believed that sexual activity was enervating and suspected that sexual exertion detracted from martial vigour.[19] Rumours circulated that the King was more concerned with satisfying his lust with a young girl than with winning the war. To Greek eyes, the indulgent royal wedding party made Antiochus appear more a Dionysian reveller than the warrior-king that the hour called for. From a political perspective, the marriage was a dismal failure.

But we should not allow ourselves to be deceived by propaganda against Antiochus transmitted through later literary sources. Polybius, who may reflect hostile Greek opinion, reports that Antiochus 'getting married in Chalcis, passed the winter there, indifferent to the affairs at hand'.[20] A brief overview of Antiochus' campaign in the winter of 192/1 BC shows this accusation to be patently untrue, as the King had filled the winter with numerous diplomatic and military successes. It seems that his marriage did not affect the ability to conduct military operations.[21]

Cultural differences around drinking habits further alienated his Greek support. The *symposium*, or drinking party, was a central part of Greek elite social life, yet these parties were also characterized by aristocratic restraint. At the start, a *symposiarch* (master of ceremonies) would set a limit to alcohol consumption and determine the proper mixture of water to wine (usually two to one). To become uncontrollably drunk at a *symposium* was shameful (e.g. Alcibiades in Plato's *Symposium*): for elite Greeks, public drinking and decorum went hand in hand.

The *symposia* of the Seleucid court, however, combined Greek drinking rituals with boisterous Macedonian court culture. Macedonian nobles drank undiluted (*akratos*) wine, and drinking frequently took on a competitive aspect, with the king pointedly outdrinking the members of his court. Thus, Macedonian royal *symposia* traditionally concluded in heavy drunkenness, leaving the Greeks to conclude that Antiochus was a man 'winesotted and revelling in strong drink', lacking the kind of self-control expected of a Greek aristocrat.[22] Drinking and partying related to the nuptial festivities was one more cultural disconnect between Antiochus and his Greek supporters.

By the start of the campaigning season in 191 BC, the Seleucid situation had further deteriorated. Tens of thousands of Roman soldiers were disembarking at Apollonia, and Antiochus' plans of using a small expeditionary force and diplomacy to win the Greek cities seemed laughable. On a diplomatic blitz through Achaea and Athens in the winter of 191, Marcus Cato sarcastically proclaimed that 'Antiochus wages war through letters, and fights with pen and ink.'[23] Here, Cato was paraphrasing the famous fourth-century orator Demosthenes in order to reassure an audience of lettered Athenian elites that the Romans were not barbarians.

The Romans began their offensive. Aided by a small force from Philip V, Acilius Glabrio assumed command of the army previously deployed to Greece, which he then supplemented with his own reinforcements; Antiochus' Anthamanian allies were quickly crushed.[24] Philip of

Megalopolis, the would-be king of Macedon, was captured and thrown into chains. Philip V taunted the pretender as he awaited transportation to Rome, calling him 'brother' and ordering Macedonian soldiers to salute him as 'king'.[25] After the campaign Athamania became Macedonian territory, Rome's gift to Philip in gratitude for his cooperation.

The Romans proceeded to mop up meagrely defended garrisons in Thessaly, effectively undoing Antiochus' previous lightning campaign. Antiochus lacked the troops to commit to a pitched battle in Thessaly. Badly outnumbered, he had only one hope of stalling the Roman onslaught into central Greece: to stop them at Thermopylae.

Thermopylae

The 'Warm Gates', named after local hot springs, had soaked up a great deal of human blood. On the road along the narrow coastal plain of eastern Greece, Thermopylae presented a natural 'choke point'. The cliffs of Mt Callidromus rose rapidly from the coast, leaving only a few hundred metres of passable flat land. (Modern visitors will be disappointed, as over two thousand years of silt deposits have significantly extended the flatlands adjacent to the sea. A national highway runs along the coastal plain, a reminder of the area's ancient importance as a trade route and military avenue.) Off the coast, turbulent seas hindered amphibious operations. At first glance, it was an ideal defensive position.

But Thermopylae had a fatal flaw for those who would defend it. While a small force could bottleneck a much larger army, shepherds' paths through the mountain made it possible for flying columns to work their way behind established blocking positions.

The first recorded battle at Thermopylae took place between the Thessalians and Phocians around the year 500 BC, when the Phocians sought to stop an invasion from Thessaly. They were outflanked through the mountain paths and forced to retreat.[26] The second and most famous battle of Thermopylae was that of King Leonidas and his '300' Spartans against the invading army of Xerxes, in 480 BC. Leonidas commanded a combined Hellenic force of roughly 7000 troops and held the position against the Persian column assaulting from the north. The Spartans built a defensive wall on the plain, and detached a contingent of Phocians to guard the path. Yet once the Persians learned of the goat trails from a local collaborator, they were able to turn the paths with overwhelming force. Leonidas ordered the majority of his Greek forces to retreat before the trap was sprung, while he waited with his Spartans to die gloriously, if foolishly. Recorded by the historian Herodotus, the legend of Leonidas was well known to Antiochus and his contemporaries,[27] and it was likely familiar to the Romans as well, particularly to Glabrio's legate Marcus Porcius Cato, a leading orator who had studied Greek literature.[28]

Subsequent battles of Thermopylae gave potential defenders mixed hopes of holding the pass. In 352 BC, the Athenians successfully defended the pass against the advancing army of Alexander's father Philip II.[29] However, Philip II had just completed a very successful campaign and may have decided that forcing the pass was not worth the trouble. The Athenians briefly held a position at Thermopylae in 323 during the Lamian War, a revolt that broke out among the Greek city-states following Alexander's death. This time, the Athenians successfully routed a Macedonian army near the pass, forcing it to retreat to the nearby Thessalian town of Lamia.[30] In 279 BC, a pan-Hellenic force attempted to hold Thermopylae against the invading army of Gauls. In a replay of 480 BC, the small force assigned to hold the goat-paths was overwhelmed, but a daring naval extraction by the Athenian fleet prevented a massacre.[31]

The lessons of history were mixed; only two of the five previous attempts to defend the pass were successful. An attacker with sufficient local knowledge – or a native guide – could use the mountain trails to flank the position of the defender, and this fact was not lost upon the Romans.

Were these history lessons lost upon Antiochus? In some respects, he had little choice. Glabrio's 22,000 man consular army outnumbered his 14,500 Seleucid-Aetolian force. He had only 500 cavalry, compared to the 2000 Roman and Italian horse, and could not afford to fight on open ground. The chokepoint at Thermopylae still offered the best chance to even the odds. For Antiochus III, the most important lesson was the critical importance of flank security, and to guard the critical mountain paths he detached his 4000 Aetolian allies. Armed with javelins and light shields, they were far more suited for mountain warfare than his heavy phalangites. He also elected not to defend the 'west gate', where

Leonidas and the Spartans made their desperate stand, but rather the 'east gate', with the hope that the eastern pass, if wider, might prove more difficult for the enemy to envelop. The King positioned his phalanx at the gates and set light troops in the high ground to the front, perpendicular to the phalanx: forming an 'L'. These would pepper the right flank of the advancing Romans with a crossfire of missiles. And like the Spartans before him, he constructed a wall for mounting catapults and ballistae: a rare example of the use of siege machines in a pitched battle.[32] From the front, his defensive position was virtually impenetrable.

A flanking manoeuvre through the heights was the obvious Roman response. Acilius Glabrio assigned Marcus Cato and Valerius Flaccus 2000 men apiece, roughly half a legion. Each detachment was to attempt a different route through the twin peaks over the Warm Gates. They were to make a midnight march, scatter any guards positioned on the flanks, and crash into the King's rear in the morning. Glabrio himself would lead the main body against the pass. If the plan worked, his main force would provide the anvil for the twin hammers of Cato and Flaccus to finish Antiochus' force. But this plan was also inherently risky, as both detachments could become disoriented and isolated in the darkness

One of the many duties of the Roman commander was to ensure the cooperation of the gods. The traditional method was the *votum*, or vow, in which the Roman gods were offered a bargain. If (and only if), Glabrio and his legions triumphed over Antiochus, then Glabrio vowed the construction of a temple to Piety (*pietas*) in Rome.[33]

Valerius Flaccus and his detachment did lose the path in the darkness and never reached the fight. Marcus Cato found the shepherds' tenuous tracks only with considerable difficulty; the prisoner of war employed as a guide became badly disoriented, and Cato broke away to locate the path, which he marked before returning to lead his troops. The path petered out again just before morning, but dawn brought the sounds of nearby Greek voices. Cato and his men were in the correct position, exactly in front of the Aetolian rearguard position. Cato unsheathed his sword, formed up his men, and attacked. Unsure of how many Romans were behind him, the panicked Aetolians fled.

Meanwhile, the consul Glabrio was failing in the attempt to force the pass. As required by the restricting terrain, his approach was in a narrow column. After an initial engagement with Antiochus' light troops, his legionary infantry encountered Antiochus' phalanx. With a flank on the mountains and a flank on the sea, the dense mass of pikes could not be budged along its narrow front, and the battle at the pass stood at a stalemate.

But Cato's legionaries soon raced down from the mountains into Antiochus' rear. The King knew that the trap had been sprung, despite his best precautions. He did not attempt to repeat the foolish gallantry of Leonidas but fled with the troops that could extract themselves. Plutarch claims that the King in retreat was hit in the face with a rock, causing the loss of even more teeth.[34] (In all likelihood Plutarch is assigning the dental incident that took place at the River Arius in Bactria to the debacle at Thermopylae.) Most of the King's 500 cavalry joined the mounted flight, galloping away before the jaws slammed shut. The survivors numbered in the hundreds: the phalanx, the flower of his expeditionary force, was surrounded, and 10,000 men were killed or captured. A mere 200 Romans and Italians fell fighting.[35]

Antiochus retreated to Chalcis with only his tiny escort of cavalry. He met his fleet, collected his bride, and sailed for Ephesus. A major reason for the failure of Antiochus' expedition in Greece lay in the fact that the Seleucids were unaccustomed to the significant logistical and infrastructure demands then required of major Mediterranean naval power. The Great King did not want for troops; his army at the time likely exceeded 100,000 men on active duty, but he was chronically short of transport for these troops. This logistical inability severely limited the numbers of his expeditionary force and gave him an unusual disadvantage in cavalry, given the space required to transport horses and their equipment.

By contrast, the Romans had over seventy-five years' experience launching elaborate overseas campaigns, ever since their first actions against Carthaginian Sicily in the 260s BC. They were experts in assembling transports and supplying large armies overseas. When compared with the logistical difficulties Antiochus experienced crossing shorter distances with smaller forces, the Romans' relative ease in moving 20,000 infantry and 2000 cavalry across the Adriatic is a testament to the rising importance of seaborne logistics.[36]

Yet Antiochus had also failed in his diplomatic efforts. His small expeditionary force might have succeeded had he been able to recruit an equal number of allied troops. For all their initial support, the Aetolians proved lukewarm allies and never mobilized their entire muster.[37] The hope that Philip V might join the anti-Roman alliance was also quickly dashed, bungled in part by Antiochus' own failed attempts at outreach to the Athamanians.

Invasion

The political unity of the Roman command team broke down after the victory at Thermopylae. Glabrio dispatched a messenger to deliver the official report of the battle. Cato, however, begged a furlough, which was granted, and he raced back to Italy to deliver a personal account of the battle before the official report arrived. In its place, Cato pronounced an entirely self-serving narrative, glorifying his own actions and sharply criticizing Glabrio's command. With Antiochus expelled from Greece, the rancour and divisiveness of Roman politics had resumed.

The Romans continued their war effort against the recalcitrant Aetolians, and the senate extended Acilius Glabrio's command to carry on the war in mainland Greece. Glabrio's high-handed actions, which involved throwing an entire Aetolian peace delegation into chains, stymied peace talks and caused the Aetolian war to drag on until 189 BC.[38]

The elections of 191 proved another great victory for the Scipionic faction. Lucius Scipio, the elder brother of Scipio Africanus, was elected consul despite a failed attempt two years before. The plebian consul was Gaius Laelius, a long-time lieutenant of Africanus during the 2nd Punic War and later an important source for Polybius. Like Acilius Glabrio, Gaius Laelius was a talented 'new man' who rose to the consulship with Scipionic patronage. He had served as Africanus' chief lieutenant in Spain and Africa from 209 to 201 BC, commanding the Roman and Italian cavalry at the Battle of Zama. Given his extensive military background, it seemed logical that Gaius Laelius be given the task of invading Asia Minor and bringing the war to an end, but Scipio Africanus interceded on behalf of his brother. He asked the senate to forego the traditional casting of lots to determine provincial responsibility, proclaiming his intention to join the conflict as a lieutenant if Lucius Scipio were given the command against Antiochus. Given the military pre-eminence of Scipio Africanus, his offer was gladly accepted, and Laelius, whose quiet competence had contributed to many of Africanus' victories, was relegated to the province of Italy.[39]

The Scipio brothers crossed to Greece to assume command of Glabrio's armies in theatre. They brought with them a *supplementum* (reinforcement) of 13,000 infantry and 500 cavalry, including 5000 clients (political dependents, often veterans) of Scipio Africans who volunteered to serve under him in the latest war. While the *supplementum* was in part designed to replace men who had been killed, injured, or taken sick, it would brought the total number of Roman troops in Illyria and Greece to well over 50,000. But most of these troops were needed to maintain the garrisons in Greece and Illyria, where the war with the Aetolians was in its final stages. The Romans continued to show a preference for modest field armies, which were easier to manage and supply. In all, the Scipios planned to take a modest expeditionary force of roughly 25,000 men as they marched toward Asia to bring the war to Seleucid territory.

First, however, the Romans confronted the problem of Antiochus' blue water navy. The Great King had energetically built up a naval presence in the Eastern Mediterranean, and his fleet of over 150 warships presented an imposing force. In 191 BC, the Romans dispatched the praetor Gaius Livius Salinator to muster a fleet of over 100 warships (81 quinqueremes and 24 triremes). Many of these ships were left over from the 2nd Punic War and were hauled out of dry dock for the first time in a decade. But Salinator's fleet was not large enough to take on Antiochus' armada by itself, though Roman diplomatic efforts helped to fill the gap. After a series of consultations, King Eumenes II joined Salinator and returned to prepare the Pergamenese fleet.

The island of Rhodes also decided to enter the war. The Rhodians had been spooked by Antiochus' naval operations off the coast of Southern Asia Minor in 197 BC, and they had previous ties to Rome as well, cooperating in the war effort against Philip V. While Rhodes was not traditionally hostile to the Seleucid Empire, the island nation questioned Antiochus' emerging ambitions on the Aegean Sea. The defeat of Antiochus and the destruction of his newly built fleet would return the Aegean to its previous status as a Rhodian lake.[40]

The Battle of Cissus

The praetor Livius Salinator and King Eumenes united fleets and sailed toward the island of Samos to rendezvous with the Rhodians. The Seleucid commander was the admiral Polyxenidas, a Rhodian mercenary with a long history of Seleucid military service. He had previously commanded a unit of Cretan archers during the engagements in the Elburz mountains during Antiochus' anabasis.[41] The opposing fleets joined battle near the small coastal town of Cissus.

In the front of Salinator's fleet were two allied Carthaginian ships. Three Seleucid warships quickly pounced on these, capturing one Carthaginian vessel and chasing the other off. Salinator, setting the tone for the entire sea-fight, quickly steered his flagship against these three ships. He caught two Seleucid ships at once with grappling hooks and swarmed them with his marines. This was the preferred manner of naval warfare for the Romans; rather than manoeuvring and ramming (standard tactics of the Eastern Mediterranean) they sought to close, grapple and board, turning a sea fight into a land battle. In the clash that followed, the Roman advantage in heavier quinqueremes proved decisive. Furthermore, Salinator deployed his line beyond the Seleucid right flank, and now his ships veered to the starboard and began to roll up the Seleucid line. The Romans destroyed ten Seleucid warships and captured thirteen more. Polyxenidas retreated with only forty-seven quinqueremes.[42]

Despite this defeat, Polyxenidas was not finished yet. He sent a series of letters to the commander of the Rhodian fleet, detailing his willingness to desert and betray the entire royal fleet. These letters were a cover to buy time to repair his fleet, drill his rowers, and recruit the aid of an arch-pirate named Nicander, who brought with him a small squadron of five ships. When these preparations were complete, Polyxenidas pounced on Samos, trapping the Rhodian fleet between his own ships and those of his pirate allies. Among the Rhodian victims was the admiral Pausistratus, a political enemy of Polyxenidas, a fact that made the victory doubly sweet.[43]

Yet the strategic effects of Polyxenidas' victory off the coast of Samos were short-lived. The Roman and Attalid fleets quickly converged against Polyxenidas, linking up with the remainder of the Rhodian fleet and hemming Polyxenidas into his base of Ephesus. Salinator himself sailed to Ilium, where he sacrificed to Athena with great fanfare.[44] This both mimicked and mocked Antiochus' sacrifice two years before. As a Roman, the praetor could claim distant mythical descent from Trojans of Ilium, yet this sacrifice, like Alexander's in 333 BC, marked an invasion that was moving in the 'proper' direction: from Greece to Asia.

While at Ephesus, Polyxenidas and his fleet succeeded in fixing Salinator's blockading force and tying up Roman and allied naval resources. In 190, a new praetor named Lucius Aemilius Regillus arrived and assumed command of the combined fleet. Salinator, however, took two Roman ships and obtained a small fleet from Smyrna and Rhodes, in the hopes of ravaging the coast of Lycia in southern Asia Minor as a diversion. This small fleet quickly suffered heavy losses, and Salinator abandoned his mission and sailed back to Italy.[45]

Skirmishes in Asia Minor

Since Eumenes had chosen to aid the Roman fleet, Antiochus' son and new crown prince Seleucus invaded the Attalid realm and attacked the city of Pergamon. Antiochus moved his army up from Sardis, sending additional forces to Seleucus and detaching 6000 soldiers to besiege Elea, the main port city of Pergamon. Eumenes was forced to rush troops to defend his capital, although he did not risk a full on battle, while the Roman fleet sailed to the defence of Elea.

As his troops raped and pillaged their way through the hinterlands of Pergamon, Antiochus had reason to be worried about the strength of the Roman fleet and the impending arrival of Scipio's army from Europe. The King sent a herald to the praetor Aemilius with a peace proposal, a prospect seriously discussed by the Roman council. Yet Eumenes advocated for rejecting the peace, as it would leave him at the mercy of Antiochus. Aemilius himself lacked the authority to offer peace terms, and told the herald that peace talks would have to wait until the consul arrived in the theatre.[46]

The arrival of a battalion of 1000 infantry and 100 cavalry from Rome's allies the Achaeans helped to turn the tide at Elea. Led by an aggressive commander named Diophanes, the Achaeans pitched into a brigade of 4000 Gallic mercenaries in a fierce skirmish and routed them completely, earning cheers from an audience of men and women watching from the walls of Pergamon.[47] Seleucus withdrew to the coast to police communities that might defect to the Romans. The Roman fleet left Elea, and Antiochus himself overran a series of cities that had until now resisted Seleucid authority: Cotton, Corylenus, Aphrodisias and Prinne.[48]

The Battle of Side

As this time, Antiochus was also assembling a new fleet in Syria out of the port of Seleucia Pieria. The commander was Hannibal Barca, who after five years as a courtier in the Seleucid court now received his first serious military command. It was an odd choice, given that Hannibal had no naval experience, despite his significant military accomplishments. Indeed, Hannibal's strategy in the Second Punic War had neglected naval affairs almost entirely, leaving the Romans to command the seas. Antiochus, however, planned to lead the land forces against Rome himself and did not want to be upstaged by a foreign commander of Hannibal's celebrity. The naval command gave Hannibal a role and prevented him from interfering in land preparations. The King likely hoped that such a military genius would flourish similarly at sea. In this task, Hannibal enjoyed one notable credential: a linguistic affinity with many of Phoenician sailors in the Seleucid fleet, who like Hannibal spoke a Phoenician dialect.

Hannibal mustered a fleet of forty-seven ships: thirty quinqueremes or quadremes, ten triremes, and seven ships larger than a quinquereme (with six or even seven decks). As he sailed north to meet the blockaded Polyxenidas, a Rhodian fleet swooped down to intercept him. The Rhodians got the best of the resulting spirited engagement, and Hannibal retired after twenty ships suffered serious damage. This defeat marked the anticlimactic end of Hannibal's storied military career. He limped the fleet back to base at Seleucia Pieria, and played no further part in the war effort.[49]

The Battle of Myonessus

Meanwhile, the praetor Aemilius Regulus, in command of the Roman fleet, had been fighting a frustrating campaign, suffering from dissensions among military tribunes as he had failed to capture the Selecid stronghold of Iasos. He had also suffered a personal setback with the death of his brother who had accompanied him on campaign.[50]

Aemilius decided to sail down the coast of Asia Minor, thus allowing Polyxenidas to finally exit the harbour of Ephesus. The Roman fleet became distracted by matters in the city of Teos, previously proclaimed 'inviolate' (*asylos*) by both Antiochus and Rome. Teos had since become an ally of the Seleucids, and a major supplier of wine to the navy. In retaliation for this betrayal, the Romans sailed into the Tean harbour and extorted some wine for themselves, disregarding the supposed inviolability of the city.

Polyxenidas, now on the prowl, had hopes to ambush the Romans along the coast. But by the time he found them at Teos, however, Aemilius had been alerted to his presence and deployed his ships in battle order. In the head-on clash, the Romans and their allies again proved victorious. Polyxenidas lost twenty-nine ships, with another thirteen captured. While both Polyxenidas and Hannibal retained rump fleets in the wake of defeat, the number of surviving ships was insufficient to challenge Roman naval superiority.[51]

Meanwhile, the Scipio brothers planned to advance north through Macedonia to Thrace, then cross the Hellespont and enter Asia Minor. Africanus warned that such an operation would require diplomatic preparations to ensure Philip V's cooperation in entering his territory, and a young military tribune named Tiberius Semperonius Gracchus was sent ahead to facilitate coordination with the Macedonian king. Gracchus arrived to find Philip V groggy after a night of heavy drinking, but the King's sloth was superficial. Philip V had made ample preparations to aid the Romans in crossing his realm: stockpiled supplies, built bridges, new roads – all were at the ready. He also personally accompanied the Scipios and their army across Macedonia and into Thrace. The King also permitted his subjects to join a 2000-strong brigade of Macedonians and Thessalians who accompanied the Roman army in the crossing.

Philip V had his own reasons for giving this generous aid to the Romans. He was in no position to deny requests from the consuls, but his enthusiastic aid also revealed a private agenda. He hoped for – and later received – material rewards for his cooperation. His son Demetrius, a hostage in Rome, was returned, and he also received certain territorial concessions. The 50-talent indemnity to the Romans was cancelled.[52] He also had reason to hope for a quick defeat of Antiochus: this would place the Great King on equal terms with his own humbled position. Furthermore, Philip likely suspected that the Romans would leave Greece after a victory, just as they had done four years earlier. With the Romans absent, he could resume his patient work of rebuilding his realm.

As the Roman army crossed the Hellespont, Antiochus suffered a diplomatic setback: the previously unaffiliated King Prusias of Bithynia sided with the Romans. Antiochus had been courting Prusias assiduously, but the King remained coyly neutral, hedging his bets until the expected outcome became clearer. With the Romans' naval triumphs and movement into Asia Minor, Prusias went with Rome, the likely victor.[53]

Kings were not the only ones trying to pick winners, but also the town councils of cities in Asia Minor. The city of Heraclea-ad-Latmos, for example, sent envoys to advancing Roman army, throwing their lot in with the Scipios. The surviving negotiations preserve an interesting hybrid of Roman and Greek diplomatic idiom. The Scipio brothers accepted what in Roman diplomatic idiom was a *deditio in fidem*, a 'surrender into the faith' of the Roman people. In return, the Scipios promised freedom and autonomy, the standard slogans of Greek relations between kings and cities.[54]

Final negotiations

Antiochus did not wish to fight a battle he might not win. The Romans had proven themselves the most dangerous enemy he had faced to date. And although military preparations had been extensive throughout the whole empire, perhaps one final attempt at negotiation could end the war without further military disaster.

Antiochus sent an envoy authorized to offer generous terms to the Romans. Rome would receive the contested cities of Lampsacus, Smyrna, and Alexandria Troas as allies, along with others that wished to leave the Seleucid sphere of influence. Furthermore, Antiochus offered to pay half of the Roman costs of war.

The envoy had additional instructions. He was to attempt to arrange a secret meeting with Scipio Africanus, and offer him a generous bribe in exchange for supporting the Seleucid position. Scipio declined. Essentially, these were the terms that the Romans had requested four years previously during the conference at Lysimacheia – before hostilities began and before the impressive string of Roman victories. Yet Antiochus had one potential trump card: he had captured Scipio Africanus' son Publius in a minor skirmish.[55]

Hearing these terms, the Romans response was the following: if he wanted peace, Antiochus must pay the full costs of the war and evacuate all of Asia Minor north of the Taurus Mountains.[56] The Scipionic family lore as recorded by Polybius suggests that Scipio Africanus also indulged in a bit of diplomatic 'trash talking'. He told the envoy that in exchange for his son, he would give Antiochus III a bit of useful advice: the King would be wise to agree to Roman terms to avoid battle with the Romans.

Given the many years Antiochus spent campaigning to secure Seleucid rights in Asia Minor, the Romans' terms proved unacceptable to the King. Negotiations ended and both sides prepared for the final, decisive battle. Antiochus did, however, release the young Publius Scipio back to his father, which can be interpreted as a chivalrous act of royal magnanimity, or perhaps an effort to bank Scipio's goodwill in the event of further military setbacks.[57]

Chapter Nine

The Battle of Magnesia

With the conclusion of peace talks, both armies sought to force a battle in a location suitable to each one's particular dispositions and strengths. Antiochus positioned himself in the Hyrcanian plain, a flat agricultural region that offered plenty of open space to deploy his overall numerical superiority and his enormous advantage in cavalry. L. Scipio, however, manoeuvred his army and constructed a camp in the narrow horseshoe formed by the confluence of the Hermus and Phyrgios Rivers. He then marched out and formed his army where the plain was only three kilometres wide, with either flank anchored on a riverbank, effectively negating Antiochus' numerical advantage. Antiochus refused to do battle here, although he dispatched detachments to raid Roman forward positions.

Yet winter was coming, bringing with it the end of the campaign season. Antiochus would still be king in the next year, but L. Scipio could not be sure of an extension to his pro-consular command. The Scipio brothers had many enemies back in the Roman senate that would gladly vote to revoke his *imperium*, and L. Scipio therefore had reason to force a decisive battle. Since the King would not fight the Romans in their cosy position with guarded flanks, L. Scipio advanced his camp forward to a position where the horseshoe widened. He now offered battle with only one flank protected by the riverbank.

In theory, Antiochus would benefit from delaying battle and sending both sides into winter camps, actions that might allow additional time for a negotiated settlement. But the debacle at Thermopylae had cost him a great deal of political capital. He needed to prove to his court that he could triumph against the Romans, especially given his overwhelming numerical advantage. Although Antiochus was enough of a tactician to refuse battle against Scipio's tidy position, now that his opponent advanced forward and exposed a vulnerable flank, the King likely felt enormous pressure from his 'friends' to commit to a fight. After all, Alexander had never backed away from a pitched battle. With such pressure mounting, Antiochus drew up his battleline and prepared for a final showdown with the Roman army.

Composition and disposition: Seleucids

The most detailed description of Antiochus' army in this effort comes from Livy (37.40), who likely uses Polybius as a source, given that his report of army strengths closely mirrors Polybius' description of the Battle of Raphia.[1] From left to right, Antiochus deployed his force as follows:

Left wing
Cyrtian singlers and Elymaean archers
4000 peltasts (light infantry)
1500 Illyrians
1500 Carians and Cilicians
1000 Neo-Cretans
2500 Galatian cavalry
(500) Tarentine cavalry
1000 royal cavalry
3000 cataphracts
2700 miscellaneous light infantry
2000 Cappadocians (light-medium infantry)

Centre
1500 Galatians
16,000 phalanx, 22 elephants
1500 Galatians

Right wing
3000 cataphracts
1000 Agema
(10,000) Silver Shields, 16 elephants
1200 Dahae cavalrymen
3000 light infantry, Cretans and Illyrians

2500 Mysian archers
Elymaean archers and Cyrtian slingers

To the front of Antiochus' main line on the left were his scythed chariots, Arab archers mounted on camelback, and sundry light infantry. The phalanx at his centre was arrayed in a double depth of thirty-two ranks rather than the traditional sixteen. It was divided into ten battalions, each 1600 strong. Between each division of the phalanx the King posted two elephants, supported by a platoon of light infantry. In addition to the twenty-two elephants supporting the phalanx, another thirty-two were held in reserve, sixteen on either wing.

Livy reports that, in all, Antiochus commanded some 60,000 infantry and 12,000 cavalry.[2] Unfortunately, Livy's own numbers do not indicate such a total; he lists strengths totalling a 45,200 infantry and 11,500 cavalry. Yet Livy does not report the strength of several units: the Silver Shields, the Tarentine cavalry, and many of the light troops. Bar Kochba offers some sensible conjectures: the Silver Shields contained 10,000 men, based on their earlier strength at Raphia, while the Tarentine numbered 500.[3] The remaining 'missing' can be accounted for by light infantry and skirmishers, including the infantry left to guard the Seleucid Camp; contingents for which Livy provides no numerical strength.

Livy's disposition has a number of major flaws, the biggest of which is the fact that there was not space in the plain for such a lengthy line of troops. The dispositions make more sense if many of the light infantry were posted ahead of the main line as skirmishers, in particular the Cyrtian slingers, Elymaean archars and Mysian bowman, who could open up the battle with their volleys. Other units listed by Livy on the extreme flanks of the Seleucid battle line were most likely held behind in reserve, or were simply squeezed out as the plain between the rivers narrowed. The placement of the Silver Shields to the right of the Seleucid cavalry on the right wing was also a highly unorthodox development, as standard Macedonian tactics positioned the elite heavy infantry to the immediate right of the main phalanx (where Antiochus had positioned the Silver Shields at Raphia, over twenty years before), in between the phalanx and the cavalry. Why Antiochus would now put his cavalry to the right of his phalanx, followed by another large unit of heavy infantry is unclear. It is quite possible that Livy has made a mistake in transcribing Polybius' description of Antiochus' battleline (or that a copyist has made a mistake transcribing Livy!), and that the Silver Shields, in fact, held the standard position to the immediate right of the phalanx, although any modification of Livy's battleline is inherently speculative.

The Seleucid army at Magnesia represented military resources from the entire empire and beyond: Psidians, Pamphylians, Lydians, Phrygians Cilicians and Carians were local levies from Asia Minor. The Cyrtians and Elymaens came from the Iranian plateau, in addition to the phalanx of citizen-soldiers mustered from the cities of Syria and Mesopotamia. The Dahae were mustered from parts of Hyrcania re-incorporated during Antiochus' anabasis, and Parthian horsemen possibly numbered among his heavy cataphracts. The 2000 Cappadocians were the result of the diplomatic match between his daughter Antiochis and King Ariarathes of Cappadocia.

Composition and disposition: Romans

Lucius Scipio's heavy infantry consisted of two legions of Roman infantry, 5400-strong apiece, and two wings (*alae*) of Italian allies, also 5400 apiece. Scipio's Roman legions were over-strength for the campaign, as the standard Roman legion consisted of 4200 infantry. To the right of the legions, Scipio stationed light troops of 3000 Pergamenese and Achaean infantry. To the right of these were 3000 cavalry, 2200 Roman and 800 Pergamenese under the command of King Eumenes. The Roman left was anchored on the Phrygios River. A mere four companies (*turmae*) of cavalry, some 120 horsemen, were posted for flank security. Some 800 Cretan and Illyrian archers were stationed to the front of the main infantry line, while 2000 Thracian and Macedonian mercenaries guarded the Roman camp.[4] In all, Lucius Scipio had 25,000 infantry and 3000 cavalry, and was therefore badly outnumbered by more than two to one.[5]

The Romans fought arranged in the *tres acies* formation, with the heavy infantry divided into three lines known in Latin as the *hastati*, *principes*, and *triarii*. Age was the primary distinction among infantry classes, with men in their late teens and early twenties as *hastati* and those in their mid twenties the *principes*. The *triarii* were the experienced veterans, generally in their thirties and beyond. The three lines of heavy infantry were screened by teenaged skirmishers called *velites*, who fought with light throwing darts.[6]

Since the soldiers of the Roman militia supplied their own equipment, body armour varied based on the resources of the individual soldier. Poorer Romans wore simple breastplates (*pectorale*), while wealthier soldiers donned expensive chain mail coats (*lorica hamata*). All soldiers sported a helmet of bronze or iron, and many wore greaves to protect their shins. All three lines of heavy infantry were also equipped with an oblong shield (*scutum*) made of plywood. Roman soldiers were universally armed with a sword, usually a vicious Spanish weapon, the *gladius hispaniensis*, which had a 24–26-inch blade well suited to cutting and thrusting.[7]

The first two lines of heavy infantry were also equipped with javelins (*pila*). They bore the brunt of the fight but might retire once exhausted. The *triarii* were the reserves of the legion, and unlike the other ranks, armed themselves with pikes and stood in the rear, ready to form a bulwark and rallying point in a crisis. Their function led to the Latin adage, denoting a desperate situation, that 'things have come down to the triarii' (*ad triarios redisse*). However, the *triarii* were rarely employed in battle, and they often kneeled or sat down to watch the younger men fight, as the comic playwright Plautus quipped to his audience at the start of a play: 'Come now, everyone sit back and relax, just like the *triarii!*'[8]

The Roman legion was not a solid mass of troops like the Hellenistic phalanx. Rather, it was divided into smaller tactical sub-units called maniples; each maniple in Lucius Scipio's legions comprised roughly 160 men (maniples of the *triarii* contained only 60 men apiece).[9] The maniples of the three lines were arranged in a checkerboard pattern (*quincunx*) with gaps of roughly 10–15 metres among them.[10] Each legion of 5400 men had a front between 400 and 500 metres.

The Roman infantry formation was therefore far more open order than Antiochus' tightly packed phalanx, in which each Seleucid phalangite occupied a frontage of three feet, with shields, elbows, and *sarissai* pressing close against each other. Scipio's legionaries could also press together in a defensive position with interlocked shields (*densatis scutis*), but in the offensive the maniples flexed forward into the open order formation (*laxare manipulos/ soluere ordines*) to give soldiers sufficient room to wield their swords. According to Polybius, each Roman soldier required six feet of space in order to fight effectively, a figure that implies approximately two feet between soldiers.[11] This open order disposition, when combined with the modularity of the manipular system, gave the Roman legion great tactical flexibility, but also made it deeply vulnerable to charges from densely massed infantry or cavalry.

Command and control

Scipio Africanus, whose tactical brilliance was expected to carry the day, fell ill in the weeks prior to the battle, and Lucius Scipio commanded at Magnesia without the benefit of his brother's proven military genius. He did rely on the tactical experience of King Eumenes II, who commanded the combined cavalry, as well as that of an energetic legate, Domitius Ahenobarbus, given control of the Roman right. The Ahenobarbi were a prominent Roman family, and their prestige would only increase over the course of the republic and early empire (the emperor Nero was an Ahenobarbus by birth). After the battle, partisans of the Ahenobarbi credited Domitius with the victory, a political move made easier by Lucius's subsequent trial for embezzlement and expulsion from the senate in 184 BC. Nonetheless, Lucius Scipio was fully in command, and his dispositions suggest military competence, if not brilliance.[12]

The Great King personally commanded his army, aided by his most loyal and experienced lieutenants. He positioned himself on his right wing, accompanied by 1000 troops of the royal *agema*, talented Iranian horsemen from Media. The King's son and designated successor, Seleucus, commanded the left wing, presumably with 1000 horsemen of the royal cavalry as his bodyguard. Young Seleucus had with him an older cousin and mentor Antipater, who had fought with Antiochus at Raphia and Panium.[13] The Seleucid centre was entrusted to Zeuxis, Antiochus' most experienced general, and to Minnio, described as Antiochus' 'first friend' (*princeps amicorum* or *protos philos*). The *elephantarchos* Philip assumed responsibility for the twenty-two elephants assigned to support the main phalanx.[14]

The weather disadvantaged Antiochus. Rain and heavy mists coming off the rivers affected the bowstrings of many of Antiochus' archers, and fog may have prevented the King from effectively controlling his lengthy battle line; the shorter line of L. Scipio would have been easier to manage under such conditions of limited visibility.[15]

Battle

Like Darius III before him, Antiochus opened the attack by deploying his scythed chariots. These were relatively novel weapons to the Romans, but Eumenes, stationed among the cavalry on the left, prepared a hasty but effective countermeasure. He sent forward Cretan archers, slingers, and other light infantry of the Pergamenese contingent to snipe at the horses and drivers of the Seleucid chariots, actions that quickly drove the chariots back to their own side. Trying to move back to the Seleucid rear, the panicked teams caused considerable confusion among the cavalry on the Seleucid left.

On the Seleucid right, the heavy cataphracts commanded by the Great King made a spirited assault, assisted by the elite Silver Shields. The heavy cavalry smashed through the open order formation of the legionaries, and the Romans were forced back toward their camp, where they were rallied by the efforts of an energetic military tribune named Aemilius Lepidus.[16] Reinforced by the Thracian and Macedonian camp guard, the Roman left wing reformed on the ramparts of the camp, still hard pressed by the cavalry and Silver Shields.

With the battle going in his favour, Antiochus again became caught in the thick of the fighting, and in the process lost his own situational awareness in the fog of war. Pressing toward the Roman camp with the enemy in disarray, he did not know of the major setback on his left flank.

The Seleucid left

Eumenes II, commanding the Roman cavalry as well as his own squadron of 800 Attalid horsemen, realized that the *kairos*, or 'right moment', had arrived. Seeing that the retreating chariots had spooked the cavalry across from him, he ordered a cavalry charge. The Roman and Attalid horse quickly infiltrated the disorganized ranks of the Seleucid cataphracts, and those who fell from their horses wallowed helplessly in their heavy mail suits until they were dispatched. Instead of pursuing the retreating enemy, the Roman cavalry wheeled around to focus on the increasingly denuded flank of the main infantry phalanx. Eumenes II rolled up the Cappadocians and Galatians screening the left flank of the Seleucid phalanx, although his horsemen were unable to penetrate the bristling hedgehog of pikes.

The Seleucid centre

By now the Roman legions and Seleucid phalanx had closed, and the light troops screening both formations hastened to make a withdrawal to the rear. The *hastati* of the legion paused to pepper the stalled phalangites with javelins, targeting the elephants Antiochus had positioned to the front of the phalanx. The Roman army contained at least 5000 veterans of Scipio Africanus' Libyan campaign, men who were familiar with fighting Hannibal's war-elephants.[17] They knew to run to the side and aim their javelins into the soft underbelly of the animal, or to run behind and hamstring it with their *gladii*.

Goading the beasts with swords and javelins had a significant effect. Several of the elephants in front ranks of the phalanx panicked. While elephant mahouts were equipped with spiked clubs to dispatch the beast if it threatened friendly ranks, the rampaging elephants managed to wreak havoc on the front ranks, confusion and destruction that rippled through the densely packed phalanx.

As long as the soldiers maintained their discipline and calm, the defensive front of the Seleucid phalanx was impenetrable. With shields tightly packed and pikes bristling forward, they remained invincible even against the most determined Roman swordsman. What use was the Roman's 26-inch *gladius* against a 16-foot pike?[18] Against an intact phalanx, the Roman infantry could do little more than stand just out of range, hurling javelins and insults.

The gaps opened by the stampede of a few wounded elephants, however, compromised the entire formation. The creatures, agonized by javelin pricks and sword gashes, bowled through the ranks, and Roman swordsmen swirled in between the discombobulated phalangites. Once they closed to fight hand to hand, the Roman soldier enjoyed an immense advantage over his Seleucid counterpart: he had a larger shield, a longer sword, and training that emphasized individual combat.[19] As small groups of men of Roman infantrymen carved a way through the ranks of the phalanx, the entire formation disintegrated into a chaotic mass. The collapse of the phalanx ended the battle, and a rout ensued. This confusion and chaos swept over the King himself, who until then believed his most glorious victory was at hand.

Livy reports the Seleucid casualties at 53,000 dead: 50,000 infantry and 3000 cavalry.[20] This implausible number may be pure invention, and it is usually dismissed as such by modern military historians. It is highly unlikely that the Romans had the physical stamina to pursue and kill 50,000 men. While the phalanx had been enveloped by Eumenes' charge, the rest of the Selucid army was in a position to escape once the retreat began.

Assuming that Livy took the figure from a more reliable source like Polybius, the 53,000 may reflect the initial 'missing in action' report in the immediate aftermath of the battle. Under this hypothesis, Antiochus rallied his forces to find a residual of only 19,000 men, and this quick calculation would indeed imply 53,000 casualties. But many soldiers fled the crumbling battleline and subsequently made their way back to homes in Anatolia or Syria; some fugitives would have eventually returned to the ranks.

There is no way to determine the actual number of Seleucid dead, but it was significant: possibly as many as 20,000 Seleucid soldiers perished at Magnesia. In addition, the Romans captured 1500 prisoners. Scipio's initial casualty report returned 349 dead, although wounded men continued to perish in the battle's aftermath.[21]

Aftermath

After the Battle of Magnesia, Lucius Scipio occupied Sardis and easily secured the citadel Antiochus had taken with great difficulty nearly twenty years earlier.[22] Antiochus attempted to rally his shattered army, but soon realized the gravity of his situation. Critical murmurs found their way back to the King, as reported by the historian Appian:

> ...his friends began to blame him for plunging headfirst into the
> dispute with the Romans, and for the incompetence and lack of
> judgement that he had displayed from the start.... They disparaged
> him in this most recent folly for rendering the strongest part of his
> army in such a narrow spot, and pinning his hopes on a huge rabble
> of green troops. (Appian, *Syrian Wars*, 37)

The defeats at Thermopylae and Magnesia had already cost Antiochus
too much political capital, and such bankruptcy made him a likely target
for assassination by disgruntled courtiers. A peace treaty with the Romans
was the best option to quickly end the war.

The King dispatched a messenger named Musaios to make initial
diplomatic contact with the Romans. The envoy received an audience
with L. Scipio and requested safe passage for an embassy to enter the
Roman camp for the purposes of peace negotiations. Scipio consented,
and Antiochus sent two trusted advisors: the general Zeuxis and his
nephew Antipater. These two met privately with King Eumenes, in order
to ensure that he would not use his pull with the Romans to sabotage their
mission. Eumenes, having picked the winning side, was magnanimous
to the Seleucid ambassadors, given that he already expected increased
influence in Asia Minor as a by-product of the peace. Shortly afterward,
Zeuxis and Antipater met with Lucius Scipio's military council, a group
that included his legates, military tribunes, and senior centurions. After
Zeuxis and Antipater spoke requesting peace and alliance, the consul's
brother Africanus, having recovered from his illness, laid down the terms
of such a peace:

> They must withdraw from Europe and from the whole of Asia on
> the near side of the Taurus. He must pay 15,000 Euboean talents to
> cover the expenses of the war, 500 immediately and 2500 once the
> people had ratified the treaty, and the rest in twelve annual payments
> of 1000 talents. He must pay Eumenes 400 talents he previously
> owed him and the undelivered grain according his treaty with
> his father (Attalus I). In addition he was to give up Hannibal the
> Carthaginian, Thoas the Aetolian, Mnasilochus the Acarnanian, and
> Philo and Eubulidas the Chalcidians. As a token of faith, Antiochus

will immediately hand over twenty stipulated hostages. (Polybius 21.17.3–9)

Zeuxis and Antipater accepted Scipio's peace offer. The treaty needed to be ratified in Rome, following the approval of the Roman senate and an official vote by the Roman assembly. Across the east, communities sent envoys to Rome to make sure the resulting treaty accommodated their interests.

L. Scipio's command ended at the end of 190, and in 189 he was replaced by Manlius Vulso. The new consul, eager for his own military glory, launched an unprovoked assault against the Galatians, on the feeble pretext that they had been allies of Antiochus. Vulso gained his glory, along with huge quantities of booty and a forced indemnity from Galatian communities. But this Gaul-bashing also was a political statement. Hellenistic kings, from Antigonus Gonatas of Macedonia to Antiochus I, had used victory over the Gauls to legitimize their right to rule. Now, with his own victory over the Gallic enemy, Vulso likewise sought to legitimize the new Roman hegemony in the Hellenistic East.

Following the terms of the proposed armistice, the Scipios required Antiochus to provide Roman armies with rations while the peace treaty awaited ratification in Rome. The King sent his oldest living son, Seleucus, to Vulso's camp near Antioch-in-Pisidia to deliver the rations, but a dispute quickly arose. Seleucus insisted that he would provide rations only to the Roman soldiers, and not the 1500 Attalid troops attached to the Roman army. While the amount of grain needed to feed these troops was relatively small when compared with the rations of 25,000 Romans, it was a humiliation for a Seleucid prince to play grocery-man to the soldiers of an Attalid king. Vulso sternly informed young Seleucus that he would accept no rations for his own forces until grain was delivered to the Attalid allies. Realizing that he was in danger of jeopardizing the terms of the peace, Seleucus acquiesced, thus bowing to the new reality of Roman military dominance.[23]

Meanwhile, Antiochus attempted to carry on as the king of his realm, exercising his routine powers as he had done before the defeat. In 189 BC, he appointed a new chief-priest (*archieros*) to the sanctuary of Apollo and Artemis at Daphne, one of the leading holy places in the empire.[24] It was through this sort of routine patronage and benefaction that Antiochus held the best hope of restoring his political position after such a crushing military defeat

The King also had to remedy a problem with refugees: what to do with the Aetolians and Euboeans who had supported him and now found life untenable in the wake of the Seleucid defeat. The late Roman historian Orosius (a contemporary of Augustine), reports that Antiochus settled an island on the Orontes River near Antioch, filling it with Aetolians, Euboeans, and Cretans. While Orosius does not provide a date for this action, it should be placed after the end of the Roman war, intended to provide homes for Aetolian and Euboean collaborators, as well as discharged Cretan mercenaries.[25]

In 188 BC, Manlius Vulso returned from his Galatian adventure, boasting of actions that freed the cities of Asia Minor from a pressing Gallic threat. In reality, however, he did little more than cause a great deal of senseless misery and enrich himself and his soldiers with Gallic treasure. On returning to Apamea, he discovered that Antiochus had diligently forwarded a payment of 1500 talents as well as a shipment of grain. This cash payment was a full 1000 talents short of the amount stipulated by the Scipios, and so Vulso dispatched his brother with a legion to demand the remaining sum. The pro-consul also learned that a Seleucid garrison still held in the city of Perga, nearly two years after the battle of Magnesia. The garrison commander asked for a month to clarify his orders, and the request was granted. On the thirtieth day, the last Seleucid troops in Asia Minor obediently evacuated the citadel. This Seleucid *archophylax*'s obstinate insistence on holding his position nearly two years after the defeat reflects both the strengths and weaknesses of the Seleucid empire; on one hand, it is a reminder of the administrative and logistical difficulties in managing so many far-flung posts. On the other, it was men like this stubborn garrison commander, oblivious to the catastrophe surrounding him, who held the Seleucid Empire together through its various political crises.[26]

Finally, after the Seleucid and Attalid envoys had spent a year petitioning the Roman senate, the peace treaty was formally promulgated in 188 BC. Polybius records the terms nearly verbatim, giving the modern reader unusual insight into the mechanics of an ancient peace:

The peace of Apamea (Polybius 21.42, LCL)

There shall be friendship between Antiochus and the Romans for all time if he fulfils the conditions of the treaty.

King Antiochus and his subjects shall not permit the passage through their territory of any enemy marching against the Romans and their allies or furnish such enemy with any supplies. The Romans and their allies engage to act likewise toward Antiochus and his subjects.

Antiochus shall not make war on the inhabitants of the islands or of Europe. He shall evacuate all cities, lands, villages, and forts on this side of Taurus as far as the river Halys and all between the valley of Taurus and the mountain ridges that descend to Lycaonia.

[With the stroke of a pen, Antiochus ceded his long standing territorial claims to Asia Minor.]

From all such places he is to carry away nothing except the arms borne by his soldiers, and if anything has been carried away, it is to be restored to the same city. He shall not receive either soldiers or others from the kingdom of Eumenes.

[Antiochus is required to evacuate Asia Minor of troops, although these are permitted leave under arms. Booty must be returned to pillaged communities. He is not allowed to accept deserters from Attalid armies.]

If there be any men in the army of Antiochus coming from the cities which the Romans take over, he shall deliver them up at Apamea. If there be any from the kingdom of Antiochus dwelling with the Romans and their allies, they may remain or depart at their good pleasure: Antiochus and his subjects shall give up the slaves of the Romans and of their allies, and any prisoners of war they have taken, if there be such.

[The military levies from now ex-Seleucid territories must be allowed to return home. The Romans are not obliged to return Seleucid deserters. Antiochus must return Roman POWs and any escaped Roman slaves taking refuge in his army.]

Antiochus shall give up, if it be in his power, Hannibal son of Hamilcar, the Carthaginian,[27] Mnasilochus the Acarnanian, Thoas the Aetolian, Eubulidas and Philo the Chalcidians, and all Aetolians who have held public office. He shall surrender all the elephants now in Apamea and not keep any in future.

*[*Antiochus must surrender key collaborators to the Romans. The most notable of these was Hannibal, who did not wait for Antiochus to hand him over. He fled, instead, and found shelter with Prusias, the King of Bithynia. In 183, the Romans pressed Prusias to surrender Hannibal, who in despair committed suicide.*]

He shall surrender his long ships with their gear and tackle and in future he shall not possess more than ten decked ships of war, nor shall he have any galley rowed by more than thirty oars, nor a skiff to serve in any war in which he is the aggressor.

His ships shall not sail beyond the Calycadnus and the Sarpedonian promontory unless conveying tribute, envoys or hostages.

*[*These two clauses utterly dashed Antiochus' ambition to reassert Seleucid naval power in the Aegean Sea.*]

Antiochus shall not have permission to hire mercenaries from the lands under the rule of the Romans, or to receive fugitives.

[*This clause was aimed primarily at the Seleucid practice of hiring Galatatian mercenaries. It was widely flouted by Antiochus' successors, who continued to use Galatians in their armies.*]

All houses that belonged to the Rhodians and their allies in the dominions of Antiochus shall remain their property as they were before he made war on them likewise if any money is owing to them they may exact payment, and if anything has been abstracted from them it shall be sought for and returned: merchandise meant for Rhodes shall be free from duties as before the war.

*[*Refers to property of Rhodian citizens seized by the King after the outbreak of hostilities with the island.*]

If any of the cities which Antiochus has to give up have been given by him to others, he shall withdraw from these also the garrisons and the men in possession of them and if any cities afterward wish to desert to him, he shall not receive them.

*[*Refers to primarily to formerly Seleucid cities in Asia which the Romans gave over to Eumenes II and Rhodes as benefits of their collaboration.*]

Antiochus shall pay to the Romans [twelve] thousand talents over a period of [twelve] years in instalments of 1000 talents, each talent shall weigh no less than eighty Roman pounds, and five hundred and forty thousand *modii* of corn. He shall pay to King Eumenes three hundred and fifty talents in the next five years, paying seventy talents a year at the same time that is fixed for his payments to the Roman and in lieu of the corn, as Antiochus estimated it – one hundred and twenty-seven talents and twelve hundred and eight drachmas, the sum Eumenes agreed to accept as a satisfactory payment to his treasury.[28]

[A modius was a volume measure, equal to roughly 2 litres. A modius of wheat weighed roughly 15 lb/ 6.8 kg. The grain indemnity was equivalent to the yearly rations of 11,250 Roman soldiers. Antiochus' total indemnity to Eumenes, with the grain requirement translated into cash, was 477.2 talents.]

Antiochus shall give twenty hostages, replacing them every three years, not below eighteen years of age and not above forty. If any of the money he pays does not correspond to the above stipulations, he shall make it good in the following year.

[The most important hostage would be Antiochus' son, the prince Antiochus, the future Antiochus IV.]

If any of the cities or peoples against which Antiochus is forbidden by this treaty to make war begin first to make war on him, he may make war on such, provided he does not exercise sovereignty over any of them or receive them into his alliance.

[The Romans granted Antiochus the right of defensive war, which was more lenient than their 201 BC treaty with Carthage, which required Carthage to request Rome's permission even to fight defensive wars.]

All grievances of both parties are be submitted to a lawful tribunal. If both parties desire to add any clauses to this treaty or to remove any by common decree, they are at liberty to do so.

The pro-consul sent two envoys, including his brother Lucius, to obtain an oath from Antiochus that he would respect the treaty as written. Q. Fabius Labeo, the commander of the Roman fleet, sailed to Patara, took possession of the Seleucid ships stationed there, and burned them.[29]

Antiochus' elephants were confiscated and handed over to Eumenes. Ten Roman commissioners arrived to determine which Seleucid territories in Asia Minor would remain independent and which would be handed over to either Eumenes or Rhodes. Ariarathes of Cappadocia, who had recently married to Antiochis, the daughter of Antiochus, now hastened to betroth his own daughter to Eumenes.[30]

At the end of the year, Manlius Vulso crossed the Hellespont with his army and ten commissioners. While battered by Thracian raids, he was still able to display lavish sums of treasure in his triumph back in Rome. While his senseless Galatian war was viewed with some cynicism in Rome, Manlius Vulso curried political favour with the plebs by using much of his loot to refund the Roman taxpayers, then groaning under the financial strains of the Seleucid–Aetolian war.[31]

The final journey East

In the wake of the disaster in the west, Antiochus looked again to the east. He travelled to Babylon in 187 BC and reaffirmed his status as King of Babylon through a lavish set of sacrifices at the great Babylonian temples: Esaglia, Erzida, and Borsippa. In return, the priests and governor of Babylon bestowed extravagant gifts on him: a gold crown worth 1000 shekels, gold bullion, and the purple robes of King Nebuchadnezzar, the greatest king of the Neo-Babylonian dynasty. Through the tested rites that predated his own dynasty by centuries, Antiochus asserted his undiminished kingship before his native subjects.[32]

From Babylon, Antiochus advanced eastward into Elam with an armed force. It is possible that he intended another grand anabasis to rebuild his royal prestige. But having paid 3000 talents to the Romans (and with another 1000 talents coming due), the King was badly cash strapped. As in Ecbatana in 210, the stored wealth of a native temple proved irresistible:

> Antiochus, short of money and hearing that the temple of Ba'al in Elam possessed much silver and gold from its votive deposits, decided to pillage it. He came to Elam and after accusing the inhabitants of starting a war, he plundered the shrine. Gathering together a great

hoard of wealth, he soon received the just retribution from the gods. (Diodorus 29.15)

The despoliation went badly awry: outraged subjects counterattacked and killed Antiochus, an inglorious death for an old king who had spent his entire adult life on military campaign.[33] He died at the age of fifty-three, having reigned for thirty-six years.[34] The priests in Babylon diligently noted his passing on the cuneiform king list:

Year 125, Month Three: The following was heard in Babylon: On the 25th Day, Antiochus the King was killed in Elam.[35]

Chapter Ten

The End of a Dynasty

The Great King was dead. Seleucus IV, the eldest son already serving as general and co-king, obtained the empire in a peaceful succession. His twelve-year reign was relatively quiet, as the substantial Roman indemnity constrained major military operations. Seleucus IV did briefly consider moving against Eumenes II, who was then attacking Pharneces, the king of Pontus, but he ultimately declined to do so. Financial problems were also evident. The Selucids failed to pay several instalments of the Roman indemnity, and his *epi ton pragmaton* Heliodorus attempted to despoil the treasures in the Temple of Yaweh in Jerusalem, a common Seleucid tactic in times of fiscal crisis.[1]

Seleucus IV was murdered in an episode of court intrigue.[2] Demetrius, Seleucus IV's adult son, was a hostage in Rome. The Romans refused to release Demetrius, instead supporting the claim of Seleucus IV's younger brother Antiochus IV, then living comfortably in Athens. Antiochus IV was an unusual character. He too spent time in Rome as a hostage following the treaty of Apamea, and there developed a passion for gladiatorial games and Roman culture in general. He exhibited gladiators in Antioch and formed a special 'legion' of 5000 men armed in the Roman fashion, soldiers who wore chainmail, carried oblong shields, and wielded javelins instead of pikes.[3]

Despite his passion for gladiators and his admiration for Roman military kit, Antiochus IV was not a Roman lackey. Rather, he was a Seleucid king with traditional ambitions, harboured particularly against Ptolemaic Egypt. Child kings and dynastic dysfunction again plagued the Ptolemaic kingdom, and by 170, the kingdom had split between two brothers, Ptolemy VI Philometer (Mother-lover) and Ptolemy VIII Euergetes (Benefactor), then twelve years old. This power sharing arrangement was not to last. In 169, Philometer invited Antiochus IV to intervene on his behalf, and the Seleucid king was more than willing to comply. After two years of campaigning, Philometer was crowned as a puppet king in Memphis while Antiochus prepared to besiege Alexandria.

At this time, Rome was engaged in a stalemated war with Macedonia. The Romans supported Euergetes, and were alarmed by the notion that Antiochus IV might become *de facto* ruler of Egypt. Additional Roman military commitments in Spain and Liguria prevented Rome from committing to military action against Antiochus IV. However, in 168, the Romans won a significant victory at the Battle of Pydna. Legionary swords butchered more than 20,000 Macedonians, and Perseus, the last Macedonian king, was removed to a Roman dungeon.[4] The swift conclusion of the war meant that more than 60,000 Roman troops stood ready for potential redeployment against Antiochus IV.

A delegation of twelve ambassadors led by the ex-consul Popilius Laenus arrived at the Alexandrian siege lines. Laenus had been dispatched earlier but lingered on the island of Cyprus waiting for definitive news from Macedonia. As long as the stalemate continued, Laenus knew his threats would be empty. As soon as the victory at Pydna was confirmed, however, he hastened to the port of Pelusium in Egypt.

The Romanophile Antiochus IV met the Roman delegation as it disembarked at Pelusium and affably offered to shake hands. This was a gesture of tremendous respect and good will. In a spectacular and arrogant gesture of showmanship, Popilius Laenus remained silent. He took his staff, drew a circle in the sand around the King, and handed him a written copy of Roman demands. Finally speaking, he told the King not to step out of the circle until he had agreed to Roman demands, demands that included the complete evacuation of Egypt. Antiochus IV was humiliated. But a fellow Hellenistic monarch had just been deposed by Rome, making manifest the potential cost of defeat. He told Laenus of his decision to comply and swiftly withdrew his forces.[5]

But an angry and humiliated king is a very dangerous thing. With his prestige shattered, Antiochus IV looked for avenues of quick and violent retribution, and while marching back through Palestine up the Gaza strip, a convenient opportunity presented itself.

Antiochus III had granted the city of Jerusalem special status and accommodated unusual Jewish practices, but the cultural and religious politics of the city had grown significantly more tense over the years. Over the past decade, a rift had opened between a 'Hellenizing' faction, Jewish elites interested in emulating Greek culture, and a more conservative faction. Following a disputed election for high priest and outbreaks of bitter street violence, the Hellenizing faction invited Antiochus IV and his passing army to intervene. Given the King's ugly mood and his desperate need to reassert his power, this invitation would turn out to be a very bad mistake.

Using the civil unrest as a pretence, Antiochus IV's army sacked Jerusalem, carried off 1800 talents of treasure from the temple, and installed a permanent garrison. Jewish ritual was forbidden within the city, although there was no attempt to ban Judaism altogether within the empire. (The prominent Jewish community in Babylon, for example, remained untouched by the King's wrath.) The conservative faction within Jerusalem soon rebelled. The leaders, Matthias and John, dubbed themselves the 'Maccabees (Hammers)' and took to the hills to wage moderately effective guerrilla war.

Antiochus IV had more important matters to attend to than the petty rebels in Judea. The Parthians were on the move in the east, while the Greek kings of Bactria were expanding at Seleucid expense. Marshalling an impressive army, Antiochus paraded it through Daphne: some 45,000 men altogether, including 26,000 phalangites and his pet Roman 'legion'. The parade stands as a potent reminder of the lingering power of the Seleucids. But such display of force costs money. Perhaps learning the lesson of his father's death, Antiochus IV attempted to mask the despoliation of native temples with a new conceit: he married himself to a native goddess in order to appropriate her treasures as a 'dowry'. This worked well enough in the Syrian town of Bambyke, where he married the goddess Atargatis and then stole all the plate in her temple, leaving the hapless deity only a single ring to symbolize their marriage.[6] A similar 'holy marriage' (*hieros gamos*) was attempted in the Temple of Nanaia in Elam, but Antiochus IV was killed in the process, much like his father before him.[7]

Antiochus IV left an infant son, Antiochus V, who was perhaps only a year old. Again, an infant's succession was complicated by the fact that one adult son of Seleucus IV was still alive: Demetrius, still a hostage in Rome. The baby 'ruled' for two years, largely through the general and regent Lysias. Eager to quell domestic problems, Lysias made major concessions to the Jews and granted them moderate autonomy; he seems to have reinstated the 'charter' of Jerusalem granted by Antiochus III.[8]

In 163 BC, a Roman delegation led by Gnaeus Octavius arrived to verify that the Seleucids were indeed in compliance with the Treaty of Apamea. It seems that the Seleucid kings, probably beginning with Antiochus III himself, had intentionally maintained ships and elephants that were banned by the treaty, and the Romans may have decided that a tenuous regency provided the perfect opportunity for a full inspection. Octavius ordered that the elephant herd of Apamea be hamstrung and killed, while the excess warships were to be set on fire. The butchery of the elephants was particularly disturbing. A man named Leptines, distraught by the animal cruelty, murdered Octavius in the gymnasium at Antioch. While the murder of an ambassador could easily justify a declaration of war (for example, the Roman invasion of Illyria in 229 BC was made under such pretences), the Romans remained uninterested in a war against an already troubled kingdom.[9]

Meanwhile, the hostage Demetrius contrived an escape from Rome. His primary accomplice was none other than the historian Polybius, who helped to provide him with a ship. Given Polybius' close ties with the Scipios, it is very likely that Demetrius' escape had the unofficial approval of a faction of the Roman aristocracy. Demetrius linked up with defecting army units and staged a coup in Antioch; the toddler Antiochus V was cruelly murdered. Lysias, the real power behind the throne, was also executed. To remain in good standing with Rome, Demetrius diligently surrendered Leptines, the murderer of the Roman envoy Octavius, to the Romans for punishment.[10]

Demetrius I turned aggressively toward two breakaway parts of the empire. He sent a series of expeditions against the rebellious Jews. Despite several setbacks, his general Bacchides eventually crushed the Maccabees, leaving the legendary Judas Maccabeus dead on the battlefield and forcing his sons to flee into exile. In Media, the satrap Timarchus had scored a major victory over the Parthians and used this victory to proclaim himself king of a breakaway kingdom centred on Babylon. Demetrius marched east, where he defeated and executed Timarchus.

The defeated Timarchus had a brother named Hereclides, who remained in the Seleucid court in a significantly reduced role. Demetrius would have been wise to execute him for good measure, as Hereclides now brought forth another pretender. He found a young man, Balas, gave him the name of Alexander, and proclaimed him the natural son of Antiochus IV. Demetrius' purges had made him unpopular in Antioch, and his military competence made him dangerous to Rome. The Roman senate threw diplomatic support behind the pretender, and Egypt and Pergamon lent material aid to the new Alexander. Demetrius fell fighting while engaged in personal combat in 150 BC. Alexander Balas was proclaimed king, and quickly gained a reputation as an adolescent voluptuary.

Prior to his death, Demetrius secured his sons in the city of Cnidus on the coast of Asia Minor, along with a substantial reserve of money. The older son, also named Demetrius, raised a small force of Cretan mercenaries and launched a stealth raid on Antioch, catching Alexander Balas entirely by surprise. The return of Demetrius II seems to have been welcomed by the population. Balas was quickly murdered; Demetrius II officially restored the legitimate line in 145 BC. He too gained a reputation as a voluptuary (it was good to be king!), but he also promptly undertook military campaigns necessary to restore faltering control of the east, where the Parthians had overrun Seleucid domains.[11] Unfortunately, Demetrius was captured by the Parthians in 139 BC and held in gentlemanly captivity for the next ten years; the Parthians then controlled much of Mesopotamia, including Babylon. For the first time, the waxing Parthian realm grew larger than the waning Seleucid Empire.

In captivity, Demetrius II was succeeded by his younger brother Antiochus VII, nicknamed Sidetes, who had just turned twenty years old. Antiochus VII moved first against the pretender Tryphon, who earlier had proclaimed the infant son of Alexander Balas king (Antiochus VI), subsequently murdered the baby, and then claimed to rule Antioch himself. Antioch fell to Antiochus VII in 138 and Tryphon was summarily executed.

The defeat of the pretender allowed Antiochus VII to turn his attentions back to the East and the Parthian threat. In 129 BC, he marched east with a sizable army that included a large contingent of Jewish troops from the semi–independent client state of Judea.[12] He enjoyed some initial successes, including the recapture of Babylon.[13] In a catastrophic battle, however, the Parthians killed Antiochus VII and annihilated his army. This was the worst military defeat in Seleucid history and proved far more consequential than the savaging suffered by Antiochus III at Magnesia. The Parthians recaptured Babylon; now only Syria remained as the pathetic rump of the Seleucid kingdom. For a military city like Antioch, contributor of so many citizens to the final expedition, the results were heart wrenching, as the Greek historian Diodorus Siculus relates (34/35.17.1–12):

> When the citizens of Antioch learned of Antiochus' (VII) death, not only did the city mourn publically, but every private household filled with gloom and lamentation. The wailing of the women especially kindled the grief. Since 300,000 had been lost, including camp followers not in the ranks, not a household could be found that was free from misfortune. Some women mourned for brothers, some for husbands, and some for sons, while many unmarried girls and boys, orphaned, grieved their desolation, until time, the best doctor for sorrow, blunted the edge off their misery.

The Parthians released Demetrius II from captivity to rule the humbled empire as a vassal king married to a Parthian princess, much in the same fashion as Antiochus had forced sisters and daughters upon defeated enemies. The Seleucid Empire was now little more than a petty kingdom in central Syria, ruled by a final succession of ineffective kings who focused their attention on tedious rounds of petty dynastic strife.[14] In 66 BC, the Roman general Gnaeus Pompeius Magnus (Pompey the Great) obtained a command in the east to conclude a drawn out war against the Pontic king Mithradites VI. With the steep decline of Seleucid power, Mithradites had transformed this previously peripheral kingdom into the last great military power of Hellenistic world and boldly challenged Rome for control of the Eastern Mediterranean. Mithradites' successes took place in the context of the civil wars between Marius and Sulla, but once these bloody distractions ceased, Rome gained the upper hand. With the defeat and suicide of Mithradates, Pompey looked to reorganize the politics of the Eastern Mediterranean. To a large extent, this involved granting new kingdoms to loyal clients and transforming large swaths of territory into Roman provinces. With little fanfare, Pompey reconfigured what remained of the Seleucid kingdom into the province of Syria, ruled by a Roman pro-consul.[15] The empire of Antiochus III was no more.

How could the mighty and expansive empire of Antiochus III decline so swiftly? First and foremost, the Seleucid Empire had the grave misfortune of physical location between two dangerous external powers: Rome and Parthia, and thus experienced military pressure from both sides. The well-organized Roman state was by far the more potent of the two external threats, but the Romans had little appetite for large-scale territorial annexation in the second century BC. Their main goal was to stymie the Seleucids so that they would not jeopardize Roman interests in the eastern Mediterranean. The Romans did not begrudge the Seleucid empire their core territories, as long as the dynasty remained weak and devoid of further Mediterranean ambitions. Yet almost as destructive as direct conquest was the senate's constant meddling in royal succession after the death of Seleucus IV, as repetitive succession crises produced a string of insecure and ineffective kings drawn from competing parallel dynasties. The ongoing Seleucid civil wars sapped the dynasty's military strength, and perhaps more dangerously, its claim of legitimacy.

Weak kings made the Seleucid Empire vulnerable to the greater menace: the Parthians. While the Parthians were not as efficiently organized as the Romans, their state was growing stronger in terms of military power and organizational sophistication. Parthian kings also had territorial designs against Mesopotamia and the Iranian plateau, vital core Seleucid territories. Antiochus III had aggressively set back Parthian state-building, but the period of dynastic instability from 160 to 145 BC allowed the waxing Parthian state to achieve a certain size and momentum. As the Parthians gathered more and more territory, the vicious cycle of military defeat weighed heavily upon the Seleucids. Lost territory meant lost tax revenue and vanished recruiting grounds. The combination of external pressures and internal instability created the death spiral of state failure so readily apparent after 145 BC.

Yet the crumbling Seleucid Empire in 145 BC was not that far removed from the troubled kingdom Antiochus III had inherited in the 220s BC.

Then, the empire was reeling from recent external defeat (in the Third Syrian War and the War of the Brothers), facing internal strife wrought by Molon and then Achaeus, and suffering from the separatist ambitions of the Parthians and Bactrians. These defeats might have reduced the Seleucid Empire to a failed state in 223 BC, but they did not. The energetic statecraft and generalship of Antiochus III were sufficient to break the cycle of defeat and overcome the constraints of geography. Antiochus III was neither a political or military genius, but he was a man driven by a simple if bold vision: to restore the empire of Seleucus Nicator. Striving relentlessly to achieve this goal, he campaigned continuously for almost thirty years in Koile Syria, the Upper Satrapies, Asia Minor and Greece. By 196 BC, he was stood triumphant, securely occupying many territories that Seleucus Nicator had only tenuously claimed.

The unforeseen events of the last five years of his life cost Antiochus dearly, and he died humbled by military defeat, trying to scrounge up cash to pay a shameful indemnity. Polybius ultimately assessed the Great King's career in a decidedly pessimistic light:

> King Antiochus in the beginning seemed full of ambition, ready to attempt great deeds, and tough and effective enough to accomplish his objectives. Advancing past middle age, however, he seemed much weaker than his usual self, and fell short of his expectations. (15.37.1–2)[16]

But even with the loss of Asia Minor and the humiliation at Magnesia, Antiochus III still left the Seleucid Empire larger and stronger than he found it, thanks largely to his conquest of Koile Syria. His constant military and administrative efforts rank him as one of the greatest Seleucid kings (perhaps second only to Seleucus I Nicator), and one of the most important kings of the Hellenistic period.

The Book of Daniel, written in the first century BC, provides an external assessment of the Seleucid king: a short moral lesson of a haughty victor punished by humiliating defeat.

> Then the king of the north shall come and throw up siege-works, and take a well-fortified city. And the forces of the south shall not stand,

not even his picked troops, for there shall be no strength to resist. But he who comes against him shall take the actions he pleases, and no one shall withstand him. He shall take a position in the beautiful land, and all of it shall be in his power. He shall set his mind to come with the strength of his whole kingdom, and he shall bring terms of peace and perform them. In order to destroy the kingdom, he shall give him a woman in marriage, but it shall not succeed or be to his advantage. Afterward he shall turn to the coastlands, and shall capture many. But a commander shall put an end to his insolence; indeed he shall turn his insolence back upon him. Then he shall turn back toward the fortresses of his own land, but he shall stumble and fall, and shall not be found. (Daniel 11.15–20, NRSV)

To this anonymous Jewish author, such was the career of Antiochus the Great: the conquest of Koile Syria, the marriage of a daughter Cleopatra to Ptolemy V, his naval operations against the south coast of Asia Minor, the defeat at Magnesia by the 'commander' L. Scipio, and the finality of his death in the east. This brief synopsis serves as a telling reminder of the fleeting impressions even powerful persons had upon the common inhabitants of their realm. To the Jewish farmers of Koile Syria, Antiochus was neither a mighty hero nor an arch-villain, but simply another passing character in the tragedy of a ruined world.

Dynasties of the Hellenistic World (to c.150 BC)

Seleucids

Seleucus I Nicator (Victor): 305–281 BC
Antiochus I Soter (Saviour): 281–265 BC
Antiochus II Theos (God): 264–246 BC
Seleucus II Callinicus (Glorious Victory): 246–225 BC
Seleucus III Soter (Saviour): 225–223 BC
Antiochus III Megas (The Great): 223–187 BC
Seleucus IV Philopater (Father-lover): 187–175 BC
Antiochus IV Epiphanes (Manifest): 175–164 BC
Antiochus V Eupator (Good father): 164–162 BC
Demetrius I Soter (Saviour): 162–150 BC
Alexander Balas: 150–145 BC
Demetrius II Nicator: 145–141 BC
Antiochus VI Epiphanes (Manifest): 141–139 BC
(Dynasty ends in 66 BC)

Antigonids of Macedonia

Demetrius I Poliorcetes (Beseiger): 294–287 BC
Antigonus II Gonatas (Knock-kneed): 277–239 BC
Demetrius II Soter (Savior): 239–229 BC
Antigonus III Doson (Giver): 229–221 BC
Philip V: 221–171 BC
Perseus: 171–168 BC
(Dynasty ends 168 BC)

The Ptolemies of Egypt

Ptolemy I Soter (Saviour): 305–283 BC
Ptolemy II Philadephus (Sister-lover): 285–246 BC
Ptolemy III: 246–221 BC
Ptolemy IV: 221–204 BC
Ptolemy V: 204–180 BC
Ptolemy VI: 180–145 BC
(Dynasty ends 31 BC)

The Attalids of Pergamon

Philetairos: 283–263 BC
Eumenes I: 263–241 BC
Attalus I: 241–197 BC
Eumenes II: 197–159 BC
Attalus II: 159–133 BC
Attalus III: 138–133 BC
(Dynasty ends 133 BC)

The Bactrian kings

Diodotids
Diodotus I: c.246–c.230 BC
Diodotus II: c. 230–c.220 BC

Euthydemnids
Euthydemos I: c. 220–c.200 BC
Demetrius I: c.200–c. 170 BC
Euthydemos II: c. 170–160 BC (contested sovereignty with Eucratides I).
Demetrius II: c.145. (limited sovereignty).
(Severe dynastic instability after 190 BC, last known rulers c.75 BC)

Roman consuls (200–187 BC): Patrician-Plebian

200: P. Sulpicius Galba and C. Aurelius Cotta
199: L. Cornelius Lentulus and P. Villius Tappalus
198: T. Quinctius Flamininus and Sex. Aelius Paetus Catus
197: C. Cornelius Cethegus and Q. Minucius Rufus
196: L. Furius Purpureo and M. Claudius Marcellus
195: L. Valerius Flaccus and Marcus Porcius Cato
194: P. Cornelius Scipio (II) and Titus Sempronius Longus
193: L. Cornelius Merula and Q. Minucius Thermus
192: L. Quinctius Flamininus and Cn. Domitius Ahenobarbus
191: P. Cornelius Scipio Nasica and M'. Acilius Glabrio
190: L. Cornelius Scipio and Gaius Laelius
189: Cn. Manlius Vulso and M. Fulvius Nobilior
188: M. Valerius Messalla and C. Livius Salinator
187: M. Aemilius Lepidus and Gaius Flaminius

Children of Antiochus III

Antiochus the Younger

Eldest son and intended successor of Antiochus the Great. Born c. 220 BC. Crowned co-king prior to his father's departure on his *anabasis* in 212 BC, he politely received a delegation from Magnesia on the Maeander requesting recognition of their Isopythian games. Commanded the right wing at the Battle of Panium. In 196 BC, he was married to his sister Laodice IV, in an attempt to mimic Ptolemaic royal incest. His sudden death in 193 BC interrupted negotiations with Roman envoys, and altered Antiochus III's succession plans.[1]

Seleucus IV

Second son of Antiochus the Great. He commanded the Seleucid left at the Battle of Magnesia, and was made co-king shortly afterward, succeeding his father in 187 BC. His power was severely constrained by 1000 talent p.a. indemnity payments. He was murdered in 175 BC.

Antiochus IV

Assumed the dynastic name Antiochus upon the death of his older brother; John Grainger hypothesizes that prior to this his name was Mithradites. Following the Peace of Apamea, he spent a comfortable stint in Rome as a hostage, where he amused himself by attending gladiatorial games and aping Roman politicians during their electoral canvass. He returned upon the death of his brother in 175 BC, determined to rebuild Seleucid power. The illegal re-construction of a new war fleet likely dates to his reign, as well as aggressive attempts to reconstitute an effective army, including the formation of a 'legion' armed with Roman equipment. In 169–168 BC, he invaded Egypt, but withdrew under Roman diplomatic pressure. Humiliated, he reasserted his royal authority by sacking Jerusalem, which had been plagued by factional unrest. In 165 BC, he mustered a 45,000-man army at Daphne, prior to setting out on an Eastern anabasis, similar in ambitions to that of his father. He died while on this campaign, supposedly trying to sack an Elamite temple.[2]

Laodice

Eldest daughter of Antiochus, she ultimately married all three of her brothers, mimicking the Ptolemaic custom of royal incest. Indeed, being married to Laodice marked a son as the designated successor: she first married Antiochus the Younger, then Seleucus IV, then Antiochus IV. Two of her children by different brothers became rival claimants to the throne: Antiochus V and Demetrias I, with the latter deposing and murdering the former.

Cleopatra 'the Syrian'

Betrothed to Ptolemy V in 196 BC, part of the treaty that ended the Fifth Syrian War. The couple married three years later, likely to allow both parties time to reach pubescence. Following the death of her husband in 180 BC, she remained a powerful force in the Ptolemaic court, as the regent to the boy-king Ptolemy VI. She died in 176 BC. Her son assumed the title Philometer, 'mother-loving' in her honour, and Cleopatra became a Ptolemaic dynastic name for girls from here onwards, culminating in the famous Cleopatra VII, lover of Julius Caesar and wife of Mark Anthony.[3]

Antiochis

She was offered in marriage to Eumenes in 193 BC, but this alliance was rejected. She was eventually married to Ariarathes IV of Cappadocia, who provided a contingent of 2000 troops at Magnesia. She died in Antioch, but was buried in Cappadocia, possibly murdered by the regents of Antiochus V.[4]

Unnamed daughter

Offered to Demetrius I of Bactria during peace negotiations in 206. It is not known if the marriage was ever accomplished. If the nuptials never, in fact, occurred, it is possible that the offer involved one of the daughters listed above.[5]

Unnamed daughter

Born to Euboea in 191 BC. Both mother and child fled with Antiochus to Ephesus following the defeat at Thermopylae, and were packed off to Apamea following the disaster at Magnesia. The girl is attested in Babylon in 187 BC.[6]

Appendix III

Seleucid Timeline to 187 BC

(dates are often approximate)

c. 241 BC:	Birth of Antiochus III
226 BC:	Death of Seleucus II (father)
223 BC:	Death of Seleucus III (brother)/ accession as king
222 BC:	Revolt of Molon
221 BC:	Marriage to Laodice
221 BC:	Antiochus' failed assaults into the Biqua Valley, start of 4th Syrian War
221 BC:	Revolt of Cyrrhus, murder of Epigenes
220 BC:	Defeat of Molon
220 BC:	Rebellion of Achaeus
220 BC:	Murder of Hermeias
219 BC:	Capture of Seleucia Pieria
219 BC:	Invasion of Koile Syria, defection of Theodotus the Aetolian
218 BC:	Storming of the Porphyrion Pass in Phonecia
217 BC:	Battle of Raphia
216 BC:	Campaign against Achaeus
214 BC:	Capture of Sardis; Achaeus holds out in citadel
213 BC:	Capture and execution of Achaeus; citadel of Sardis falls
212 BC:	Campaign against Xerxes of Armenia.
211 BC:	Musters forces in Ecbatana, loots temple to Aina
211 BC:	'Anabasis' begins: capture of Hecatompylos, invasion of Hyrcania
209 BC:	Nicanor appointed high priest of Asia Minor
210–208 BC:	Seige of Bactra
208–207 BC:	March to the Indus River Valley
206 BC:	Return journey to Babylon
205 BC:	Campaign against the Gerrhae of the Arabian coast
204 BC:	Antiochus in Asia Minor, *asylia* agreement with Teos
203 BC:	So-called 'Pact between the kings'. Antiochus and Philip V agree to divide Ptolemaic holdings
202 BC:	New invasion of Koile Syria, start of the 5th Syrian War.
201 BC:	Scopas counterattacks
200? BC:	Battle of Panium (dated anywhere from 201–198 BC)
197 BC:	Campaigns in Asia Minor and the Thracian Chersonese
196 BC:	Meeting with Roman envoys in Lysimacheia

196 BC:	Rumour of death of Ptolemy V; expedition against Cyprus thwarted by storms
196/5 BC:	Laodice makes benefaction of grain to city of Iasus
196/5 BC:	Peace with Ptolemy V, end of 5th Syrian War
195 BC:	Marriage of Antiochus the Younger with sister Laodice
195 BC:	Hannibal arrives in Tyre
194 BC:	Seleucid delegation in Rome
194/3 BC:	Roman delegation visits Ephesus and Apamea
194/3 BC:	Antiochus establishes royal cult for Laodice (now deceased?)
193 BC:	Death of Antiochus the Younger. Negotiations with Rome halted
193 BC:	Marriage of Cleopatra Syra to Ptolemy V
192 BC:	Aetolians invite Antiochus to invade Greece
191 BC:	Antiochus marries 'Euboea'
191 BC:	Battle of Thermopylae
190 BC:	Battle of Magnesia
188 BC:	Peace of Apamea
187 BC:	Visit to Babylon, death of Antiochus III in Elam while despoiling a temple of Ba'al

International Timeline: 220–187 BC

223 BC:	Ptolemy IV becomes king of Egypt upon death of Ptolemy III
221 BC:	Philip V becomes king of Macedonia with the death of Antigonus III Doson
221 BC:	'Social War' between Macedonia and Achaea vs the Aetolians
219 BC:	Romans invade Illyria in response to organized Illyrian piracy
219 BC:	Hannibal captures Saguntum in Spain
218 BC:	Hannibal Invades Italy, start of 2nd Punic War; Battle of Trebia, Hannibal annihilates two consular armies
217 BC:	Peace of Naupactus ends Social War
217 BC:	Battle of Transemene. Hannibal annihilates another consular army
216 BC:	Battle of Cannae: Hannibal annihilates 8-legion Roman army
215 BC:	Alliance between Philip V and Carthage; war between Philip V and Rome
212 BC:	Romans capture Syracuse
211 BC:	Aetolians declare war against Philip V, as allies of Rome
210 BC:	P. Scipio captures New Carthage in Spain
206 BC:	P. Scipio expels Carthaginians from Spain
206 BC:	Aetolians make peace with Philip V
205 BC:	Romans make peace with Philip V
204 BC:	P. Scipio invades Africa
202 BC:	Battle of Zama: P. Scipio defeats Hannibal
204? BC:	Death of Ptolemy IV
202 BC:	Riots in Alexandria, murder of regent Agathocles
201 BC:	End of 2nd Punic War
200 BC:	Start of 2nd Macedonian War between Rome and Macedon
200? BC:	Death of Euthydemos I in Bactria
197 BC:	Battle of Cynoscephalae: Flamininus defeats Philip V
197 BC:	Death of Attalus I, Eumenes II becomes king of Pergamon
196 BC:	Flamininus declares 'freedom for the Greeks' at Corinth
196 BC:	Teos makes *asylia* agreement with Rome
195 BC:	War between Rome and Nabis of Sparta
195 BC:	Hannibal *suffet* in Carthage, subsequently exiled and flees to Tyre
189 BC:	Manlius Vulso campaigns against the Galatians
187 BC:	Trial of the Scipio brothers in Rome on charges of extortion

Notes

Chapter 1

1. Aphergis, *Royal Economy*: 57 (population), 201 (military strength), 251 (revenues).
2. Strabo 16.2.10.
3. Kuhrt and Sherwin-White, *From Samarkhand to Sardis A New Approach to the Seleucid Empire* (UC Press, 1993). This remains the essential overview of the Seleucid Empire. Their optimistic vision of the Seleucid Empire put forward in this monograph is not universally shared. Wolski, Jozef, *Seleucid and Arsacid Studies* (Polish Academy of Science, 2003) presents a far more negative view of the extent and benevolence of Seleucid power, while Lerner, Jeffery *The Impact of Seleucid Decline on the Eastern Iranian Plateau* (Franz Steiner Verlag, 1999) emphasizes the collapse of Seleucid power following the reign of Antiochus III.
4. Thapar, Romila, *Asoka and the Decline of the Mauryas* (Oxford, 1997 {1961}), 255–257.
5. Library of Antioch: Suda s.v. Euphorion. Gladiatorial Games: Livy 41.20, who reports that the games were initially unpopular due to their violence, but that the crowds of Antioch soon developed a taste for them.
6. Ma, John, *Antiochus III and the Cities of Western Asia Minor* (Oxford University Press, 1999), 28–52.
7. For an old fashioned narrative of Seleucid dynastic history, see Bevan, E.R., *The House of Seleucus* (Edward Arnold, 1902). Grainger, John, *Seleukos Nikator* (Routledge, 1990) provides a scholarly biography of the dynasty's founder. For an overview of the political developments of the Hellenistic world: Rostovetzeff, SEHHW, 1–73, Green, Peter, *From Actium to Alexander: The Evolution of the Hellenistic World*, Berkeley (UC Berkeley Press, 1990), Shipley, Graham, *The Greek World After Alexander: 323–30 BC* (Routledge, 2000) and Walbank, Frank. *The Hellenistic World, Revised Edition* (Harvard, 1993).
8. Ptolemy I, founder of the last dynasty of Egypt and biographer of Alexander the Great. For a biography, see Ellis, Walter, *Ptolemy of Egypt* (Routledge, 1994); an old fashioned narrative of the dynasty is provided by Bevan, Edwyn, *House of Ptolemy: A History of Hellenistic Egypt under the Ptolemaic Dynasty* (Argonaut, 1927).
9. These eight years of internecine war are compellingly narrated by Romm, James *Ghost on the Throne: The Death of Alexander the Great and the War for Crown and Empire* (Knopf, 2011).
10. For a complete biography of this important successor see Billows, Richard, *Antigonus One-Eyed and the Creation of the Hellenistic State* (University of California Press, 1990).
11. On the Seleucid anchor: Antela-Bernardez, Borja, 'The Anchor and the Crown. Seleucos' use of the "Anchor" Coin Type in 305 BC', *Athenaeum: Studi di letteratura e Stori*a, January, 2009. Anchor on a siege bullet: UC Berkeley Excavation Report, Tel Dor. Area F (1992), available online at: www.arf.berkeley.edu/projects/teldor/reports/index.htm.
12. Diodorus Siculus 19.90.

13. Strabo 15.2.9.
14. Justin 15.2.5, Jacoby, FGrH 155, 1.6, Diodorus 19.105.4. The exact date of the event is uncertain.
15. Gruen, Erich. 'The Coronation of the Diadochoi', in Eadie and Ober (eds.) The Craft of the Ancient Historian: Essays in Honor of Chester Starr (University Press of America, 1985), pp. 253–271.
16. On Lysimachus, an often ignored successor. Lund, Helen, Lysimachus: A Study in Early Hellenistic Kingship (Routledge, 1992).
17. Battle of Ipsus and aftermath: Plutarch, Demetrias, 29–30. Griffith, G.T., The Mercenaries of the Hellenistic World (Cambridge University Press, 1935), 54–56.
18. Plutarch, Demetrias 30.1 ὥσπερ μέγα σῶμα κατακόπτοντες.
19. For a 'biography' of Antioch see Downey, Glanville, A History of Antioch in Syria: from Seleucus to the Arab Conquest (Princeton University Press, 1961).
20. John Malalas 8.201.
21. On the city-building program of Seleucus I, see Grainger, John, The Cities of Seleukid Syria (Clarendon Press, 1990).
22. Polybius 5.67.4–10.
23. Grainger, John, A Seleukid Prosopography and Gazetteer (Brill, 1997), 9–13.
24. Demetrias' fortunes temporarily improved, as he seized power in Macedonia in 294 BC.
25. On this very important point for understanding Hellenistic dynastic politics, see Ogden, Daniel Polygamy, Prostitutes and Death: The Hellenistic Dynasties (Duckworth: Classical Press of Wales, 1997).
26. Retold romantically in the Second Sophistic by Lucian, De Dea Syria, 17–18; Appian, Syrian Wars, 60–61.
27. Grainger, Prosopography, 67.
28. Last days of Demetrias: Plutarch, Demetrias, 46–50.
29. Deaths of Lysimachus and Seleucus: Appian, 62–64. Gallic Invasion: Justin 24.4–8, Pausanias 1.4.1.
30. Suda, s.v. Simonides, which provides one of the few mentions of elephants.
31. Pausanias, 10.22.4. On Hellenistic propaganda concerning Guals, see Strootman, Rolf. 'Kings Against Celts: Deliverance from Barbarians as a Theme in Hellenistic Royal Propoganda', The Manipulative Mode: Political Propaganda in Antiquity (Mnemosyne Supplement) (Brill, 2005), pp. 101–141.
32. Grainger, Syrian Wars is the most in depth study of this long series of conflicts.
33. Grainger, Prosopography, 13–15.
34. Trogus, Prologue, 26, John of Antioch fr. 55 (Jacoby FHG iv, p 558.) Ogden, Polygamy, 125.
35. Polyaenus 8.50. Ogden, Polygamy, 124
36. The 'Laodice Dossier', OGIS 224; Austin #173; Aphergis, Royal Economy: 315; Wells RC 18.
37. Seleucus II: Grainger, Prosopography, 60–63.
38. FGrH 160 (Austin, # 266.).
39. Lerner, Jeffery, The Impact of Seleucid Decline on the Eastern Iranian Plateau (Steiner Verlag, 1999), 13–43.
40. Strabo 13.4.2.
41. Polybius 5.90.
42. Grainger, Prosopography, 63.

43. The so-called 'Seleucus III chronicle', provides an intriguing hint that Antiochus III may have originally had a different name prior to his accession. The chronical reports that the king's brother named Ly[sias?] is in the city overseeing a judicial case. Antiochus III is the only attested brother of Seleucus III, and he is known to have been in Babylon at this time. It is possible therefore, that Antiochus III went by another name, until he succeeded to the throne and adopted a dynastic name (Seleucus III himself was originally named Alexander). See commentary by Bert van der Spek on the website: www.livius.org.

44. On the epithets of Hellenistic kings, Van Nueffelen, Peter, 'The Name Game: Hellenistic Historians and Royal Epithets' in *Faces of Hellenism* (Van Nueffelen, ed.) (Peeters, 2009).

45. The Roman emperor Hadrian (117–138) seems to have been a pivotal figure in the return of bearded faces to ancient Mediterranean fashion.

46. Ma, *Asia Minor*, 272–273. It is unclear when it became common to refer to Alexander as 'the Great'. Our earliest reference to Alexander the Great in fact comes from a Roman play by Plautus, which refers to *Alexandrus Magnus*. (*Mostellaria*, Act 3, Scene 2, ln 88). However, it is unclear whether this should be seen as a Roman invention, or rather a reflection of contemporary Hellenistic practice. (Pace Beard, 'Alexander: How Great', *New York Review of Books*, Oct. 27, 2011, who suggests that 'the Great' is a Roman coinage).

47. From the funeral inscription of Darius I at Naqs-i-Rustam, translation by R.T. Hallock. For the use of the term by Antiochus III, see Ma, *Asia Minor*, 273–276.

48. These ratios are based upon the price edict of Diocletian, but were likely valid for much of antiquity.

49. For comparison to the Roman *cursus publicus*, see Ramsay, A.M., 'The Speed of the Roman Imperial Post', *Journal of Roman Studies*, Vol. 15 (1925).

50. Grainger, *Prosopography*, 811, 814 (s.v.satrap/strategos). The precise relationship between *strategoi* and *eparchoi* is unclear.

51. On satrapies and *strategoi*, see Carsana Chiara, *Le Dirigenze Cittadine Nello Stato Seleucidico*, (Biblioteca di Athenaeum, 1996), pp. 15–28.

52. On the importance of merchants as sources of intelligence see Woolmer, Mark, 'Tinker, Tailor, Sailor, Spy? The Role of the Mercantile Community', in Bragg, Hau and Macaulay-Lewis (eds) *Beyond Battlefields* (Cambridge Scholars Publishing, 2008).

53. On the image of Alexander in the Hellenistic World, Stewart, Andrew, *Faces of Power: Alexander's Images and Hellenistic Politics* (UC Press, 1993).

54. The so-called Chremonidean War.

55. Populations estimates of Hellenistic Macedonia fluctutate between 300,000 and one million. I believe estimates closer to the lower end of this spectrum are closer, based largely on evidence of Macedonian military mobilizations, which as a rule of thumb seldom exceed 10 per cent of the total population. For a high estimate of Macedonian population, see Billows, Richard, *Kings and Colonists: Aspects of Macedonian Imperialism* (Brill, 1995), 7–8, although Billow's estimate of one million is not nearly as high as Beloch's improbable estimate of three to four million Macedonians.

56. Philip's mining revenues: Diodorus, 16.8. This numbers is likely rounded up to begin with, and must represent peak production in the reign of Philip V.

57. 12,000: Strabo 17.1.13, 14,800: Jerome, *Commentary on Daniel 15.1*. It is unclear whether these figures have been converted to Attic talents, or remain in the somewhat lighter Ptolemaic standard (roughly 80 per cent of an Attic talent). For the workings of the Ptolemaic economy, based largely on papyrological evidence, Manning, J.G., *The Last Pharaohs: Egypt Under the Ptolemies, 305–30 BC* (Princeton University Press, 2010).

58. Fredricksmeyer, E.A., 'The Origins of Alexander's Royal Insignia', *Transactions of the American Philological Association*, Vol. 127 (1997) pp. 97–109.
59. E.g. 2 Maccabees 3.38.
60. E.g. Herodotus, 3.80, Polybius 6.7.
61. Gruen, Erich, 'The Coronation of the Diadochoi' (op.cit.), 253–262.
62. Pliny the Elder, Natural History 33.97.
63. Polybius 2.25. The classic study remains Brunt, P.A., *Italian Manpower* (Oxford, 1971), also Schiedel Walter 'Human Mobility in Roman Italy: The Free Population', *Journal of Roman Studies, Vol. 94, (2004)*. Both reflect the orthodoxy of the 'low count' of classical Italian population.
64. Aristotle, *Politics*, 2.11.
65. Polybius 6.11–18.
66. Polybius 5.104.10 νῦν ἀπὸ τῆς ἑσπέρας νέφη προσδέξηται.
67. Gruen, *Hellenistic World* , 359–373.
68. Surus: Pliny, *Natural History*, 8.11, Plautus, Pseudolus, 1215. Indian elephants, with their distinctive 'batwing' ears also appear on Hannibal's coins.
69. Suetonius, Life of Claudius, 25.3.
70. Grainger, *Roman War*,11; Gruen, *Hellenistic World*, 612–613.
71. Dmitriev, Sviatoslav, *The Greek Slogan of Freedom and Early Roman Politics in Greece* (Oxford, 2011), 112–141.
72. Polybius 5.88–90.
73. On Greek 'federal' states J.A.O. Larsen *Greek Federal States* (Oxford 1968) is dated but worth reading, see also Mackil, Emily, *Creating a Common Polity: Religion, Economy, and Politics in the Making of a Greek Koinon* (University of California Press, 2013). On the Aetolians, Grainger, John. *League of the Aotolians* (Brill, 1999) and Scholten, Joseph, *The Politics of Plunder: The Aitolians and their Koinon in the Early Hellenistic Era* (UC Press, 2000).
74. An overview of literary sources for the Seleucid Empire is provided by Edson, Charles, 'Imperium Macedonicum. The Seleucid Empire and the Literary Evidence', *Classical Philology*, Vol. 53, No. 3 (1958), pp. 153–170.
75. The bibliography on Polybius is vast. The essential commentary remains F.W. Walbank, *Historical Commentary on Polybius*, 3 vols. (Oxford, 1957). Worthwhile monographs include F.W. Walbank, *Polybius* (University of California Press, 1990), Arthur Eckstein, *Moral Vision in the Histories of Polybius* (UC Press, 1995) and Craig Champion, *Cultural Politics in Polybius' Histories* (UC Press, 2004).
76. An English translation of Plutarch is available online at: http://penelope.uchicago.edu/Thayer/E/Roman/Texts/Plutarch/Lives/home.html, courtesy of William Thayer.
77. An English translation of Appian is available online at www.livius.org, courtesy of Jona Lendering. For Appian and the Seleucids, see Marasco, Gabriele, *Appiano e La Storia dei Seleucidi* (Florence: Giorgio Pasquali Institute of Classical Philology, 1982).
78. The text of Justin with an English translation is available online at www.forumromanum.org, courtesy of David Camden.
79. Royal letters are collected and translated in Wells, Bradford, *Royal Correspondence in the Hellenistic Period: A Study in Greek Epigraphy* (Ares, 1974 {London, 1934]). The best epigraphic study of Antiochus III is Ma, John, *Antiochus III and the Cities of Western Asia Minor* (Oxford, 1999).

80. Collected in Sachs, Alfred and Hunger, Herbert, *Astronomical Diaries and Related Texts from Babylon* (Austrian Academy of Sciences, 1988).
81. Seleucid coins: Newell, E.T., *The Coinage of the eastern Seleucid Mints from Seleucus I to Antiochus III* (American Numismatic Society, 1938) and *The Coinage of the western Seleucid Mints from Seleucus I to Antiochus III* (American Numismatic Society, 1941).

Chapter 2
1. BM 35603. Text and English translation by Bert Van Der Spek can be found on: www.livius.org, s.v. 'Babylonian Kinglist from the Hellenistic Period'.
2. On Antiochus' birth and accession: Schmitt, Hatto H., *'Untersuchungen Zur Geschichte Antiochos'des Grossen und seiner Zeit'*, *Historia*, vol 6. 1964; 1–7. Fifty years old in 191: Polybius 20.8.1 (Athenaeus 10.439); Diodorus 29.2.1.
3. Polybius 5.40.5, Schmitt, 108–109.
4. Grainger *Syrian Wars*,183, postulates that Molon and Alexander were in fact sent to replace Antiochus as governors of the upper satrapies; in all likelihood they already held their posts, but assumed new prominence once Antiochus left Babylon. Polybius 5.41.1.
5. Strootman, Rolf. 'Hellenistic Court Society: Seleukid Imperial Court Under Antiochus The Great, 2230187 BCE.' (in Duindam, et al., 2011), 73.
6. Polybius 4.48 1–12; Grainger, John, *A Seleukid Prosopography and Gazetteer* (Brill, 1997), 5 (Achaeus).
7. The continuation of Macedonian polygamy in Hellenistic dynasties is argued by Daniel Ogden, *Polygamy, Prostitutes and Death* (Duckworth, 1999).
8. The constant recycling of royal names is a source of frequent consternation to students of Hellenistic history.
9. Polybius 5.43.1–3.
10. Polybius 5.43.7 καταπλαγέντες.
11. Theodotus' future service: Spearheading into the Biqua Valley, Polybius 5.59.2 and commanding the main phalanx at Raphia, Polybius 5.79.5. Both these subsequent endeavours also ended in failure. He does not appear to hold major commands after 217 BC.
12. Polybius 5.45.4.
13. The Xenoitas debacle: Polybius 5.45.4–5.49.16.
14. Polybius 5.46.7.
15. Polybius 5-45.7–5.46.6.
16. Polybius 5.49.
17. Polybius 5.50.8.
18. Polybius 5.50.
19. Polybius 5.51–52.
20. The battle narrative: Polybius 5.52.4–5.54.5, cf. Bar Kochba, *Seleucid Army*, 117–123.
21. Polybius 5.54. 1–7.
22. Polybius 5.54.8 δοὺς δεξιὰν.
23. Wolski, 1999: 64–65.
24. Polybius 5.54.11; Aphergis, *Royal Economy*, 250.
25. Polybius 5.54.12. Grainger, *Prosopography*, 87.
26. Polybius 5.55.1–10.
27. The fall of Hermeias: Polybius 5.56. 1–15.
28. Grabowski, 'Achaeus, the Ptolemies and the Fourth Syrian War', *Electrum*, 2010: 116.

29. Achaeus' rebellion: Polybius 5.57.1–8. Coinage of Achaeus: Newell, *Coinage of the Western Seleucid Mints*, (American Numismatic Society, 1977) 267–270.
30. Polybius 5.53.3. Grainger, *Prosopography*, 81.
31. Recapture of Seleucia Pieria: Polybius 5.59–60.
32. Polybius 5.61.6
33. Polybius 5.40.1–3.
34. Campaign in Koile Syria: Polybius 5.61.3– 5.63.1

Chapter 3

1. For the Seleucid Army, see Bar Kochba, *Seleucid Army*, passim, and Bickerman, *Institutions*, 51–105
2. Polybius 18.29.2: 14 cubits; Markle, M.M. 'The Macedonian Sarissa, Spear, and Related Armor', *American Journal of Archaeology*, Vol. 81, No. 3 (1977) pp. 323–339.
3. On the Macedonian shield, see Markle, M.M. 'A Shield Monument from Veria and the Chronology of Macedonian Shield Types,' *Hesperia*, Vol. 1999, also Anderson, J.K. 'Shields Eight Palms Width', *California Studies in Classical Antiquity*, Vol. 9 (1976). pp. 1–6.
4. Web resource: Greg Aldrete's 'Linothorax project': http://www.uwgb.edu/aldreteg/ Linothorax.html
5. The *loci classici* for the Macedonian style Phalanx are Polybius 18.28–18.30.5, and Asclepiodotus *Tactica* 1–5.
6. AJ 12.147.
7. 3000 cavalry from Antioch: Polybius 30.25.6. Diodorus indicates that after catastrophic defeat to the Parthians in 129 BC, 'there was not a household (in Antioch) that was exempt from misfortune' (Diodorus 34.17).
8. Raphia (217): 20,000, Magnesia (190): 16,000. Daphne (168): 20,000.
9. On the cataphract, Rattenbury, R.M. 'An Ancient Armoured Force.' *Classical Review*, Vol. 56, No.3 (1942), pp. 113–116., Glover, R.F. 'Some Curiosities of Ancient Warfare', *Greece and Rome*, Vol. 19, No. 55 (January 1950), pp. 1–3; and Eadie, John W. 'The Development of Roman Mailed Cavalry.' Journal of Roman Studies, Vol. 57, no. ½ (1967), pp.163–4.
10. e.g. Polybius 30.25.5.
11. Bar Kochba, *Seleucid Army*, 9.
12. Herodotus 7.83.
13. Livy, 37.40.7–12 : *agema eam uocabant; Medi erant, lecti uiri, et eiusdem regionis mixti multarum gentium equites…et mille alii equites, regia ala leuioribus tegumentis suis equorumque, alio haud dissimili habitu; Syri plerique erant Phrygibus et Lydis immixti.*
14. H.H. Schullard's *The Elephant in the Greek and Roman World*, 60–63.
15. Seleucid Elephant Corps: Bikerman, *Institutes*, 61–63.
16. Nefiodkin, Alexander. 'On the Origin of the Scythed Chariots', *Historia: Zeitschrift fur Alte Geschichte*. Band 53, H. 3 (2004), pp. 376–378. Scythed Chariots against Alexander: Arrian *Anabasis Alexandrou* 3.11.7.
17. For recent studies on the Seleucid court of Antiochus III see Dreyer, Boris 'How to Become a 'Relative' of the King: Careers and Hierarchy at the Court of Antiochus III', *American Journal of Philology*, Vol. 132, No. 1, Spring 2011, pp. 45–57. and Strootman, Rolf. 'Hellenistic Court Society: Seleukid Imperial Court Under Antiochus The Great, 2230187 BCE', in Duindam, et al., 2011. On *philoi*, Habicht, *Hellenistic Monarchies*, 26–40. See also Bikerman, *Institutions*, 31–50.
18. Polybius 5.82.13. Grainger, *Prosopography*, 107.

19. See Pownall, 2011:55–65 for the role of drinking in the Argead court. Persians: Herodotus 1.133, 3–4.

20. Athenaeus 14.27, although this may be the dance performed by Philip in 338, after the battle of Chaironaia (Demosthenes 20.3; Grainger, *Prosopography*: 806). On the use of Athenaeus as a source for the Seleucid Court, see Cecarelli, Paulo. 'Kings Philosophers and Drunkards: Athenaeus' Information on the Seleucids', in Erickson and Ramsey (eds.) *Seleucid Dissolution. The Sinking of the Anchor*, (Wiesbaden: Harrassowitz Verlag, 2011), pp. 162–179.

21. Athenaeus 4.155.

22. Livy 34.57.6

23. Grainger suggests that dancing in armour was a Macedonian courtly custom, although the evidence for this is extremely thin, and limited to the image of Philip II dancing on the graves of slain enemy at Chaeronaea.

24. AJ 12.147.

25. Livy 35.15.

26. 1 Maccabees 3:38.

27. Lucian, *De Dea Syria*.

28. See various references in Grainger, *Prosopography*, in 'Institutions of the Kingdom'.

29. Pliny, *Natural History* 22.59, Galen 14.183.

30. Athenaeus 6.246.d.

31. Wallace Hadrill, Andrew. CAH II, Vol. 10, 289 (in comparison to the Roman Imperial court).

32. Inge, Nielsen, *Hellenistic Palaces: Tradition and Renewal* (Aarhus University Press, 1994) 111–115.

33. Ibid, 115. For elements of the Seleucid palace at Apamea, see Plutarch *Demetrius* 50. On hunting in the Macedonian court tradition, Carney, Elizabeth, 'Hunting and the Macedonian Elite: Sharing the Rivalry of the Chase', in Ogden (ed.) *The Hellenistic World* (The Classical Press of Wales, 2002).

34. Nielsen (op. cit. above), 111–115.

35. Athenaeus 4.145. This figure is accepted by Aphergis (2001: 82). The massive rations required by the Persian court complex, to feed courtiers and bodyguards, are listed in Polyaenus 4.3.31–32.

36. Aphergis, *Royal Economy*, 207.

37. On the library of Alexandria, see Bagnall, Roger. 'Alexandria: Library of Dreams', *Proceedings of the American Philosophical Association*, Vol. 146 (2002), 348–362.

38. *Suda* s.v. Euphorion.

39. Athenaios 15.697; πλεῖστον ἰσχύσαντος; Grainger *Prosopography*, 107.

40. Ibid. κἀγὼ παιδοφιλήσω· πολύ μοι κάλλιον ἢ γαμεῖν/παῖς μὲν γὰρ παρεὼν κἢν πολέμῳ μᾶλλον ἐπωφελεῖ.

41. For an 'ecological' view of the Mediterranean, Horden, Peregrin and Purcell, Nicholas *The Corrupting Sea: A Study in Mediterranean History* (Oxford, Blackwell, 2000). The best overview of the economy of the Seleucid realm remains Rostovetzeff, *SEHHW*, 422–551. For an overview of modern scholarship on the problems in the Hellenistic Economy, see Archibald, Zofia (ed.) *Hellensitic Economies* (Routledge, 2001).

42. Austin, *Hellenistic World*, No. 198. Ma, *Asia Minor*, 329–35.

43. For the Mnesimachos inscription see Austin, Aphergis, *Royal Economy*: 137, Document 5.

44. Rostovtzeff, SEHHW, 443–446.

45. Diodorus 19.56.5

46. Assumes military pay of 1 drachma per day, combined pay in coin and the cash value of rations.
47. Austin, *Hellenistic World*, 461; Aphergis, *Royal Economy*, 260.
48. Lucian, *De Dea Syria*, 17–18.
49. The so-called Borsippa cylinder, Austin, *Hellenistic World*, no. 166.
50. I hope to publish soon on the topic of Seleucid Temple pillaging.
51. Justin 15.4
52. Wells, RC 44.
53. Erickson, Kyle. 'Apollo-Nabu: the Babylonian Policy of Antiochus I.' in *Seleucid Dissolution: the Sinking of the Anchor*. 2011. pp. 51–66.
54. Antiochus IV and Zeus: Rigsby, K.J. 'Seleucid Notes', *Transactions of the American Philological Association*, Vol. 110 (1980), 233-238.
55. Plutarch, *Lysander*, 18.3–4.
56. Hyperides *Contra Demosthenes* 5.31–5.32 discusses a statue raised in Athens of 'Alexander, king and invincible god', and implies debate in Athens about worshiping Alexander as such, presumably in response to a royal order.
57. Athenaeus 4.353B.
58. Austin, *Hellenistic World*, No. 200.

Chapter 4
1. An alternative reading of Polybius (e.g. Griffith G.T., *Mercenaries of the Hellensitic World*, (Cambridge, 1935), pp. 118–122) suggesting that Ptolemy IV could only muster 5000 hoplites is surely incorrect, as it is unclear how Ptolemaic Egypt had even been a military power with such a limited pool of heavy infantry.
2. Spyridakis, Stylianos. 'Cretans and Neocretans', *The Classical Journal*, Vol. 72, No. 4 (April–May 1977), pp. 299–307 argues instead that Neocretans were, in fact, members of the underclass in Cretan cities, similar to the *neodamodeis* in Sparta. His argument is intriguing, but not fully convincing.
3. On Egyptians in Ptolemaic service, see Fischer Bovet, Christelle, 'Egyptian Warriors: the machimoi of Herodotus and the Ptolemaic army', *Classical Quarterly*, Vol. 61, No. 2, New Series, 2011.
4. Ptolemy's Army: Polybius 5.65
5. Polybius 5.70.10–11.
6. Polybius 5.70–71.
7. Polybius 5.81
8. The Battle of Raphia: Polybius 5.82–5.86.7. Bar Kochba, *Seleucid Army*, 124–141, Galili, E. 'Raphia, 217 BCE, Revisited', *Scripta Classica Israelica*, Vol. III (1976–77), pp. 52–127.
9. Scullard, H. H., *The Elephant in the Greek and Roman World*.
10. Polybius 5.82.8; Grainger, *Syrian Wars*, 212-216.
11. Polybius 5.58.13. τὸ μὲν καθ' αὑτὸν μέρος πεπεισμένος νικᾶν, διὰ δὲ τὴν τῶν ἄλλων ἀγεννίαν καὶ δειλίαν ἐσφάλθαι νομίζων τοῖς ὅλοις.
12. Keegan, John, *The Mask of Command* (Viking, 1987), 13–91.
13. Text and Translation: Austin, *Hellenistic World*, No. 276.

Chapter 5
1. Polybius 5.72–77.
2. Polybius 5.72.3

3. Polybius 5.61.9; Grainger, *Prosopography*: 100.
4. The relationship between the Silver Shields and the hypaspists is unclear. At Raphia, they were brigaded together under the command of Theodotus the Aetolian. The linkage with Dionyius and Theodotus again suggests a close relationship between the two units. Likely, the 2000 hypaspists were an elite subset of the larger unit.
5. The confusion of Hellenistic dynastic names is apparent here. Achaeus had an aunt named Laodice, then married Laodice, the daughter of King Mithdrates of Pontus. Mithradites had another daughter named Laodice, the wife of Antiochus III.
6. Polybius 8.15–21.
7. Ma, *Asia Minor*, 61–62. Text and translation, ibid, Epigraphic Dossier I (pp. 284–289).
8. Translation by Aphergis, *Royal Economy*, 326 (Document 9). See also Ma, *Asia Minor*, 284 (No. 1).
9. Ma, *Asia Minor*: 288(I.3).
10. Ibid.
11. Zeuxis' exact title is obscure. Polybius describes him as the governor (*hyparchos*) of Lydia (21.16.4), while Josephus (*Jewish Antiquities* 12.147) refers to him a general (*strategos*) and another inscription refers to him as 'prime minster' (*epi ton pragmaton*).

Chapter 6
1. Justin, 41.5.7. Bar Kochba, *Seleucid Army*, 10 is cautious in dismissing these figures all together.
2. BM 35603. Text and translation by Bert Van Der Speck available online at www.livius.org, s.v. 'Babylonian Kinglist of the Hellenistic Period' .
3. Polybius 8.23.3 οἱ μὲν οὖν πιστοὶ τῶν φίλων.
4. Grainger, *Prosopography*, 8–9.
5. The Armenian Campaign: Polybius 8.23. Murder of Xerxes: John of Antioch *FGH* 4.557.
6. John of Antioch, *FHG* iv. 557.
7. Aphergis, *Royal Economy*, 202–203. See also Sherwin-White 1982: 55-61, for the pay rates of the Seleucid garrison in Babylon, and Griffith, G.T., *Mercenaries in the Hellenistic World* (Cambridge, 1935), 300–306 for general mercenary pay rates in the Hellenistic world.
8. Arrian *Anababis* 7.14.5 may describe Alexander's sack of the temple, possible related to his grief over the death of Hephaistion.
9. The major work on logistics in Hellenistic armies remains Engles, Donald, *Alexander the Great and the Logistics of the Macedonian Army* (UC Press, 1980). Two other books on ancient military logistics, focused on the Roman army, are nonetheless worth reading when taking into account Hellenisitic warfare: Roth, Jonathan, *The Logistics of the Roman Army at War (264 BC–AD 235)* (Brill, 1999) and Erkamp, Paul, *Hunger and the Sword, warfare and food supply in the Roman Republican Wars (264–30 BC)* (Brill, 1998).
10. The standard Greek military ration was a *choinix* of grain, a measure of volume roughly equivalent to a modern litre, or roughly 1.5 pounds (.628 kg) of wheat. Scheidel, Walter, Morris, Ian, and Sallers, Richard, *The Cambridge Economic History of the Ancient World* (Cambridge Universiry Press, 2007), 403, note 96.
11. Van Nuffelen. 'Le Culte Royal de L'Empire des Seleucides: une reinterpretation', *Historia*, Vol. 53 (2004), pp. 278–301.
12. SEG, 1987, 1010; Malay, Hasan. 'Letter of Antiochus III to Zeuxis with two Covering Letters (209BC)', *Epigraphica Anatolia*, Vol. 10 (1987), pp. 7–15.

13. On the speed of the Roman Imperial post, A.M. Ramsay, 'The Speed of the Roman Imperial Post', *Journal of Roman Studies*, Vol. 15 (1925), pp. 60–74.
14. Josephus, *Jewish Antiquities*, 12.147–151. The first century AD Jewish historian Josephus here relates the contents of the letter, which had probably been inscribed. While some historians have doubted the authenticity of this document, I see no reason to doubt that Josephus gives a relatively faithful transcription of what must have been a still extant inscription.
15. Polybius 29.12.8.
16. We do not know whether he was referring to Magnesia in Thessaly, Magnesia-ad-Syphlium, the site of the famous battle, or Magnesia ad Maeander in Lydia. Euthydemos did not likely himself come from Magnesia. He was probably the descendant of a Greek settler previously settled by either Alexander or Seleucus I. See Lerner, 1999:53–54.
17. Holt, Frank, *Thundering Zeus: the Making of Hellensitic Bactria* (University of California Press, 1999), 132.
18. Austin, *Hellenistic World*, no. 178.
19. Polybius 11.39.12; Grainger, *Prosopography*, 77.
20. On the Greek diplomatic status of Asylia, see Rigsby, Kent, *Asylia: Territorial Inviolability in the Hellenistic World* (University of California Press, 1996).
21. Hellenistic colonization produced a series of cities sharing the same name, often named after a city in mainland Greece (the habit of naming North American sites after British towns is analogous). Thus there were three major Magnesias: Magnesia in Thessaly, Magnesia on the Maeander and Magnesia on the Siphlum; the last will be the site of the epic battle between Antiochus and Rome.
22. Austin, *Hellenistic World*, # 189.
23. Kuhrt/Sherwin-White, *Samarkhand*, 130–131.
24. *hiera, asylos, aphorologetos.*
25. *Austin, #191.*
26. Ma, *Asia Minor*, 297 (E.D. 8).
27. Wells, RC, No. 39. The exact violations against the temple are unclear, as only the first part of the inscription surivives.
28. Green, *Alexander to Actium*, 295–296.
29. Rostovtzeff, M. SEHHW, 696.
30. The earliest reference to Alexander the Great is in fact Roman, dating from the Plautine play *Mostellaria* (775), which refers to *Magnus Alexandrus*. It is highly unlikely, however, that the Romans invented this title out of whole cloth. Indeed, if they had, a more likely Roman title would perhaps be *Alexandrus Maximus.*

Chapter 7
1. Eckstein, *Mediterranean Anarchy, The Greek East, passim.*
2. Ibid. *passim.*
3. Eckstein, Arthur, 'The Pact Between the Kings, Polybius 15.20.6 and Polybius' View of the Outbreak of the 2nd Macedonian War', *Classical Philology*, Vol. 100, No. 3, July 2005.
4. Grainger, *Syrian Wars*, 242.
5. Grainger, *Roman War*, 249; Polyaenus 4.15.
6. Polybius 16.22.
7. I must emphasize that these estimates are extremely speculative.
8. Polybius 15.25.16, Livy 31.43.5–7.

9. Polybius 16.39.3/Josephus AJ 12.3.3.

10. Bar Kochba, *The Seleucid Army*: 154.

11. Justin 30.3.3. *Mittuntur itaque legati qui Philippo et Antiocho denuntient regno Aegypti abstineant.*

12. Jerome, Commentary on Daniel, 11.15.

13. Porphery, Fragment 46.

14. Grainger, 1997: 115; Gera, 1987: 63–73, Habicht, *Hellenistic Monarchies*, 264–274.

15. Translations following Aphergis, *Royal Economy*, 320.

16. Presumably the silver piece in question is a tetradrachma (=1 shekle), putting the value of this royal allowance (essentially a tax break) at roughly 13 talents p.a.

17. A medimnos was a measure of volume equivalent of about six quarts.

18. The council of elders, derived from the Greek *gerontes*, meaning 'old men'.

19. Josephus AJ 12.138–144, LCL.

20. Polybius 16.2–8.

21. Polybius 16.24.9 (Athanaeus 3.78C).

22. On the transfer of the naval stone: Ando, Clifford, *The Matter of the Gods* (UC Press, 2008), 22–27.

23. Eckstein, *Mediterranean Anarchy* and *Rome Enters the Greek East, passim*, both works which have fundamentally shaped my understanding of the Mediterranean in the early second century BC.

24. Livy 30.26.3 Dorey, T.A., 'Macedonian Troops at the Battle of Zama', *The American Journal of Philology*, Vol. 78 No. 2 (1957) pp. 185–187.

25. Polybius 18.46.

26. Hegesianax is almost certainly the court poet who previously refused to dance with Antiochus, preferring to recite his works instead.

27. Livy 33.19.9–10. Livy is certainly incorrect in calling Ardys a son of Antiochus. Grainger *Prosopography*, 22–27 and 81.

28. Polybius 18.40.

29. Polybius 21.20.5.

30. Austin 197 (Syll.(3) 591/I Lampsakos, no. 4).

31. Livy 33.38.

32. Badian Ernst. 'Rome and Antiochus the Great: A Study in Cold War', *Classical Philology*, Vol. 54, No. 2 (April 1959) pp. 81–99.

33. Porphyry, *FGH* 260, Fr. 47.

34. Grainger, *Syrian Wars*: 107–108. I concur with his reconstruction of the baffling statement in Josephus AJ 12.154, that 'Cleopatra brought Koile Syria as a dowry', to mean that revenues from Koile Syria supported the necessarily lavish lifestyle of the new Queen of Egypt.

35. Livy 33.41; Appian, *Syrian Wars* 4.

36. Appian, *Syrian Wars*, 4. Appian is wrong about the chronology, placing Hannibal's arrival in 196, prior to Hannibal's magistry in Carthage.

37. Livy 33.47–49.

38. Polybius 3.11. Livy (35.14) reports a delightful story that Scipio Africanus was a member of this delegation, and engaged in a long conversation with his old adversary, but this story is most likely apocryphal.

39. Harris, William V., *War and Imperialism in Republican Rome: 327–70 BC* (Oxford, 1979). Much scholarship since has been a response to Harris' grim view of Roman war motives,

Notes   179

including Gruen, *Coming of Rome,* which stresses Rome's desire to become of full-fledged player in Hellenistic diplomacy, and Eckstein's *Mediterranean Anarchy*, which stresses 'realist' factors as the driving force behind Roman policy.

40. The Seleucid history lesson: Ma, *Asia Minor*, 29.
41. Livy 34.59.7: *quo decreto turbaturi orbem terrarum essent.*
42. Livy 34.57–59, Appian Syrian Wars 6, Diodorus 28.15.
43. Austin, *Hellensitic World*, No. 199. (SEG 601).
44. Livy 35.15.4–5. *grauem successorem eum instare senectuti suae patrem credentem.*
45. Grainger, *Roman War*, 157 (*contra* Eckstein, *Rome Enters the Greek East*, 137).
46. Grainger, *Prosopography*, 22. Grainger's elegant solution (that the otherwise unattested son Mithradites is Antiochus IV) explains the otherwise puzzling issue of how Antiochus III could have two sons named Antiochus.
47. Livy 35.12–13.1.
48. The Aetolian Council of 192: Livy 35.32–33.
49. Livy 35.33.8–9 *quo accerseretur Antiochus ad liberandam Graeciam disceptandumque inter Aetolos et Romanos.*
50. This figure represents the Aetolian strength at Cynoscephalae (Plutarch *Flamininus*, 7), and probably the maximum muster of the Aetolian League.
51. e.g. Polybius 3.11.1–2, Livy 36.6.
52. The Ptolemaic dynasty in particular was plagued by foreign generals turning against their masters. The exiled Spartan king Cleomenes had planned a coup against Ptolemy III, using Peloponnesian mercenaries in the Alexandrian garrison, while the Scopas the Aetolian, backed by Aetolian mercenary forces, had likewise plotted against the crown.
53. Death of Nabis: Livy 35.35–36. Cartledge, Paul and Spawforth, Anthony, *Hellenistic and Roman Sparta: A Tale of Two Cities*, 2nd edition (Routledge, 2002), pp. 70–72.

Chapter 8

1. While the canonically version of the Aeneid was composed by Vergil during the Augstan age, Cato the Elder already made Aeneas central to his Latin history of Rome. (Servius on the *Aeneid* 1.267, 4.620, 6.760). The mid-Republican Roman poets Naevius and Ennius also made Aeneas the grandfather of Romulus: *Naevius et Ennius Aeneae ex filia nepotem Romulum conditorem urbis tradunt.* (Servius on the *Aeneid* 1.273). While mid-Republican poets differed from the later Vergilian account on the details, the basic Trojan connection was well established.
2. Appian *Syrian Wars*, 46. Livy 35.45.9.
3. For the relationship between Antiochus III and Athens, and the possibility of Seleucid benefactions to the city, see Habicht, *Hellenistic Monarchies*, 157–164.
4. Livy 35.50.4
5. Livy 35.23-24
6. Antiochus takes Chalcis: Livy 35.50–51.
7. Thessalian blitz: Livy 36.9
8. Burial of Macedonian skeletons at Cynoscephalae: Livy 36.8
9. Further Thessalian operations: Livy 36.10.
10. Livy 30.40.9.
11. The Latin term 'province,' *provincia*, at this point referred less to a specific geographic region with set , than to a specific 'tasking' or 'area of operations.'
12. The standard biography is Astin, A.E., *Cato the Censor* (Oxford, 1978).

13. Fabius Maximus and Scipio Africanus had been two of Rome's greatest generals during the 2nd Punic War, but had clashed vehemently about military strategy. The elderly Fabius wished to maintain a defensive strategy of attrition. Scipio favoured an aggressive invasion of Africa (commanded by himself, of course). Scipio's policy prevailed, but the ensuing popularity and prestige attached to the victorious Africanus excited significant jealousies in rival factions.

14. Cicero (*De Senectute* 32) explicitly states that Cato was a military tribune, not a legate. The imperial author Frontinus (Strategems, 2.4.4) also describes him as an 'elected military tribune (*tribunus militium a populo*). In the future, senior advisors to Republican generals would usually serve as 'picked' *legati*, rather than elected military tribunes.

15. Livy 36.14, Appian, Syr. 17.1.

16. Ogden, *Polygamy* argues that Laodice was still very much alive, although some scholars point to the emphasis of Laodice in the establishment of the royal cult may suggest that she passed sometime before 194 BC.

17. Ibid. 137–138.

18. Ibid.

19. For an overview of ancient sexuality, based largely on Roman medical texts, see Rousselle, Aline, *Porneia: On Desire and the Body in Antiquity* (Blackwell, 1993).

20. Polybius 20.8.4 (Athenaeus 10.439.c-f.) καὶ τοὺς γάμους συντελῶν ἐν τῇ Χαλκίδιαὐτόθι διέτριψε τὸν χειμῶνα, τῶν ἐνεστώτων οὐδ᾿ἡντινοῦν ποιούμενος πρόνοια.

21. On the marriage with Euboea: Polybius 20.8. 1–5; Livy 36.11.1-4; Appian Syrian Wars, 16; Diodorus 29.2. Plutarch Flameninus 16.1–2. Gruen, *Coming of Rome*, 637.

22. Athenaeus 10.439 C οἰνοπότης ὢν καὶ μέθαις χαίρων.

23. ORF(3), Fragment 20. Astin, Cato the Censor (op.cit), 149. *Antiochus epistulis bellum gerit, calamo et atramento militat.*

24. Baebius had a force of approximately 25,000 men, to which Acilius added 10,000 infantry and 2000 cavalry. (Livy 36.14.1) Some soldiers, however, would have subsequently returned to Rome for discharge, while others would have been assigned to garrison duty. Acilius' field army consisted of 22,000 men, 20,000 infantry and 2000 cavalry.

25. Livy 36.14.

26. Herodotus 7.215.

27. Herodotus 7.200–7.238.

28. This despite Cato's own hostility toward Greek culture. Cato had served in Sicily, and was good friends with the trilingual poet Ennius, who according to one source tutored him in Greek. Plutarch (Cato the Elder 12.5) indicates that Cato spoke to Greek audiences in Latin through an interpreter, but could have, if he wished, addressed them in fluent Greek.

29. Diodorus 16.37–38.

30. Diodorus 18.12.2–4.

31. Pausanians, 10.19-20.

32. Bar Kochba, *Seleucid Army*, 161.

33. Livy 40.34.5; Valerius Maximus 2.5.1. The Temple was dedicated ten years later in 181 BC.

34. Plutarch, *Cato the Elder*, 14.1.

35. Battle of Thermopylae: Appian, Syrian Wars, 18-20, Plutarch, *Cato Maior*, 13–14. Livy. 36. 15–19.11, Polybius 20.8.6. Bar Kochba, *Seleucid Army* 158–163.

36. For Roman Logistics, see Roth, Jonathan, *The Logistics of the Roman Army at War* (Brill, 1999) and Erdkamp, Paul, *Hunger and the Sword* (Brill 1998).

37. Livy 36.15.

38. Polybius 20.10.
39. There is no evidence that Laelius was bitter for the loss of his command, as he later praised Scipio's character to Polybius. The Laelii and Cornelii Scipiones maintained close ties, so that two generations later, Scipio's adopted grandson Aemilianus was close friends with the Laelius' grandson, also called Gaius Laelius.
40. The best book on the naval history of the Republic remains Theil, J.H., *Studies on the History of Roman Sea-Power in Republican Times* (North Holland Publishing Company, 1946) and Grainger, *Roman War*: 247–306, both upon which the following sections of naval affairs are heavily indebted. See also Grainger, John, *Hellenistic and Roman Naval Wars: 336-31 BC* (Pen and Sword, 2011).
41. Polybius 10.29.3. Grainger, *Prosopography*:114.
42. Battle of Cissus: Livy 37.4
43. Polyxenidas assault on Samos: Livy 37.10–13.
44. Livy 37.9.7
45. Salinator attacks Lycia: Livy 37.16.
46. Aemilius war council: 37.19.
47. Achaean moment of glory: Livy 37.20.
48. Livy 37.21.
49. Battle of Side: Livy 37.23–24.
50. Livy 37.22.2.
51. Battle of Myonnesus: Livy 37.27–30. For a more detailed discussion of the naval aspects of the Syrian War, see Theil, J. H., *Studies on the History of Roman Sea-Power in Republican Times* (North Holland Publishing Company, 1946), 293–372.
52. Appian, *Syrian Wars*, 23.
53. Ibid.
54. Heraclea ad Latmos: Austin *Hellenistic World*, No. 202. Ma, *Asia Minor*, 366–67.
55. Appian, Syrian Wars 29 is incorrect in identifying this son as Scipio Aemilianus, who destroyed Carthage. This Publius Cornelius Scipio obtained the office of praetor, but his political career was derailed by ill health. He did, however, adopt the son of Aemilius Paullus, the future Scipio Aemilianus 'Africanus'. Appian is merely off by a generation.
56. Livy 37.34–35, Polybius 21.13–15. Appian Syr, 29. Gruen, *Coming of Rome*, 639.
57. Livy 37.34.

Chapter 9
1. Cf. Appian *Syrian Wars* 32.
2. Livy 37.37. Appian, who is either summarizing Livy, or possibly Livy's source Polybius, rounds Antiochus' strength up to 70,000 (Syrian Wars 32).
3. Bar Kochba, *Seleucid Army*, 9, 168.
4. Livy, 37.39.
5. Appian (*Syrian Wars*, 31) generally confirms these numbers, rounding them to 30,000 altogether, including 3000 Achaean peltasts and 3000 cavalry. Bar Kochba Seleucid Army: 165.
6. Sekunda, Nicolas, *The Republican Roman Army* (Osprey, 1996) provides a well-illustrated but still substantial introduction to the army of the Roman Republic. Erdkamp, Paul (ed.) *A Companion to the Roman Army* (Wiley Blackwell, 2007) provides a summary of current scholarly work. The *locus classicus* for the equipment of a Roman soldier is Polybius 6.19–23.

7. On the archaeological evidence for the Roman sword, Quesada-Sanz, Fernando. 'Gladius Hispaniensis: an Archaeological View from Iberia', *Journal of Roman Military Equipment Studies*, Vol. 8, 1997 (pp. 251–270).

8. Varro, *de Lingua Latina*, 5.89. *Agite nunc, subsidite omnes quasi solent triarii.*

9. I hope to publish my thoughts soon on the tactical arrangement of the Roman legions.

10. Livy 8.8.5–9.

11. Polybius 18.30.8. The passage in Polybius has been variously interpreted, but the best reading would mean that each Roman soldier has a frontage of six feet, some of which is shared with the soldier next to him. The 'file width' of each Roman soldier in open order was therefore approximately 4.5 feet (.1.35 m).

12. Harl, Kenneth. 'Legion Over Phalanx' in Howe, Timothy and Reames, Jeanne (eds) *Macedonian Legacies: Studies in Ancient History and Culture in Honor of Eugene N. Borza* (Regina Books, 2008), 275 correctly assigns credit for command to L. Scipio.

13. Livy 37.41.

14. Ibid.

15. Ibid.

16. Justin 38.8.6. Bar Kochba, *Seleucid Army*, 170.

17. Livy 37.4.3

18. For the confrontation of legion and phalanx, Polybius 18.29–32. Taylor, Michael 'Fear the Phalanx' *MHQ: The Quarterly Magazine of Military History*, Winter 2011, Sabin, Philip, 'The Face of Roman Battle', *Journal of Roman Studies*, Vol. 90, 2000, pp. 1–17.

19. Livy 26.51.

20. Livy 37.44.1.

21. Grainger, *Roman War*, 328 estimates a minimum of 10,000 KIA on the Seleucid side. However, Antiochus suffered 10,000 KIA at Raphia against the Ptolemies, and the Romans proved more aggressive than most ancient armies at pursuing slaughtering survivors once enemy formations were shattered. For comparison, Hannibal suffered 20,000 KIA at Zama, while Perseus lost some 20,000 KIA at Pydna. Although these numbers are rounded, they are generally considered accurate.

22. Polybius 21.16.1.

23. Livy 38.13.8–10.

24. Wells, RC # 44.

25. Orosius 11.119, Cohen, Getzel, *The Seleucid Colonies: Studies in Founding, Administration and Organization* (Steiner, Franz Verlag, 1971), 82.

26. Livy 38.37. Ma, *Asia Minor*.

27. Hannibal fled the Seleucid court to that of Prusius of Bithynia, where he committed suicide in 183 BC.

28. Antiochus' total indemnity to Eumenes was therefore 477.2 talents.

29. Polybius 21.43.

30. Livy 38.39.

31. It is possible to view the so-called 'trial of the Scipios,' supposedly for embezzlement, as a Roman tax revolt, as Scipio's political enemies were emboldened by a populace weary from the costs of on-going wars, as well as a expensive program of road building in Italy itself. The refund effected by Vulso can perhaps be seen as the conclusion of the 'tax revolt'.

32. Sachs and Hungar *AD* # 187. Kurht and Sherwin White, *Samarkhand*, 216.

33. Diodorus 28.3.1, Strabo 16.1.8, Justin 32.2.1.

34. Because of imprecision about Antiochus' precise regnal years, sources vary at the total length of his reign. Appian (*Syrian Wars*, 66), claims thirty-seven years. The Babylonian King list (below), reports of a reign of thirty-five years, although this dates from the formal proclamation in Babylon, and not Antiochus actual assumption of rule two years previously.
35. BM 35603. Text and translation by Bert Van Der Spek, available online at www.livius.org, s.v. 'Babylonian Kinglist from the Hellenistic World.'

Chapter 10
1. Late payment: Livy 42.6.7. Attempt to despoil Temple of Yaweh: 2 Maccabees 3.11–13.
2. Appian, *Syrian Wars* 45.
3. Sekunda, Nicholas, *Hellenistic Infantry Reform in the 160s BC* (Foundation for the Development of Gdansk University, 2006), 84–86.
4. On the Battle of Pydna, Hammond, NGL 'The Battle of Pydna', *The Journal of Hellenic Studies*, Vol. 104, (1984) 31–47.
5. On the 'day in Eleusis' Polybius 29.2, Livy 44.19.13, Diadorus 31.1.1, Justin 34.3. Gruen, *Coming of Rome*, 689–692.
6. Granius Licinianus 28.6.1 (Critini).
7. Appian, *Syrian Wars* 66; Polybius 31.9; Diodorus Siculus 31.18; 2Mac. 1.14.
8. Josephus, *AJ*, 12.258.
9. Polybius 31.2, Appian *Syrian Wars*, 46–47.
10. Polybius 32.2–3.
11. Even Demetrius' friend Polybius admitted that he was often drunk for much of the day (Polybius 33.19/Athenaeus 10.440B).
12. Army size: Justin suggests 80,000 soldiers, which if rounded up is not implausible (compare 72,000 at Magnesia and 68,000 at Raphia). Reports of hundreds of thousands of camp followers are undoubtedly false exaggerations.
13. Kurht and Sherwin White, *Samarkhand*, 222.
14. For a political history of the collapse of the dynasty, see Bellinger, Alfred. 'The End of the Seleucids', *Transactions of the Connecticut Academy of Arts and Sciences*, Vol. 38, 1949, also Habicht, *Hellenistic Monarchies*, 174-242 (=CAH II, vol. 8 324–87).
15. Diodorus 40.2-4, Appian *Syrian Wars*, 70.
16. Ὅτι Ἀντίοχος ὁ βασιλεὺς ἐδόκει κατὰ μὲν τὰςἀρχὰς γεγονέναι μεγαλεπίβολος καὶ τολμηρὸς καὶτοῦ προτεθέντος ἐξεργαστικός, προβαίνων δὲ κατὰτὴν ἡλικίαν ἐφάνη πολὺ καταδεέστερος αὐτοῦ καὶτῆς τῶν ἐκτὸς προσδοκίας.

Appendix II
1. Grainger, *Prosopography*, 36–37.
2. Grainger *Prosopography*, 22–26.
3. Grainger, *Prosopography*, 45.
4. Ibid, 8.
5. Ibid, 71.
6. Grainger, *Prosopography*, 44, 71; Livy 37.44.6.

Selected Bibliography

Adcock, F.E., *The Greek and Macedonian Art of War*, Berkeley: University of California Press, 1957.

Ager, Shiela, 'Familiarity Breeds: Incest and the Ptolemaic Dynasty', *Journal of Hellenic Studies*, Vol 125 (2005), 1–24.

Allen, R.E., *The Attalid Kingdom*, Oxford: Clarendon Press, 1983.

Aperghis, Makis, *The Seleukid Royal Economy*, Cambridge: Cambridge University Press, 2004.

Archibald, Zofia H., Davies, John, Gabrielsen, Vincent and Oliver, Graham (eds.) *Hellenistic Economies* New York: Routledge, 2001.

Astin, Alan E., *Cato the Censor*, Oxford: The Clarendon Press, 1978.

Austin, Michael, *The Hellenistic World from Alexander to the Roman Conquest* (2nd Edition), Cambridge: Cambridge University Press, 2006.

— 'War and Culture in the Seleucid Empire' in *War as a Cultural and Social Force*, (Tonnes Becker Nielsen and Lise Hannestad, eds.), Det kongelige Danske Videnskabernes Selskab, 2001.

Badian, Ernst, 'Rome and Antiochus the Great: A Study in Cold War', *Classical Philology*, Vol 54 No 2. (April 1959) pp. 81–99.

Bagnall, Roger S., *The Administration of the Ptolemaic Possessions Outside Egypt*, Leiden: Brille, 1976.

Bagnall, Roger, 'Alexandria: Library of Dreams', *Proceedings of the American Philosophical Association*, Vol. 146, No. 4 (2002), 348–362.

Bar Kochba, Bezalel, *The Seleucid Army: Organization and Tactics in the Great Campaigns*, Cambridge: Cambridge University Press, 1979.

Bevan, Anthony, *The House of Seleucus: A History of the Hellenistic Near East*, Edward Arnold, 1902.

Bevan, E.R., 'Antiochus III and His Title 'Great King', *The Journal of Hellenic Studies*, Vol. 22 (1922), pp. 241–244.

Bickerman, E.J., *Institutions Des Seleucides*, Paris, 1938.

Bilde, Per, et al., *Religion and Religious Practice in the Seleucid Kingdom*, Aarhus: Aarhus University Press, 1990.

Billows, Richard, *Antigonus the One-Eyed and the Creation of the Hellenistic State*, Berkeley, University of California Press, 1990.

—*Kings and Colonists: Aspects of Macedonian Imperialism*, Berkeley: UC Press, 1995.

Brunt, P.A., *Italian Manpower: 225 BC–AD 14*, Oxford: Oxford University Press, 1971.

Bugh, Glenn R. (ed.) *The Cambridge Companion to the Hellenistic World*, Cambridge: Cambridge University Press, 2006.

Burton, Paul, *Friendship and Empire*, Cambridge: Cambridge University Press, 2011.

Carney, Elizabeth and Ogden, Daniel (eds.) *Philip II and Alexander: Lives and Afterlives*, Oxford: Oxford University Press, 2010.

Carsana, Chiara, *Le Dirigenze Cittadine nello Stato Seleucidico*, Como: Bibloteca di Athenaeum, 1996.

Ceccarelli, Paola, 'Kings, Philosophers and Drunkards: Athenaeus' Information on the Seleucids', in K. Erickson and G. Ramsey (eds.) *Seleucid Dissolution The Sinking of the Anchor*, Wiesbaden: Harrassowitz Verlag, 2012.

Champion, Craige Brian, *Cultural Politics in Polybius' Histories*, Berkeley: University of California Press, 2004.

Chaniotis, Angelos, *War in the Hellenistic World: A Social and Cultural History*, Oxford: Malden, 2005.

Cohen, Getzel, *The Seleucid Colonies: Studies in Founding, Administration and Organization*, Steiner: Franz Verlag, 1971.

Coudry, Marianne and Humm, Michel, *Praeda. Butin de guerre et société dans la Rome Republicaine / Kriegsbeute und Gesellschaft im republikanischen Rom*, Stuttgart: Franz Steiner Verlag, 2009.

Dabrowa, Edward (ed.) *Orbis Parthicus: Studies in Memory of Professor Jozef Wolski*, Krakow: Wydawnictwo Uniwersytetu Jagiellonskiego, 2010.

Debevoise, Neilson, *A Political History of Parthia*, Chicago: The University of Chicago Press, 1938.

Dmitriev, Sviatoslav, *The Greek Slogan of Freedom and Early Roman Politics*, Oxford: Oxford University Press, 2011.

— 'Antiochus III: A Friend and Ally of the Roman People', *Klio*, Vol. 1 No. 1 (2011). pp 104–130.

Downey, Glanville, *A History of Antioch in Syria: from Seleucus to the Arab Conquest*, Princeton: Princeton University Press, 1961.

Dreyer, Boris *Die romische Nobilitatsherrschaft und Antiochus III: (205 bis 188 v.Chr)*, Hennef: Buchverlag Marthe Clauss, 2007.

—How to Become a 'Relative' of the King: Careers and Hierarchy at the Court of Antiochus III. *American Journal of Philology*, Vol 132, no 1. Spring 2011, pp 45–57.

Duindam, Jeroen, Artan, Tulay, and Kunt, Metin (eds.) *Royal Courts in Dynastic States and Empires: A Global Perspective*, Brill, 2011.

Eckstein, Arthur, *Senate and General: Individual Decision Making and Roman Foreign Relations, 264–194 BC*, Berkeley, University of California Press, 1987.

—*Moral Vision in the Histories of Polybius*, Berkeley: University of California Press, 1995.

—*Mediterranean Anarchy*, Berkeley: University of California Press, 2006.

—*Rome Enters the Greek East: From Anarchy to Hierarchy*, Berkeley: University of California Press, 2008.

Eddy, Samuel K., *The King is Dead: Studies in the Near Eastern Resistance to Hellenism. 334–31 BC*, Lincoln: University of Nebraska Press, 1961.

Ehling, Kay, 'Der Tod des Usurpators Achaeus', *Historia: Zeitschrift fur Alte Geschichte*, Bd. 56. H.4 (2007). pp 497–501.

Errington, R.M., *The Dawn of Empire: Rome's Rise to World Power*, London: Hamish Hamilton, 1971.

Grabowski, Thomas, 'Achaeus, the Ptolemies and the Fourth Syrian War', *Electrum*, Vol. 18, 2010.

Grainger, John D., *Cities of Seleukid Syria*, Oxford: Clarendon Press, 1990.

— *Seleukos Nikator: Constructing a Hellenistic Kingdom*, Routledge, 1990.

— *A Seleukid Prosopography and Gazetteer*, Leiden: Brill, 1997.

— *The Roman War of Antiochos the Great*, Boston, Brill, 2002.

— *The Syrian Wars*, Boston: Brill, 2010.

Griffith, G.T., *The Mercenaries of the Hellenistic World*, Cambridge: Cambridge University Press, 1935.

Green, Peter, *Alexander to Actium: The Historical Evolution of the Hellenistic Age*, Berkeley: University of California Press, 1995.

Gruen, Erich, *The Hellenistic World and the Coming of Rome (II vol)*, Berkeley: University of California Press, 1984.

Habicht, Christian, *Hellensitic Monarchies: Selected Papers*, Ann Arbor: University of Michigan Press, 2002.

Holt, Frank L., *Thundering Zeus: The Making of Hellenistic Bactria*, Berkeley, University of California Press, 1999.

Harl, Kenneth, 'Legion v. Phalanx: The Battle of Magnesia, 190 BC', in T. Howe and J. Reames (eds.) *Macedonian Legacies: Studies in Ancient Macedonian History and Culture in Honor of Eugene N. Borza*, Claremont: Regina Books, 2008.

Harris, William V., *War and Imperialism in Republican Rome: 327–70 BC*, Oxford, Clarendon Press, 1979.

Howe, Timothy and Reames, Jeanne, (eds.) *Macedonian Legacies: Studies in Ancient Macedonian History and Culture in Honor of Eugene N. Borza*, Claremont: Regina Books, 2008.

Inge, Nielsen, *Hellenistic Palaces: Tradition and Renewal*, Aarhus University Press, 1994.

Jouget, Pierre, *Macedonian Imperialism and the Hellenization of the East*, New York: Knopf, 1932.

Keegan, John, *The Mask of Command*, New York: Viking, 1988.

Kincaid, C.A., *Successors of Alexander the Great*, Chicago: Argonaut Publishers, 1969.

Kuhrt, Amelie and Sherwin-White, Susan, *From Samarkhand to Sardis: A New Approach to the Seleucid Empire*, Berkeley: UC Press, 1993.

Larsen, J.A.O., *The Greek Federal States: Their Institutions and History*, Oxford: Clarendon Press, 1968.

Lerner, Jeffery D., *The Impact of Seleucid Decline on the Eastern Iranian Plateau: The Foundations of Arsacid Parthia and Graeco-Bacrtia*, Stuttgart: Historia, Zeitschrift fur Alte Geschichte (#123), 1999.

Ma, John, *Antiochus III and the Cities of Western Asia Minor*, Oxford: Oxford University Press, 1999.

Macurdy, Grace Harriet, *Hellenistic Queens: A Study of Woman Power in Macedonia, Seleucid Syria and Ptolemaic Egypt*, Westport: Greenwood Press, 1932.

Magie, David, 'The "Agreement" between Philip V and Antiochus III for the Partition of the Egyptian Empire', *The Journal of Roman Studies*, Vol. 29, Part 1 (1939), pp. 32–44.

Marasco, Gabriele, *Appiano e La Storia dei Seleucidi*, Florence: Giorgio Pasquali Institute of Classical Philology, 1982.

Markle, Minor M., 'The Macedonian Sarissa, Spear and Related Armor', *American Journal of Archaeology*, Vol. 81, No. 3 (Summer), 1977, pp 323–339.

— 'A Shield Monument from Veria and the Chronology of Macedonian Shield Types', *Hesperia*, Vol. 68, No. 2 (April–June) 1999, pp. 219–254.

McKechnie, Paul and Guillaume, Phillippe (eds) *Ptolemy II Philadelphus and his World*, Boston: Brill, 2008.

Mittag, Peter Franz, 'Blood and Money: On the Loyalty of the Seleucid Army', *Electrum*, Vol. 14 (2008), pp 48–54.

Ogden, Daniel, *Polygamy, Prostitutes and Death: The Hellenistic Dynasties*, London: Duckworth, 1999.

— (ed.) *The Hellenistic World: New Perspectives*, The Classical Press of Wales, 2002.

Pownell, Frances, 'The Symposia of Philip II and Alexander: The View from Greece', in E. Carney and D. Ogden (eds.), *Philip II and Alexander: Lives and Afterlives*, Oxford: Oxford University Press, 2010.

Rajak, Tessa; Pearce, Sarah; Aitken, James and Dines, Jennifer, *Jewish Perspectives on Hellenistic Rulers*, Berkeley: University of California Press, 2007.

Rigsby, Kent J., *Asylia*, Berkeley: University of California Press, 1996.

Rostovtzeff, Michael, *A Social and Economic History of the Hellenistic World*, 2nd Edition, Oxford: Clarendon Press, 1953.

Sabin, Philip, 'The Face of Roman Battle', *Journal of Roman Studies*, Vol. 90 (2000).

Scullard, H.H., *Roman Politics: 220–150 BC*, Oxford: Clarendon Press, 1951.

— *Scipio Africanus: Soldier and Politician*, Cornell University Press, 1970.

— *The Elephant in the Greek and Roman World*, Thames and Hudson, 1974.

Scheidel, Walter, Morris Ian, and Sallers, Richard, *The Cambridge Economic History of the Ancient World*, Cambridge: Cambridge University Press, 2007.

Sellwood, David, *An Introduction to the Coinage of Parthia*, London: Spink and Son Ltd, 1971.

Schmitt, Hatto H., 'Untersuchungen Zur Geschichte Antiochos'des Grossen und seiner Zeit', *Historia*, vol 6. 1964.

Shipley, Graham, *The Greek World After Alexander*, New York: Routledge, 2000.

Strootman, Rolf, 'Hellenistic Court Society: Seleukid Imperial Court Under Antiochus The Great, 2230187 BCE', in J. Duindam, T. Artan and M. Kunt (eds.) *Royal Courts in Dynastic States and Empires: A Global Perspective*, Brill, 2011, pp. 63–89.

— 'Kings Against Celts: Deliverance from Barbarians as a Theme in Hellenistic Royal Propoganda', *The Manipulative Mode: Political Propaganda in Antiquity (Mnemosyne Supplement)*, Brill, 2005.

Theil, J. H., *Studies on the History of Roman Sea Power in Republican Times*, Amsterdam: North Holland Publishing Company, 1946.

Van Nueffelen, Peter, 'The Name Game: Hellenistic Historians and Royal Epithets' in *Faces of Hellenism*, Van Nueffelen (ed.) Walpole: Peeters, 2009.

Walbank, Frank W., *Commentary on Polybius* (3 Vol.) Oxford University Press, 1957–1979.

— *Polybius, Rome and the Hellenistic World: Essays and Reflections*, Cambridge: Cambridge University Press, 2002.

Wolski, Jozef, *The Seleucids: The Decline and Fall of their Empire*, Krakow: Polskiej Akademii Umieijetnosci, 1999.

Index